D0824660

Cold War
Almanac

Cold War
Almanac

Volume 2

Sharon M. Hanes
and Richard C. Hanes

Lawrence W. Baker,
Project Editor

Detroit • New York • San Diego • San Francisco • Cleveland • New Haven, Conn. • Waterville, Maine • London • Munich

Cold War: Almanac

Sharon M. Hanes and Richard C. Hanes

Project Editor
Lawrence W. Baker

Editorial
Sarah Hermsen, Matthew May, Allison McNeill, Diane Sawinski

Permissions
Margaret Chamberlain, Shalice Shah-Caldwell

Imaging and Multimedia
Mary Grimes, Lezlie Light, Mike Logusz, Kelly A. Quin

Product Design
Pamela A. E. Galbreath, Jennifer Wahi

Composition
Evi Seoud

Manufacturing
Rita Wimberley

Library of Congress Control Card Number: 2003019223

ISBN 0-7876-9089-9 (2-volume set); 0-7876-7662-4 (volume 1); 0-7876-9087-2 (volume 2)

Printed in the United States of America
10 9 8 7 6 5 4

Contents

Volume 1

Volume 2

Introduction

Sometimes single events alter the course of history; other times, a chain reaction of seemingly lesser occurrences changes the path of nations. The intense rivalry between the United States and the Soviet Union that emerged immediately after World War II (1939–45) followed the second pattern. Known as the Cold War, the rivalry grew out of mutual distrust between two starkly different societies: communist Soviet Union and the democratic West, which was led by the United States and included Western Europe. Communism is a political and economic system in which the Communist Party controls all aspects of citizens' lives and private ownership of property is banned. It is not compatible with America's democratic way of life. Democracy is a political system consisting of several political parties whose members are elected to various government offices by vote of the people. The rapidly growing rivalry between the two emerging post–World War II superpowers in 1945 would dominate world politics until 1991. Throughout much of the time, the Cold War was more a war of ideas than one of battlefield combat. Yet for generations, the Cold War affected almost every aspect of American life and those who lived in numerous other countries around the world.

The global rivalry was characterized by many things. Perhaps the most dramatic was the cost in lives and public funds. Millions of military personnel and civilians were killed in conflicts often set in Third World countries. This toll includes tens of thousands of American soldiers in the Korean War (1950–53) and Vietnam War (1954–75) and thousands of Soviet soldiers in Afghanistan. National budgets were stretched to support the nuclear arms races, military buildups, localized wars, and aid to friendly nations. On the international front, the United States often supported oppressive but strongly anticommunist military dictatorships. On the other hand, the Soviets frequently supported revolutionary movements seeking to overthrow established governments. Internal political developments within nations around the world were interpreted by the two superpowers—the Soviet Union and the United States—in terms of the Cold War rivalry. In many nations, including the Soviet-dominated Eastern European countries, basic human freedoms were lost. New international military and peacekeeping alliances were also formed, such as the United Nations (UN), the North Atlantic Treaty Organization (NATO), the Organization of American States (OAS), and the Warsaw Pact.

Effects of the Cold War were extensive on the home front, too. The U.S. government became more responsive to national security needs, including the sharpened efforts of the Federal Bureau of Investigation (FBI). Created were the Central Intelligence Agency (CIA), the National Security Council (NSC), and the Department of Defense. Suspicion of communist influences within the United States built some individual careers and destroyed others. The national education priorities of public schools were changed to emphasize science and engineering after the Soviets launched the satellite *Sputnik,* which itself launched the space race.

What would cause such a situation to develop and last for so long? One major factor was mistrust for each other. The communists were generally shunned by other nations, including the United States, since they gained power in Russia in 1917 then organized that country into the Soviet Union. The Soviets' insecurities loomed large. They feared another invasion from the West through Poland, as had happened through the centuries. On the other hand, the West was highly suspicious of the harsh closed society of Soviet communism. As a result, a move by one nation would bring a response by the other. Hard-liners on both sides believed long-term coexistence was not feasible.

A second major factor was that the U.S. and Soviet ideologies were dramatically at odds. The political, social, and economic systems of democratic United States and communist Soviet Union were essentially incompatible. Before the communist (or Bolshevik) revolution in 1917, the United States and Russia competed as they both sought to expand into the Pacific Northwest. In addition, Americans had a strong disdain for Russian oppression under their monarchy of the tsars. Otherwise, contact between the two growing powers was almost nonexistent until thrown together as allies in a common cause to defeat Germany and Japan in World War II.

It was during the meetings of the allied leaders in Yalta and Potsdam in 1945 when peaceful postwar cooperation was being sought that the collision course of the two new superpowers started becoming more evident. The end of World War II had brought the U.S. and Soviet armies face-to-face in central Europe in victory over the Germans. Yet the old mistrusts between communists and capitalists quickly dominated diplomatic relations. Capitalism is an economic system in which property and businesses are privately owned. Prices, production, and distribution of goods are determined by competition in a market relatively free of government intervention. A peace treaty ending World War II in Europe was blocked as the Soviets and the U.S.-led West carved out spheres of influence. Western Europe and Great Britain aligned with the United States and collectively was referred to as the "West"; Eastern Europe would be controlled by the Soviet Communist Party. The Soviet Union and its Eastern European satellite countries were collectively referred to as the "East." The two powers tested the resolve of each other in Germany, Iran, Turkey, and Greece in the late 1940s.

In 1949, the Soviets successfully tested an atomic bomb and Chinese communist forces overthrew the National Chinese government, and U.S. officials and American citizens feared a sweeping massive communist movement was overtaking the world. A "red scare" spread through America. The term "red" referred to communists, especially the Soviets. The public began to suspect that communists or communist sympathizers lurked in every corner of the nation.

Meanwhile, the superpower confrontations spread from Europe to other global areas: Asia, Africa, the Middle East, and Latin America. Most dramatic were the Korean and Vietnam wars, the Cuban Missile Crisis, and the military standoffs in Berlin, Germany. However, bloody conflicts erupted in many other areas as the United States and Soviet Union sought to expand their influence by supporting or opposing various movements.

In addition, a costly arms race lasted decades despite sporadic efforts at arms control agreements. The score card for the Cold War was kept in terms of how many nuclear weapons one country had aimed at the other. Finally, in the 1970s and 1980s, the Soviet Union could no longer keep up with the changing world economic trends. Its tightly controlled and highly inefficient industrial and agricultural systems could not compete in world markets while the government was still focusing its wealth on Cold War confrontations and the arms race. Developments in telecommunications also made it more difficult to maintain a closed society. Ideas were increasingly being exchanged despite longstanding political barriers. The door was finally cracked open in the communist European nations to more freedoms in the late 1980s through efforts at economic and social reform. Seizing the moment, the long suppressed populations of communist Eastern European nations and fifteen Soviet republics demanded political and economic freedom.

Through 1989, the various Eastern European nations replaced long-time communist leaders with noncommunist officials. By the end of 1991, the Soviet Communist Party had been banned from various Soviet republics, and the Soviet Union itself ceased to exist. After a decades-long rivalry, the end to the Cold War came swiftly and unexpectedly.

A new world order dawned in 1992 with a single superpower, the United States, and a vastly changed political landscape around much of the globe. Communism remained in China and Cuba, but Cold War legacies remained elsewhere. In the early 1990s, the United States was economically burdened with a massive national debt, the former Soviet republics were attempting a very difficult economic transition to a more capitalistic open market system, and Europe, starkly divided by the Cold War, was reunited once again and sought to establish a new union including both Eastern and Western European nations.

Reader's Guide

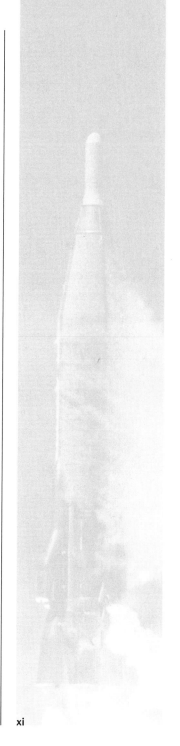

C*old War: Almanac* presents a comprehensive overview of the Cold War, the period in history from 1945 until 1991 that was dominated by the rivalry between the world's superpowers, the United States and the Soviet Union. The *Almanac* covers the origins of the Cold War, including the fierce divisions created by the differences between American democracy and capitalism and Soviet communism; the key programs and treaties, such as the Marshall Plan, Berlin Airlift, and Strategic Defense Initiative (SDI); how the general public coped with the rivalry and consequent nuclear buildup; government changes designed to make society feel more secure; the end of the Cold War, brought about by the fall of communism in Eastern Europe and the dissolution of the Soviet Union; and the aftereffects of the Cold War, still felt in the twenty-first century.

Coverage and features

Cold War: Almanac is divided into fifteen chapters, each focusing on a particular topic or time period, such as the origins of the Cold War, the beginning of the nuclear age, the arms race, espionage, anticommunist campaigns and political purges on the home fronts, détente, the Cuban Missile Crisis, the Berlin Airlift and the Berlin Wall, the Korean and Vietnam wars, and the ending of the Cold War. Each chapter contains three types of sidebars: "Words to Know" and "People to Know" boxes, which define important terms and individuals discussed in the chapter; and boxes that describe people, events, and facts of special interest. Each chapter concludes with a list of additional sources students can go to for more information. More than 140 black-and-white photographs and maps help illustrate the material.

Each volume of *Cold War: Almanac* begins with a timeline of important events in the history of the Cold War; "Words to Know" and "People to Know" sections that feature important terms and people from the entire Cold War era; and a "Research and Activity Ideas" section with suggestions for study questions, group projects, and oral and dramatic presentations. The two volumes conclude with a general bibliography and a subject index so students can easily find the people, places, and events discussed throughout *Cold War: Almanac*.

U•X•L Cold War Reference Library

Cold War: Almanac is only one component of the three-part U•X•L Cold War Reference Library. The other two titles in this set are:

- *Cold War: Biographies* (two volumes) presents the life stories of fifty individuals who played key roles in the Cold War superpower rivalry. Though primarily a competition between the United States and the Soviet Union, the Cold War is a story of individual personalities that critically influenced the direction of the rivalry at various crossroads and in different regions of the world. Profiled are well-known figures such as Joseph Stalin, Harry Truman, Nikita Khrushchev, Henry Kissinger, John F. Kennedy, Mao Zedong, and Mikhail Gorbachev, as well as lesser-known individuals such as physicist and father of the Soviet atomic bomb Igor Kurchatov, British foreign minister Ernest Bevin, and longtime U.S. foreign policy analyst George F. Kennan.

- *Cold War: Primary Sources* (one volume) this book tells the story of the Cold War in the words of the people who lived and shaped it. Thirty-one excerpted documents provide a wide range of perspectives on this period of history. Included are excerpts from presidential press conferences; addresses to U.S. Congress and Soviet Communist Party meetings; public speeches; telegrams; magazine articles; radio and television addresses; and later reflections by key government leaders.

• A cumulative index of all three titles in the U•X•L Cold War Reference Library is also available.

Acknowledgments

Special thanks to Catherine Filip, who typed much of the manuscript. Much appreciation also goes to copyeditor Jane Woychick, proofreader Wyn Hilty, indexer Dan Brannen, and typesetter Marco Di Vita of the Graphix Group for their fine work.

Dedication

To Aaron and Kara Hanes, that their children may learn about the events and ideas that shaped the world through the latter half of the twentieth century.

Comments and suggestions

We welcome your comments on *Cold War: Almanac* and suggestions for other topics to consider. Please write: Editors, *Cold War: Almanac,* U•X•L, 27500 Drake Rd., Farmington Hills, Michigan 48331-3535; call toll free: 1-800-877-4253; fax to 248-699-8097; or send e-mail via http://www.gale.com.

Words to Know

A

Alliance for Progress: A program designed to block the spread of communism by improving the overall quality of life for Latin Americans. The Alliance attempted to reduce disease, increase literacy, and ease poverty throughout Latin America.

Allied Control Council: An organization of military governors from each of the four zones of Germany.

Allies: Alliances of countries in military opposition to another group of nations. In World War II, the Allied powers included Great Britain, the United States, and the Soviet Union.

Annihilation: Complete destruction.

Armistice: A temporary agreement to end fighting in a war; a cease-fire.

Arms race: A key aspect of superpower rivalry in which one superpower amasses weapons, particularly nuclear weapons, to keep up with another superpower or to gain an edge.

Asymmetrical response: The potentially much harsher retaliation of a nation already attacked.

Atomic bomb: An explosive device that releases nuclear energy (energy that comes from an atom's core). All previous explosive devices were powered by rapid burning or decomposition of a chemical compound; they only released energy from the outermost electrons of an atom. Nuclear explosives are energized by splitting an atom, a process called fission.

Atomic Energy Commission (AEC): A unit established by Congress in July 1946 that managed the nuclear research facilities in Oak Ridge, Tennessee; Hanford, Washington; and Los Alamos, New Mexico.

Authoritarian: A political system in which authority is centered in a ruling party that demands complete obedience of its citizens and is not legally accountable to the people.

B

Bay of Pigs: The failed U.S.-backed invasion of Cuba at the Bay of Pigs by fifteen hundred Cuban exiles opposed to Fidel Castro, on April 17, 1961.

Berlin airlift: Massive shipments of food and goods, airlifted into the Western sector of Berlin, organized by the Western powers, after the Soviets halted all shipments of supplies and food from the eastern zone into West Berlin. The Americans nicknamed the airlift Operation Vittles, while the British dubbed the effort Operation Plain Fare.

Berlin blockade: A ten-and-a-half-month stoppage by the Soviets of shipments of supplies and food through East Germany into West Berlin. The Soviets also cut all coal-generated electricity supplied from East Germany to Berlin's western sectors, and land and water routes from West Germany into Berlin were closed.

Berlin Wall: A wall dividing the Soviet-controlled sector of Berlin from the three Western-controlled zones, built in an attempt to stem the tide of refugees seeking asylum in the West.

Big Three: The trio of U.S. president Franklin D. Roosevelt, British prime minister Winston Churchill, and Soviet leader Joseph Stalin; also refers to the countries of the United States, Great Britain, and the Soviet Union.

Blacklisting: Denying employment to anyone found connected to a group that in any way had anything to do with subversive activities, real or imagined.

Bolshevik: A member of the revolutionary political party of Russian workers and peasants that became the Communist Party after the Russian Revolution of 1917; the terms Bolshevik and communist became interchangeable, with communist eventually becoming more common.

Brinkmanship: An increased reliance on nuclear weapons as a deterrent to threats of communist expansion in the world; an international game played between the Soviet Union and the United States of who had the highest number of and the most powerful weapons with which to threaten the enemy.

Bugs: Listening devices planted in such places as telephones and in walls to allow eavesdropping on conversations.

C

Capitalism: An economic system in which property and businesses are privately owned. Prices, production, and distribution of goods are determined by competition in a market relatively free of government intervention.

Central committee: The important administrative body in the Communist Party overseeing day-to-day party activities.

Cold War: A prolonged conflict for world dominance from 1945 to 1991 between the two superpowers—the democratic, capitalist United States and the communist Soviet Union. The weapons of conflict were commonly words of propaganda and threats.

Collectivism: A system that combines many local holdings, such as farms or industry, into a single unit that is supervised by the government.

Colonialism: An economic system in which Western European nations controlled various underdeveloped countries located around the world.

Communism: A system of government in which the nation's leaders are selected by a single political party that controls all aspects of society. Private ownership of property is eliminated and government directs all economic production. The goods produced and accumulated wealth are, in theory, shared relatively equally by all. All religious practices are banned.

Containment: A key U.S. Cold War policy to restrict the territorial growth of communist rule.

Counterculture: A rebellion of Americans, mostly youth, against the established U.S. social values largely spawned by opposition to the Vietnam War.

Counterinsurgency: A military strategy to fight guerilla forces rising against established governments.

Coup d'état: The violent and forceful act of changing a government's leadership.

Covert: Secret.

Cryptosystems: Secret code systems that protect countries' communications; also called cipher; a cryptonologist "deciphered" the secret codes.

Cuban Missile Crisis: A showdown in October 1962 that brought the Soviet Union and the United States close to war over the existence of Soviet nuclear missiles in Cuba.

D

Decolonization: When a country's people subjected to rule by a foreign power seek to overturn that rule and gain national independence.

Deficit spending: When a government spends more money than the revenue coming in; a key feature of the Cold War arms race with high military expenses.

Democracy: A system of government that allows multiple political parties. Their members are elected to various government offices by popular vote of the people.

Destalinization: Soviet leader Nikita Khrushchev's effort to introduce social reforms to the Soviet Union by providing greater personal freedoms, lessening the powers of the secret police, closing concentration and hard-labor camps, and restoring certain legal processes.

Détente: A lessening of tensions between nations.

Deterrence: An attempt to discourage another nation from initiating hostile activity by threatening severe retaliation such as nuclear war.

Dictatorship: A form of government in which a person wields absolute power and control over the people.

Disarmament: The reduction of weapons and armed forces of a nation.

Dissidents: Those who actively disagree with the ruling authority.

Doctrine: A particular idea or policy embraced by a state or group.

Domino theory: The belief that if one country falls to communism then nearby nations will be taken over one after another.

E

Eisenhower Doctrine: A doctrine giving the U.S. president the right to use force in the Middle East against any form of communist aggression.

Espionage: The act of spying on others to discover military or political secrets.

Expansionism: The policy of a nation to gain more territory by taking over control of other countries.

F

Fascism: A dictatorship based on strong nationalism and often racism.

Fifth Amendment: An amendment to the U.S. Constitution that protects people from having to testify against themselves in formal hearings.

Fission: A process in which the nucleus of an atom of a heavy element is split into two nuclei, resulting in lighter elements releasing a substantial amount of energy; the process utilized in atomic bombs such as that dropped on Hiroshima, Japan, in 1945.

Flexible response: The military strategy to maintain both sufficient conventional and nuclear weapons so that hostile actions by another nation may be met with a similar level of force.

Fusion: The joining together of atomic nuclei of the element hydrogen, generating an incredible amount of heat; the process utilized in hydrogen bombs.

G

Glasnost: A plan for greater freedom of expression put into place by Soviet president Mikhail Gorbachev in the mid-1980s.

H

Hollywood Ten: Ten producers, directors, and screenwriters from Hollywood who were called before the House Un-American Activities Committee (HUAC) to explain their politics and reveal what organizations they were part of. Eight of the ten had communist affiliations.

House Un-American Activities Committee (HUAC): A congressional group established to investigate and root out any communist influences within the United States.

Human rights: A broad notion that all people, simply by being human, deserve certain economic and political freedoms of opportunity such as freedom from various kinds of deprivations including freedom from oppression, unlawful imprisonment and execution, torture, persecution, and exploitation.

Hydrogen bomb: A bomb more powerful than the atomic bomb that derives its explosive energy from a nuclear fusion reaction.

I

Ideology: A body of beliefs.

Imperialism: A policy of expanding the rule of one nation over foreign countries.

Industrialization: A large-scale introduction of industry into an area, normally replacing agriculture to some degree.

Intercontinental ballistic missile: A missile that has a range of over 3,500 nautical miles.

Intermediate-range ballistic missile: A missile that has a range of between 800 and 1,500 nautical miles.

Internationalist: A person who promotes cooperation among nations.

Isolationism: A policy of avoiding official agreements with other nations in order to remain neutral.

J

Junta: A group of military leaders in political control.

K

Kiloton: Approximately equal to the amount of explosive force (energy released) of 1,000 tons of TNT, a conventional (non-nuclear) explosive.

Korean War (1950–53): A conflict that began when North Korean communist troops crossed the thirty-eighth parallel into South Korea.

L

Land reform: A common feature of nationalist movements that often involves taking away large land holdings owned by foreigners and parceling them out to its citizens for small farming operations.

M

Manhattan Project: A project begun in 1942—during World War II (1939–45)—with the goal of building an atomic weapon before scientists in Germany or Japan did.

Marketplace: The world of commerce operating relatively free of government interventions where demand and availability of goods and materials determine prices, distribution, and production levels.

Marshall Plan: A massive U.S. plan to promote Europe's economic recovery from the war; officially known as the European Recovery Program for Western Europe, it was made available to all nations, though the communist regime rejected it.

McCarthyism: A term used to describe a person who makes accusations of disloyalty supported by doubtful evidence; it originated during the 1950s anticommunism campaign of U.S. senator Joseph R. McCarthy of Wisconsin.

Megaton: Approximately equals the explosive force of 1,000,000 tons of TNT.

Military industrial complex: A politically powerful alliance of the military services and industry that provides materials to the military.

Moles: Spies who betray the agency they worked for by quietly funneling top secret information to the enemy.

Molotov Plan: A Soviet series of trade agreements—made after the rejection of the Marshall Plan—designed to provide economic assistance to eastern European countries.

Most-favored-nation status: An economic and political program that lowers taxes on goods exported by a foreign nation to the United States, making it much easier to sell goods to the U.S. public and businesses.

Mutual assured destruction (MAD): A military strategy in which the threat of catastrophic damages by a nuclear counterstrike would deter any launch of a first-strike attack.

N

Nation building: Installing friendly governments wherever feasible around the world by the United States and the Soviet Union.

National Security Act: An act that created the National Security Council, which advises the president on national security policy.

National Security Agency (NSA): The United States' prime intelligence organization that listens to and analyzes foreign communications.

National Security Council Document 68, or NSC-68: A plan for keeping Soviet influence contained within its existing areas; the strategy required dramatic increases in U.S. military spending.

Nationalism: A strong loyalty to one's own nation and the quest to be independent from other nations.

Nationalize: To place land or industry under ownership of the state.

Ninjas: Highly skilled spies who can move in and out of buildings without keys, find entrance into forbidden places, or easily slip in and out of personal relationships.

Nonproliferation: The halt of the spread of nuclear weapons to previously non-nuclear countries.

Normalization: Improved relations between two countries to more usual diplomatic conditions.

North Atlantic Treaty Organization (NATO): A peacetime alliance of the United States and eleven other nations, and a key factor in the attempt to contain communism; the pact meant that the United States became the undisputed global military leader.

O

Overt: Open; not secret.

P

Parity: The act of maintaining an equal amount of something, such as similar levels of nuclear weapons between the two superpowers.

Peace Corps: A U.S. program designed to promote world peace and friendship by having citizens travel abroad and assist developing nations.

Peaceful coexistence: A state of living peacefully and accepting other ideologies that widely differ; with regard to military competition, the United States and the Soviet Union sought to coexist peacefully.

Perestroika: A 1980s Soviet plan for recovery by restructuring the Soviet Union's economic and social systems.

Philosophies: Certain principles or bodies of knowledge that are followed by a group.

Plutonium: A radioactive element capable of explosive fission.

Politburo: The important policy making body of the Communist Party.

Prague Spring: A brief thaw in Cold War communist policies when in 1968 Czechoslovakia's Communist Party leader, Alexander Dubcek, sought to modernize communism with certain democratic reforms, including greater freedom of the press.

Propaganda: The spread of information or ideas to promote a certain organization or cause.

Purge: To remove undesirable persons from a group, such as mass executions of Communist Party members by Soviet leadership.

R

Red scare: A great fear among U.S. citizens in the late 1940s and early 1950s that communist influences were infiltrating U.S. society and government and could eventually lead to the overthrow of the American democratic system.

Reparations: Payments made by a defeated nation for war damages it inflicted on the winning nations.

Resistance movement: Underground forces within a nation organized to defeat an occupying force.

Revolutionaries: Those seeking change by forceful overthrow of the existing government.

S

Sabotage: An illegal interference of work or industrial production such as by enemy agents or employees.

Satellite: A country under domination by another; also, a man-made object that is launched into orbit around Earth.

Second strike capability: A military strategy in which a sufficiently large nuclear arsenal would ensure enough U.S. missiles would survive a Soviet first strike to effectively destroy the Soviet Union in an automatic second strike.

Silent majority: The segment of society in the 1970s that quietly supported the nation's war efforts in Vietnam as opposed to the more visible anti-war protesters.

Southeast Asia Treaty Organization (SEATO): An alliance of nations created to combat the expansion of communism in the Southeast Asian region, specifically Vietnam, Cambodia, and Laos. Member nations included the United States, Great Britain, France, New Zealand, Thailand, Australia, Pakistan, and the Philippines.

Space race: A key feature of the Cold War rivalry between the two superpowers in their quest to gain dominance in space technology and achievements.

Sphere of influence: An area over which a nation holds domination over other nations, such as the United States and Soviet Union during the Cold War holding influence over major areas of the world.

Strategic Air Command (SAC): A unit established by the U.S. military with the goal of identifying targets in the Soviet Union and being ready to deliver nuclear weapons to those targets.

Strategic arms: Military weapons key to the strategy of making the enemy incapable of conducting war; generally refers to long-ranging weapons.

Strategic Triad: The United States' trio of weapons aimed at the Soviet Union; the arsenal consisted of long- and intermediate-range missiles fitted with nuclear warheads, long-range bombers carrying nuclear weapons, and nuclear-powered submarines with onboard nuclear-tipped missiles.

Subversive: An individual who attempts to overthrow or destroy an established political system.

Superpowers: Nations capable of influencing the acts or policies of other nations; during the Cold War, the United States and Soviet Union were considered the superpowers.

T

Tactical arms: Military weapons that allow flexibility and skillful maneuverability in combat; generally referring to short-range weapons.

Thermonuclear: A nuclear fusion reaction releasing tremendous heat and energy as utilized in the hydrogen bomb.

Third World: Poor underdeveloped or economically developing nations in Africa, Asia, and Latin America. Many were seeking independence from political control of Western European nations.

Totalitarianism: A highly centralized form of government that has total control over the population.

Tradecraft: The tricks and techniques used by spies in their covert, or secret, operations.

Treaty: A formal agreement between two nations relating to peace or trade.

Truman Doctrine: A Cold War–era program designed by President Harry S. Truman that sent aid to anticommunist forces in Turkey and Greece. The Soviet Union had naval stations in Turkey, and nearby Greece was fighting a civil war with communist-dominated rebels.

U

United Nations: An international organization, comprised of most of the nations of the world, created to preserve world peace and security.

Uranium: A metallic natural element used primarily in atomic bombs and in nuclear power plants.

V

Vietcong: Vietnamese communists engaged in warfare against the government and people of South Vietnam.

W

Warsaw Pact: A mutual military alliance between the Soviet Union and the Eastern European nations under Soviet influence, including East Germany.

Y

Yalta Conference: A 1944 meeting between Allied leaders Joseph Stalin, Winston Churchill, and Franklin D. Roosevelt in anticipation of an Allied victory in Europe over Adolf Hitler and Germany's Nazi Party. The leaders discussed how to manage lands conquered by Germany, and Roosevelt and Churchill urged Stalin to enter the Soviet Union in the war against Japan.

People to Know

A

Jacobo Arbenz Guzmán (1913–1971): Guatemalan president, 1950–54.

Clement R. Attlee (1883–1967): British prime minister, 1945–51.

B

Fulgencio Batista y Zaldívar (1901–1973): Cuban dictatorial leader, 1933–44, 1952–59.

Lavrenty Beria (1899–1953): Leader of the Soviet secret police (KGB) and manager of the Soviet bomb project.

Anthony F. Blunt (1907–1983): One of the KGB's famed Cambridge Spies.

Willy Brandt (1913–1992): West German chancellor, 1969–74.

Leonid Brezhnev (1906–1982): Leader of the Soviet Union Communist Party, 1964–82.

Zbigniew Brzezinski (1928–): U.S. national security advisor, 1977–81.

Guy Burgess (1910–1963): One of the KGB's famed Cambridge Spies.

George Bush (1924–): Forty-first U.S. president, 1989–93.

James F. Byrnes (1879–1972): U.S. secretary of state, 1945–47.

C

Jimmy Carter (1924–): Thirty-ninth U.S. president, 1977–81.

Carlos Castillo Armas (1914–1957): Guatemalan president, 1954–57.

Fidel Castro (1926–): Cuban premier/president, 1959–.

Whittaker Chambers (1901–1961): A journalist who admitted at the House Un-American Activities Committee (HUAC) hearings that he had once been a communist but had later denounced communism; he named Alger Hiss as a communist.

Chiang Kai-shek (1887–1975): Ruler of China's Nationalist (Kuomintang) party, 1943–49.

Winston Churchill (1874–1965): British prime minister, 1940–45, 1951–55.

D

Charles de Gaulle (1890–1970): French president, 1958–69.

Deng Xiaoping (1905–1997): Leader of Communist China, 1976–90.

Martin Dies (1900–1972): U.S. representative from Texas, 1931–44, 1953–58; chairman of the House Un-American Activities Committee (HUAC), often called the Dies Committee.

Anatoly Dobrynin (1919–): Soviet ambassador to the United States, 1962–86.

Alexander Dubcek (1921–1992): Czechoslovakian Communist Party leader, 1968.

John Foster Dulles (1888–1959): U.S. secretary of state, 1953–59.

E

Dwight D. Eisenhower (1890–1969): Thirty-fourth U.S. president, 1953–61.

F

Gerald R. Ford (1913–): Thirty-eighth U.S. president, 1974–77.

Klaus Fuchs (1911–1988): British scientist who worked on the U.S. Manhattan Project and began passing detailed notes to the Soviets about the work being done on the development of a nuclear bomb.

G

Mikhail Gorbachev (1931–): Soviet president, 1985–91.

Andrey Gromyko (1909–1989): Soviet foreign minister, 1957–85.

Leslie R. Groves (1896–1970): U.S. Army officer in charge of the Manhattan Project.

H

Alger Hiss (1904–1996): U.S. State Department official who was accused of being a communist; he served three years and eight months in prison after being convicted of perjury.

Adolf Hitler (1889–1945): Nazi party president, 1921–45; German leader, 1933–45.

J

Lyndon B. Johnson (1908–1973): Thirty-sixth U.S. president, 1963–69.

K

John F. Kennedy (1917–1963): Thirty-fifth U.S. president, 1961–63.

Robert F. Kennedy (1925–1968): U.S. attorney general, 1961–64.

Nikita Khrushchev (1894–1971): Soviet premier, 1958–64.

Martin Luther King Jr. (1929–1968): African American civil rights leader.

Henry Kissinger (1923–): U.S. national security advisor, 1969–75; secretary of state, 1973–77.

Igor Kurchatov (1903–1960): The Soviet Union's premier nuclear physicist who led the building of the Soviet's atomic bomb in 1948.

L

Vladimir I. Lenin (1870–1924): Leader of the Bolshevik Revolution, 1917; head of the Soviet government, 1918–24; founder of the Communist Party in Russia, 1919.

Patrice Lumumba (1925–1961): Congolese nationalist movement activist; prime minister, 1960.

M

Douglas MacArthur (1880–1964): Supreme commander of occupational forces in Japan, 1945–51, and UN forces in Korea, 1950–51.

Donald Maclean (1913–1983): One of the KGB's famed Cambridge Spies.

Georgy M. Malenkov (1902–1988): Soviet premier, 1953–55.

Mao Zedong (1893–1976): Chairman of the People's Republic of China and its Communist party, 1949–76.

George C. Marshall (1880–1959): U.S. secretary of state, 1947–49; secretary of defense, 1950–51.

Joseph R. McCarthy (1908–1957): U.S. senator from Wisconsin, 1947–57; for four years, he sought to expose American communists by manipulating the public's fear of communism and by making false accusations and claims that a massive communist conspiracy threatened to take over the country.

Mohammad Mosaddeq (1880–1967): Iranian premier, 1951–53.

N

Gamal Abdel Nasser (1918–1970): Egyptian president, 1958–70.

Ngo Dinh Diem (1901–1963): Republic of Vietnam president, 1954–63.

Richard M. Nixon (1913–1994): Republican congressman from California, 1947–50; member of the House Un-American Activities Committee (HUAC), and closely involved with the investigation of accused communist Alger Hiss; U.S. senator from California, 1950–53; vice president, 1953–61; and thirty-seventh U.S. president, 1969–74.

O

J. Robert Oppenheimer (1904–1967): A theoretical physicist who led the building of the U.S. atomic bomb during World War II.

P

Kim Philby (1911–1988): One of the KGB's famed Cambridge Spies.

R

Ronald Reagan (1911–): Fortieth U.S. president, 1981–89.

Franklin D. Roosevelt (1882–1945): Thirty-second U.S. president, 1933–45.

S

Eduard Shevardnadze (1928–): Soviet foreign minister, 1985–90.

Joseph Stalin (1879–1953): Dictatorial Russian/Soviet leader, 1924–53.

T

Harry S. Truman (1884–1972): Thirty-third U.S. president, 1945–53.

U

Walter Ulbricht (1893–1973): Head of the East German government, 1949–71.

V

Cyrus Vance (1917–2001): U.S. secretary of state, 1977–80.

Y

Boris Yeltsin (1931–): Russian president, 1989–99.

Cold War Timeline

September 1, 1939 Germany invades Poland, beginning World War II.

June 30, 1941 Germany invades the Soviet Union, drawing the Soviets into World War II.

December 7, 1941 Japan launches a surprise air attack on U.S. military installations at Pearl Harbor, Hawaii, drawing the United States into World War II.

November 1943 U.S. president Franklin D. Roosevelt, British prime minister Winston Churchill, and Soviet premier Joseph Stalin meet in Tehran, Iran, to discuss war strategies against Germany and Italy.

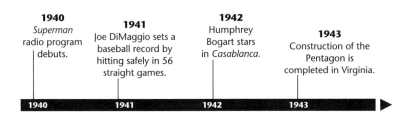

1940
Superman radio program debuts.

1941
Joe DiMaggio sets a baseball record by hitting safely in 56 straight games.

1942
Humphrey Bogart stars in *Casablanca.*

1943
Construction of the Pentagon is completed in Virginia.

1940   1941   1942   1943

August-October 1944 An international conference held at Dumbarton Oaks in Washington, D.C., creates the beginning of the United Nations.

February 1945 The Yalta Conference is held in the Crimean region of the Soviet Union among the three key allied leaders, U.S. president Franklin D. Roosevelt, British prime minister Winston Churchill, and Soviet premier Joseph Stalin to discuss German surrender terms, a Soviet attack against Japanese forces, and the future of Eastern Europe.

April-June 1945 Fifty nations meet in San Francisco to write the UN charter.

May 7, 1945 Germany surrenders to allied forces, leaving Germany and its capital of Berlin divided into four military occupation zones with American, British, French, and Soviet forces.

July 16, 1945 The first successful U.S. atomic bomb test occurs in Alamogardo, New Mexico.

July-August 1945 U.S. president Harry S. Truman, Soviet premier Joseph Stalin, and British prime minister Winston Churchill meet in Potsdam, Germany, to discuss postwar conditions of Germany.

August 14, 1945 Japan surrenders, ending World War II, after the United States drops two atomic bombs on the cities of Hiroshima and Nagasaki.

December 2, 1946 The United States, Great Britain, and France merge their German occupation zones to create what would become West Germany.

March 12, 1947 U.S. president Harry S. Truman announces the Truman Doctrine, which says the United States

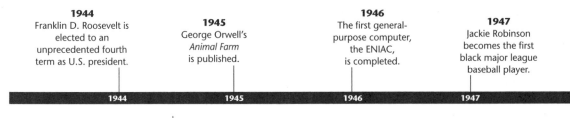

1944
Franklin D. Roosevelt is elected to an unprecedented fourth term as U.S. president.

1945
George Orwell's *Animal Farm* is published.

1946
The first general-purpose computer, the ENIAC, is completed.

1947
Jackie Robinson becomes the first black major league baseball player.

1944   1945   1946   1947

will assist any nation in the world being threatened by communist expansion.

June 5, 1947 U.S. secretary of state George C. Marshall announces the Marshall Plan, an ambitious economic aid program to rebuild Western Europe from World War II destruction.

July 26, 1947 Congress passes the National Security Act, creating the Central Intelligence Agency (CIA) and the National Security Council (NSC).

October 23, 1947 Actor Ronald Reagan testifies before the House Un-American Activities Committee (HUAC), a Congressional group established to investigate and root out any communist influences within the United States.

December 5, 1947 The Soviets establish the Communist Information Bureau (Cominform) to promote the expansion of communism in the world.

February 25, 1948 A communist coup in Czechoslovakia topples the last remaining democratic government in Eastern Europe.

March 14, 1948 Israel announces its independence as a new state in the Middle East.

June 24, 1948 The Soviets begin a blockade of Berlin, leading to a massive airlift of daily supplies by the Western powers for the next eleven months.

April 4, 1949 The North Atlantic Treaty Organization (NATO), a military alliance involving Western Europe and the United States, comes into existence.

May 5, 1949 The West Germans establish the Federal Republic of Germany government.

1947
Tennessee Williams's *A Streetcar Named Desire* opens on Broadway.

1948
The Baskin-Robbins ice cream chain opens.

1949
The first Emmy Awards ceremony is held.

1947   1948   1949

May 12, 1949 The Soviet blockade of access routes to West Berlin is lifted.

May 30, 1949 Soviet-controlled East Germany establishes the German Democratic Republic.

August 29, 1949 The Soviet Union conducts its first atomic bomb test.

October 1, 1949 Communist forces under Mao Zedong gain victory in the Chinese civil war, and the People's Republic of China (PRC) is established, with Zhou Enlai as its leader.

January 1950 Former State Department employee Alger Hiss is convicted of perjury but not of spy charges.

February 3, 1950 Klaus Fuchs is convicted of passing U.S. atomic secrets to the Soviets.

March 1, 1950 Chiang Kai-shek, former leader of nationalist China, which was defeated by communist forces, establishes the Republic of China (ROC) on the island of Taiwan.

April 7, 1950 U.S. security analyst Paul Nitze issues the secret National Security Council report 68 (NSC-68), calling for a dramatic buildup of U.S. military forces to combat the Soviet threat.

June 25, 1950 Forces of communist North Korea invade pro-U.S. South Korea, starting the Korean War.

October 24, 1950 U.S. forces push the North Korean army back to the border with China, sparking a Chinese invasion one week later and forcing the United States into a hasty retreat.

June 21, 1951 The Korean War reaches a military stalemate at the original boundary between North and South Korea.

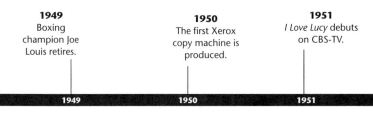

1949
Boxing champion Joe Louis retires.

1950
The first Xerox copy machine is produced.

1951
I Love Lucy debuts on CBS-TV.

1949   1950   1951

September 1, 1951 The United States, Australia, and New Zealand sign the ANZUS treaty, creating a military alliance to contain communism in the Southwest Pacific region.

October 3, 1952 Great Britain conducts its first atomic weapons test.

November 1, 1952 The United States tests the hydrogen bomb on the Marshall Islands in the Pacific Ocean.

March 5, 1953 After leading the Soviet Union for thirty years, Joseph Stalin dies of a stroke; Georgy Malenkov becomes the new Soviet leader.

June 27, 1953 An armistice is signed, bringing a cease-fire to the Korean War.

August 12, 1953 The Soviet Union announces its first hydrogen bomb test.

May 7, 1954 Vietminh communist forces defeat the French at Dien Bien Phu, leading to a U.S. commitment to containing communist expansion in Vietnam.

September 8, 1954 The Southeast Asia Treaty Organization (SEATO) is formed.

February 8, 1955 Nikolai Bulganin replaces Georgy Malenkov as Soviet premier.

May 14, 1955 The Warsaw Pact, a military alliance of Soviet-controlled Eastern European nations, is established; the countries include Albania, Bulgaria, Czechoslovakia, East Germany, Hungary, Poland, and Romania.

October 31, 1956 British, French, and Israeli forces attack Egypt to regain control of the Suez Canal.

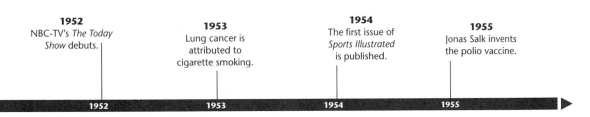

1952
NBC-TV's *The Today Show* debuts.

1953
Lung cancer is attributed to cigarette smoking.

1954
The first issue of *Sports Illustrated* is published.

1955
Jonas Salk invents the polio vaccine.

1952   1953   1954   1955

November 1, 1956 In Hungary, the Soviets crush an uprising against strict communist rule, killing many protestors.

March 7, 1957 The Eisenhower Doctrine, offering U.S. assistance to Middle East countries facing communist expansion threats, is approved by Congress.

October 5, 1957 Shocking the world with their new technology, the Soviets launch into space *Sputnik,* the first man-made satellite.

November 10, 1958 Soviet leader Nikita Khrushchev issues an ultimatum to the West to pull out of Berlin, but later backs down.

September 17, 1959 Soviet leader Nikita Khrushchev arrives in the United States to tour the country and meet with U.S. president Dwight D. Eisenhower.

May 1, 1960 The Soviets shoot down over Russia a U.S. spy plane piloted by Francis Gary Powers, leading to the cancellation of a planned summit meeting in Paris between Soviet leader Nikita Khrushchev and U.S. president Dwight D. Eisenhower.

April 15, 1961 A U.S.-supported army of Cuban exiles launches an ill-fated invasion of Cuba, leading to U.S. humiliation in the world.

June 3, 1961 U.S. president John F. Kennedy meets with Soviet leader Nikita Khrushchev at a Vienna summit meeting to discuss the arms race and Berlin; Kennedy comes away shaken by Khrushchev's belligerence.

August 15, 1961 Under orders from Soviet leader Nikita Khrushchev, the Berlin Wall is constructed stopping the flight of refugees from East Germany to West Berlin.

1957
West Side Story opens on Broadway.

1959
Alaska and Hawaii become the 49th and 50th U.S states.

1961
Soviet cosmonaut Yuri Gagarin becomes the first man to orbit Earth.

1962
Jim Beatty becomes the first person to run the mile in less than four minutes.

1956   1958   1960   1962

October 1962 The Cuban Missile Crisis occurs as the United States demands that the Soviets remove nuclear missiles from the island.

January 1, 1963 Chinese communist leaders denounce Soviet leader Nikita Khrushchev's policies of peaceful coexistence with the West; the Soviets respond by denouncing the Chinese Communist Party.

August 5, 1963 The first arms control agreement, the Limited Test Ban Treaty, banning above-ground nuclear testing, is reached between the United States, Soviet Union, and Great Britain.

August 7, 1964 U.S. Congress passes the Gulf of Tonkin Resolution, authorizing U.S. president Lyndon B. Johnson to conduct whatever military operations he thinks appropriate in Southeast Asia.

October 16, 1964 China conducts its first nuclear weapons test.

March 8, 1965 The first U.S. ground combat units arrive in South Vietnam.

June 23, 1967 U.S. president Lyndon B. Johnson and Soviet prime minister Aleksey Kosygin meet in Glassboro, New Jersey, to discuss a peace settlement to the Vietnam War.

January 30, 1968 The communist Vietcong forces launch the Tet Offensive, convincing the American public that the Vietnam War is not winnable.

July 15, 1968 Soviet leader Leonid Brezhnev announces the Brezhnev Doctrine, which authorizes the use of force where necessary to ensure maintenance of communist governments in Eastern European nations.

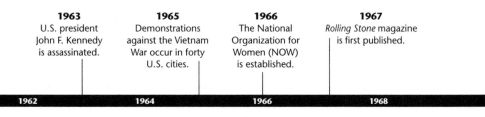

1963
U.S. president
John F. Kennedy
is assassinated.

1965
Demonstrations
against the Vietnam
War occur in forty
U.S. cities.

1966
The National
Organization for
Women (NOW)
is established.

1967
Rolling Stone magazine
is first published.

1962   1964   1966   1968

August 20, 1968 The Warsaw Pact forces a crackdown on a Czechoslovakia reform movement known as the "Prague Spring."

August 27, 1968 Antiwar riots rage in Chicago's streets outside the Democratic National Convention.

March 18, 1969 The United States begins secret bombing of Cambodia to destroy North Vietnamese supply lines.

July 20, 1969 The United States lands the first men on the moon.

April 16, 1970 Strategic arms limitation talks, SALT, begin.

April 30, 1970 U.S. president Richard Nixon announces an invasion by U.S. forces of Cambodia to destroy North Vietnamese supply camps.

May 4, 1970 Four students are killed at Kent State University as Ohio National Guardsmen open fire on antiwar demonstrators.

October 25, 1971 The People's Republic of China (PRC) is admitted to the United Nations as the Republic of China (ROC) is expelled.

February 20, 1972 U.S. president Richard Nixon makes an historic trip to the People's Republic of China to discuss renewing relations between the two countries.

May 26, 1972 U.S. president Richard Nixon travels to Moscow to meet with Soviet leader Leonid Brezhnev to reach an agreement on the strategic arms limitation treaty, SALT I.

January 27, 1973 After intensive bombing of North Vietnamese cities the previous month, the United States and North Vietnam sign a peace treaty, ending U.S. involvement in Vietnam.

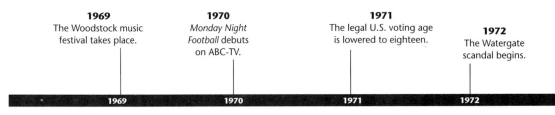

1969 The Woodstock music festival takes place.

1970 *Monday Night Football* debuts on ABC-TV.

1971 The legal U.S. voting age is lowered to eighteen.

1972 The Watergate scandal begins.

1969   1970   1971   1972

September 11, 1973 Chilean president Salvador Allende is ousted in a coup in Chile.

June 27, 1974 U.S. president Richard Nixon travels to Moscow for another summit conference with Soviet leader Leonid Brezhnev.

August 9, 1974 Under threats of impeachment due to a political scandal, Richard Nixon resigns as U.S. president and is replaced by Vice President Gerald R. Ford.

November 23, 1974 U.S. president Gerald R. Ford and Soviet leader Leonid Brezhnev meet in the Soviet city of Vladivostok.

April 30, 1975 In renewed fighting, North Vietnam captures South Vietnam and reunites the country.

August 1, 1975 Numerous nations sign the Helsinki Accords at the end of the Conference on Security and Cooperation in Europe.

December 25, 1977 Israeli prime minister Menachim Begin and Egyptian president Anwar Sadat begin peace negotiations in Egypt.

September 17, 1978 Israeli prime minister Menachim Begin and Egyptian president Anwar Sadat, meeting with U.S. president Jimmy Carter at Camp David, reach an historic peace settlement between Israel and Egypt.

January 1, 1979 The United States and the People's Republic of China (PRC) establish diplomatic relations.

January 16, 1979 The shah of Iran is overthrown as the leader of Iran and is replaced by Islamic leader Ayatollah Ruhollah Khomeini.

June 18, 1979 U.S. president Jimmy Carter and Soviet leader Leonid Brezhnev sign the SALT II strategic arms limitation agreement in Vienna, Austria.

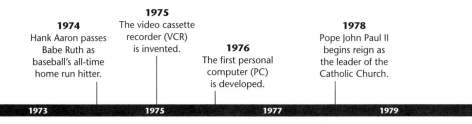

1974 Hank Aaron passes Babe Ruth as baseball's all-time home run hitter.

1975 The video cassette recorder (VCR) is invented.

1976 The first personal computer (PC) is developed.

1978 Pope John Paul II begins reign as the leader of the Catholic Church.

1973   1975   1977   1979

July 19, 1979 Sandinista rebels seize power in Nicaragua with Daniel Ortega becoming the new leader.

November 4, 1979 Islamic militants seize the U.S. embassy in Tehran, Iran, taking U.S. staff hostage.

December 26, 1979 Soviet forces invade Afghanistan to prop up an unpopular pro-Soviet government, leading to a decade of bloody fighting.

April 24, 1980 An attempted military rescue of American hostages in Iran ends with eight U.S. soldiers dead.

August 14, 1980 The Solidarity labor union protests the prices of goods in Poland.

January 20, 1981 Iran releases the U.S. hostages as Ronald Reagan is being sworn in as the new U.S. president.

November 12, 1982 Yuri Andropov becomes the new Soviet leader after the death of Leonid Brezhnev two days earlier.

March 23, 1983 U.S. president Ronald Reagan announces the Strategic Defense Initiative (SDI).

September 1, 1983 A Soviet fighter shoots down Korean Airlines Flight 007 as it strays off-course over Soviet restricted airspace.

October 25, 1983 U.S. forces invade Grenada to end fighting between two pro-communist factions.

February 13, 1984 Konstantin Chernenko becomes the new Soviet leader after the death of Yuri Andropov four days earlier.

February 1985 The United States issues the Reagan Doctrine, offering assistance to military dictatorships in defense against communist expansion.

1980
Former Beatle John Lennon is murdered.

1981
MTV makes its debut.

1982
The compact disc (CD) is introduced.

1985
Microsoft releases Windows.

1979   1981   1983   1985

March 11, 1985 Mikhail Gorbachev becomes the new Soviet leader after the death of Konstantin Chernenko the previous day.

October 11–12, 1986 Soviet leader Mikhail Gorbachev and U.S. president Ronald Reagan meet in Reykjavik, Iceland, and agree to seek the elimination of nuclear weapons.

October 17, 1986 Congress approves aid to Contra rebels in Nicaragua.

November 3, 1986 The Iran-Contra affair is uncovered.

June 11, 1987 Margaret Thatcher wins an unprecedented third term as British prime minister.

December 8–10, 1987 U.S. president Ronald Reagan and Soviet leader Mikhail Gorbachev meet in Washington to sign the Intermediate Nuclear Forces Treaty (INF), removing thousands of missiles from Europe.

February 8, 1988 Soviet leader Mikhail Gorbachev announces his decision to withdraw Soviet forces from Afghanistan through the following year.

May 29, 1988 U.S. president Ronald Reagan journeys to Moscow for a summit meeting with Soviet leader Mikhail Gorbachev.

January 11, 1989 The Hungarian parliament adopts reforms granting greater personal freedoms to Hungarians, including allowing political parties and organizations.

January 18, 1989 The labor union Solidarity gains formal acceptance in Poland.

March 26, 1989 Open elections are held for the new Soviet Congress of People's Deputies, with the communists suffering major defeats; Boris Yeltsin wins the Moscow seat.

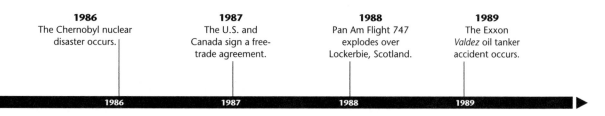

1986	**1987**	**1988**	**1989**
The Chernobyl nuclear disaster occurs.	The U.S. and Canada sign a free-trade agreement.	Pan Am Flight 747 explodes over Lockerbie, Scotland.	The Exxon *Valdez* oil tanker accident occurs.

May 11, 1989 Soviet leader Mikhail Gorbachev announces major reductions of nuclear forces in Eastern Europe.

June 3–4, 1989 Chinese communist leaders order a military crackdown on pro-democracy demonstrations in Tiananmen Square, leading to many deaths.

June 4, 1989 The first Polish free elections lead to major victory by Solidarity.

October 7, 1989 The Hungarian communist party disbands.

October 23, 1989 Massive demonstrations begin against the East German communist government, involving hundreds of thousands of protesters and leading to the resignation of the East German leadership in early November.

November 10, 1989 East Germany begins dismantling the Berlin Wall; Bulgarian communist leadership resigns.

November 24, 1989 Czechoslovakia communist leaders resign.

December 1, 1989 U.S. president George Bush and Soviet leader Mikhail Gorbachev begin a three-day meeting on a ship in a Malta harbor to discuss rapid changes in Eastern Europe and the Soviet Union.

December 20, 1989 Lithuania votes for independence from the Soviet Union.

December 22, 1989 Romanian communist leader Nicolae Ceausescu is toppled and executed three days later.

March 1990 Lithuania declares independence from Moscow.

March 14, 1990 Mikhail Gorbachev is elected president of the Soviet Union.

March 18, 1990 Open East German elections lead to a major defeat of Communist Party candidates.

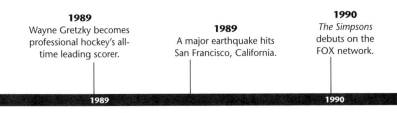

1989
Wayne Gretzky becomes professional hockey's all-time leading scorer.

1989
A major earthquake hits San Francisco, California.

1990
The Simpsons debuts on the FOX network.

1989

1990

May 29, 1990 Boris Yeltsin is elected president of the Russian republic.

June 1990 Russia declares independence as the Russian Federation.

October 15, 1990 Soviet leader Mikhail Gorbachev is awarded the Nobel Peace Prize for his reforms that ended the Cold War.

November 14, 1990 Various nations sign the Charter of Paris for a New Europe, ending the economic and military division of Europe created by the Cold War.

July 1, 1991 The Warsaw Pact disbands.

August 19, 1991 Soviet communist hardliners attempt an unsuccessful coup of Soviet leader Mikhail Gorbachev, leading to the banning of the Communist Party in Russia and other Soviet republics.

August 20–September 9, 1991 The various Soviet republics declare their independence from the Soviet Union, including Estonia, Latvia, Lithuania, Ukraine, Belorussia, Moldovia, Azerbaijan, Uzbekistan, Kirgizia, and Tadzhikistan.

October 3, 1991 West and East Germany reunite as one nation.

December 8, 1991 Russia, Ukraine, and Belorussia create the Commonwealth of Independent States organization as an alliance replacing the Soviet Union.

December 25, 1991 Soviet leader Mikhail Gorbachev resigns as the Soviet president, and the Soviet Union ceases to exist.

January 28, 1992 In his Annual State of the Union Address, U.S. president George Bush declares victory in the Cold War.

1990
The Hubble Space Telescope is deployed in space.

1991
The Persian Gulf War takes place.

1992
Hurricane Andrew causes $15 billion in damage in Florida.

1990   1991   1992

Research and Activity Ideas

The following research and activity ideas are intended to offer suggestions for complementing social studies and history curricula, to trigger additional ideas for enhancing learning, and to provide cross-disciplinary projects for library and classroom use.

- **Newspaper search:** Old issues of local newspapers are likely available at your public library, a nearby college or university library, or from the local newspaper office itself. Locate and review newspapers for the following events using the approximate dates given. Assess if reporters grasped the major points of the crisis. Choose interesting accounts to read to the class. The events are: Cuban Missile Crisis (October 23, 1962, through the end of October 1962); Berlin, Germany, Airlift (mid-July 1948 to mid-May 1949); Building the Berlin Wall (August 14, 1961, through the end of August 1961); and Tearing Down the Berlin Wall (November 10, 1989, through the end of November 1989).

- **The bomb scare:** At the height of the Cold War (1945–91), many individuals attempting to protect family members considered building bomb shelters in case of nuclear attack. At your local library, secure an old copy of the September 15, 1961, issue of *Life* magazine. Look for an article titled "Fallout Shelters." Also note the preceding letter to the American public from President John F. Kennedy.

- **Make an important decision:** Would you choose to build a shelter or rely on public bomb shelters being identified at that time by the Civil Defense? If you decide you would build, consider the same issues as those 1960s families did in the article. Where would you place your shelter, what kind would you build, could you afford to build it, and what and how many provisions would you stock it with? In the event of an attack warning, how long would it take to gather your family at the shelter?

- **Pretend you are a 1960s teenager:** Would a family shelter represent comfort and security, or a constant reminder of a possible doomsday event? Write what your thoughts might have been as the shelter was constructed.

- **Arms control treaties:** Create a timeline of nuclear weapons control treaties. Briefly describe the substance of each treaty and indicate which countries signed onto them. Begin with the 1963 Limited Test Ban Treaty. In addition to information found in books, check out information on the Internet at www.atomicarchive.com.

- **Strategic Triad:** To defend the United States from a nuclear attack, the U.S. government and military developed a system known as the Strategic Triad. Triad, meaning three, incorporated: (1) long-range bombers carrying nuclear weapons; (2) land-based intercontinental ballistic missiles; and (3) missile-carrying submarines. The reasoning behind the Triad was that an enemy could not hope to destroy all three systems in a first attack—at least one system would be left to retaliate. Hence, an enemy should be discouraged from launching an attack. Choose one of the three systems and report to the class. To learn more about the history of these systems, go to these Web sites on the Internet: U.S. Strategic Air Command, http://www.stratcom.af.mil; Titan Missile Museum, http://www.pimaair.org/titan_01. htm; Ballistic Missile Submarines (SSBNs), http://www. stratcom.af.mil/factsheetshtml/submarines.htm; and U.S. Navy Fact File, http://chinfo.navy.mil/navpalib/factfile/ships/ship-ssn.html.

- **At the movies:** Watch one of the following movies, each of which have Cold War overtones: *I Married a Communist* (1950); *My Son John* (1952); *Storm Center* (1956); *On the Beach* (1959); *The Manchurian Candidate* (1962); *Dr. Strangelove* (1963); *The Russians Are Coming, the Russians Are Coming* (1966); *The Deer Hunter* (1978); *Red Dawn* (1984); and *The Hunt for Red October* (1990). Applying your knowledge of the Cold War, how was the superpower rivalry portrayed in the movie? Whether the movie was dramatic and suspense-filled or a comedy spoof, what ideas about the Cold War did it relay to the audiences?

- **Map project:** Create the two following maps, then compare and contrast them. First, create a map of Europe and the Soviet Union as the countries existed in the late 1960s. Include the democratic Western European countries and the communist Eastern European countries and the Soviet Union. Second, create a map of the same geographical area in 2000 after the breakup of the Soviet Union during the 1990s.

- **U.S. Cold War military sites:** On a map of the western United States, locate the following sites involved in top secret Cold War military activities. Using a numbered key, on the map briefly describe the mission charged to each site. Using your favorite Internet search engine, enter these terms: Los Alamos, White Sands, Titan II Museum, Trinity Site, Nevada Test Site, Long Beach Navy Yard, Mare Island Naval Shipyard, North American Air Defense Command (NORAD) Headquarters, and Strategic Air Command (SAC) Headquarters.

- **Spying from above:** Research and report on aircraft and satellite spies. Include the U-2, Corona Satellite project, SR71 Blackbird (succeeded the U-2), and drone-type aircraft such as the U.S. Air Force Predator.

- **International Spy Museum, Washington, D.C.:** Go to the website of the International Spy Museum (http://www.spymuseum.org) and find out about such fascinating topics as the tools of the trade of spying, lives of the spies of the Cold War, the Berlin Tunnel, or any other topic that catches your imagination at this exciting site.

- **VENONA Project:** Research the VENONA Project, which was the U.S. Army's Signal Intelligence Service's attempt, beginning in 1943, to decode the encrypted messages of the Soviet intelligence agencies, the KGB and GRU. The National Security Agency (NSA) ended a fifty-year silence on VENONA when it released documents in 1995 for the general public to study. The intelligence secrets uncovered by deciphering codes helped expose Soviet espionage activities carried out in the United States. For information, go to the National Security Agency's Web site, http://www.nsa.gov/docs/VENONA and the Public Broadcasting Service's *NOVA Online* Web site at http://www.pbs.org/wgbh/nova/venona.

- **CNN's "Cold War Experience":** Media giant CNN produced a documentary series on the Cold War for television broadcast in 1998. It won the prestigious George Foster Peabody Award for an excellent documentary series. To coincide with the programming, CNN developed an Internet interactive website, the *Cold War Experience,* that allows you to explore many facets of key situations and events of the Cold War. Go to this website at http://www.cnn.com/SPECIALS/cold.war/ for spellbinding information about the bomb, culture, technology, espionage, and more.

- **Development of nuclear weapons:** Divide the class into two groups, the Americans and the Soviets. Research and then write a class play on the development of the early nuclear technology. First act: The successful American development of an atomic bomb by 1945 with leading characters J. Robert Oppenheimer and Brigadier General Leslie R. Groves. Second act: The successful Soviet development of an atomic bomb by 1949 with leading characters Igor Kurchatov (physicist) and Lavrenti Beria (head of the KGB, the Soviet secret police). Third act: Follow Oppenheimer and Kurchatov until their deaths. What conclusions did they both independently come to concerning nuclear development, and how did they promote their views?

- **Coded or encrypted messages:** Divide the class into small groups for creating secret codes. Have each group make up an encrypted message using three letters for one letter, such as "abc" standing for "t." Make a tiny code deciphering book. Exchange code books and messages with another group. All students then become codebreakers employed by the National Security Agency and break the code. Remember, in real situations, code books changed from week to week and month to month, making deciphering very difficult.

- **Fission and fusion:** Explore the scientific basis of and difference between the nuclear reactions of fission and fusion. Explain the difference in destructive force between the atomic bomb based on fission and the hydrogen bomb based on fusion. Define what is meant by strategic and tactical nuclear weapons.

- **Terrorist thievery:** In the era of terrorists in the early twenty-first century, why do government officials fear that plutonium and uranium isotopes (two or more forms of an element that differ from each other according to their mass number) might be stolen. Which type of bomb, fission or fusion, might a terrorist produce with the stolen material? Would that bomb destroy a large part of the world or would it be, however devastating, limited in its destructive effects?

- **Interviews:** Make a list of persons who students know lived during much of the Cold War. Parents or grandparents born in the 1940s would be good candidates. Develop questions ahead of time. Tape record the interview if possible or take careful notes. Transcribe the recording or notes into a clear written retelling of the interview. This process is known as taking and recording an oral history. Share the oral history with the class.

- **Cartoon creation:** Cartoons are common features in newspapers and magazines. Used to illustrate the artist's viewpoint of an occurrence or common issue of the day, cartoons draw reactions from readers ranging from laughter to quiet agreement with the artist to howls of disgust. Use your imagination and artistic skills to create a cartoon about some aspect of the Cold War. Take either the side of the United States or of the Soviets. Suggestions for topics are Winston Churchill's phrase the "Iron Curtain," the Berlin Airlift, the Berlin Wall, the nuclear arms race, the space race, Senator Joseph R. McCarthy, the mutual assured destruction policy, détente, and President Ronald Reagan's "Star Wars" program. Be sure to convey an emotion such as humor, fear, or surprise. Write a caption for the cartoon that captures the essential message or spirit of the cartoon.

- **Debate #1:** Divide the class into two groups: (1) democratic, capitalists of Western Europe and the United States and (2) the communists of the Soviet Union. Debate thoroughly the differences in the two systems of government and economies. In reality, both sides believed their system was best. So staunchly defend what you think is right about your respective system. Were there any similarities or common ground in the two systems, or were they hopelessly incompatible?

- **Debate #2:** Divide the class into two groups: U.S. government officials and Soviet government officials. Set the debate in the time frame of 1945 to approximately 1949, post–World War II. Remember, the two groups were becoming more distrustful of each other with each passing day. Explore the reasons why, then debate over a "summit" table such issues as why the Soviets insisted on occupying Eastern European countries, why German reunification was such a stumbling block, and why Americans were suspicious of a communist conspiracy to take over the world and therefore began a policy of "containment."

- **Debate #3:** Divide the class into two groups: one in favor of a massive arms buildup to deter the Soviets and the other opposed to an arms buildup and instead vigorously pressing for arms control talks. Debate the advantages and problems with mutual assured destruction (MAD).

- **Debate #4:** Research and debate the ideas of the domino theory, particularly relating it to China, Korea, and Vietnam. How did it impact tensions of the Cold War?

- **Debate #5:** Study and debate President Ronald Reagan's "Star Wars" project. How did Reagan's insistence on the program affect the Soviets and did it prolong or hasten an end to the Cold War?

- **The image of Nikita Khrushchev:** At your public library, or a nearby college or university library, locate *Nikita Khrushchev and the Creation of a Superpower* (2000) by the late Soviet leader's son, Sergei Khrushchev. In the 1960s, most Americans thought of Nikita Khrushchev as an evil, stubborn Soviet leader determined to blow up the United States with nuclear weapons. From your reading of the book, construct your own personality and leadership profile of Nikita Khrushchev.

- **Mikhail Gorbachev:** Study in depth the life and ideologies of the Soviet Union's final president, Mikhail Gorbachev. Why was he chosen for the Nobel Peace Prize in 1990?

Cold War
Almanac

Renewed Tensions

8

"We will bury you!" Soviet premier Nikita Khrushchev (1894–1971) shouted these dramatic words in a speech in Moscow in 1956. His language struck fear in many U.S. citizens and contributed to Cold War paranoia. However, the line was misinterpreted; the statement referred to a Russian phrase meaning "We will outlast you and attend your funeral [or burial]." Khrushchev himself later complained about the negative reaction: "I once said, 'We will bury you,' and I got into trouble with it. Of course we will not bury you with a shovel. Your own working class will bury you." But the damage had been done, and the line has been quoted out of context for years and years.

Four years later, at a United Nations meeting on September 20, 1960, the Soviet leader lashed out again. (The United Nations is an international organization, composed of most of the nations of the world, created to preserve world peace and security.) After British prime minister Harold Macmillan (1894–1986) made a speech that was critical of the Soviet Union, the red-faced Soviet leader angrily responded by taking off his shoe and banging it on the table and waving it at Macmillan.

Words to Know

Capitalism: An economic system in which property and businesses are privately owned.

Cold War: A prolonged conflict for world dominance from 1945 to 1991 between the two superpowers, the democratic, capitalist United States and the communist Soviet Union. The weapons of conflict were commonly words of propaganda and threats.

Communism: A system of government in which the nation's leaders are selected by a single political party that controls almost all aspects of society. Private ownership of property is eliminated and government directs all economic production. The goods produced and accumulated wealth are, in theory, shared relatively equally by all. All religious practices are banned.

Democracy: A system of government in which several political parties compete.

Eisenhower Doctrine: A doctrine giving the U.S. president the right to use force in the Middle East against any form of communist aggression.

These two images of Khrushchev are among the more memorable moments of the Cold War, a forty-five-year rivalry between the two world superpowers, the communist Soviet Union and the capitalist democracy of the United States. Communism is a system of government in which a single political party, the Communist Party, controls nearly all aspects of society. Government leaders are selected by the party leadership. The communist system prohibits private ownership of property; goods produced and resulting wealth are, in theory, shared equally by all citizens. A communist government controls all economic production and does not allow religious practices. A democracy is a system of government in which several political parties compete. Their members are elected to various government offices through general public elections. Capitalism is an economic system in which property and businesses are privately owned. Economic activity operates relatively free of government interventions; competition determines the prices, production, and distribution of goods. Religious freedom is one of the cornerstones of the United States; it is guaranteed in the Bill of Rights.

In February 1956, Khrushchev, the Soviet leader, made a lengthy historic speech setting a new course for his nation. Khrushchev strongly denounced the past practices of former Soviet premier Joseph Stalin (1879– 1953), calling them crimes against the people. Stalin's crimes included mass killings of Eastern Europeans in the 1930s. Khrushchev condemned Stalin for placing his own quest for power above the welfare of the people. Breaking from Stalin's precedent, Khrushchev called for peaceful competition with the West.

The speech gave U.S. president Dwight D. Eisenhower (1890–1969; served 1953–61) some hope that tensions between the United States and the Soviet Union could be eased; it even seemed that the Soviets might loosen their hold on Eastern Europe. However, Khrushchev's speech triggered a dramatic and unexpected outcry against the Soviets by Eastern Europeans. Revealing the truth about the Stalin era sparked a backlash against Soviet rule in Eastern Europe.

Despite the seemingly optimistic prospects in early 1956, Eisenhower's second term as president, beginning in January 1957, coincided with increased tensions worldwide. European crises erupted, and in the Third World—from the Congo in Africa to Cuba in Latin America—the Cold War between noncommunist and communist factions intensified. Third World is a term used to refer to poor underdeveloped or developing nations in Africa, Asia, and Latin America. Most Third World countries are former colonies whose economies are primarily based on agriculture. Latin America includes the entire Western Hemisphere south of the United States. It includes Central and South America as well as Mexico and the islands of the West Indies.

People to Know

Fidel Castro Ruz (1926–): Cuban premier/president, 1959–.

Dwight D. Eisenhower (1890–1969): Thirty-fourth U.S. president, 1953–61.

Nikita S. Khrushchev (1894–1971): Soviet premier, 1958–64.

Patrice Lumumba (1925–1961): Congolese nationalist movement activist; prime minister, 1960.

Gamal Abdel Nasser (1918–1970): Egyptian president, 1958–70.

Joseph Stalin (1879–1953): Dictatorial Russian/Soviet leader, 1924–53.

European unrest

Following the horrific revelations about the Stalin era, Eastern Europeans boldly demonstrated their disdain for communist rule. In June 1956, riots broke out in Poland after workers went on strike; they were protesting wage cuts imposed by the government and harsh working conditions. In an effort to peacefully resolve the crisis, Khrushchev ousted the Stalin-era Polish leaders. He installed a new communist leader, Wladyslaw Gomulka (1905–1982), who promised

worker reforms. Khrushchev quickly became uncomfortable with the reforms and asked Gomulka to limit his efforts. Gomulka had pressed for more expansive social reforms, including greater personal freedoms, than Khrushchev was willing to accept. The new Polish leader refused to back down, and Khrushchev chose not to force the issue.

Seeing Soviet rule being successfully challenged in Poland, students in Hungary decided to press for even greater change in their country. They wanted to eliminate communism altogether and turn Hungary toward neutrality. On October 23, 1956, student demonstrations turned violent in the growing rebellion against the Soviet presence. One week later, Hungarian leader Imre Nagy (1896–1958) announced that Hungary would pull out of the Warsaw Pact and drop the ban on political parties within Hungary. Orchestrated by the Soviet Union, the Warsaw Pact was a military alliance of Eastern European nations, designed to protect them in case of Western European aggression. The pact also served anoth-

er purpose: It gave the Soviets firmer control over the internal affairs of the member countries.

Khrushchev decided events in Hungary had gone too far, and on November 4 he responded with force. Some two hundred thousand Soviet troops and fifty-five hundred tanks launched a bloody surprise attack. Before the revolt, the United States had been encouraging Eastern European nations to follow independent communist paths, much like Yu-

Soviet tanks roll into Budapest, Hungary, to break up anticommunist revolts in 1956. *Reproduced by permission of the Corbis Corporation.*

goslavia. However, Eisenhower did not want to risk nuclear war, so he chose not to assist the Hungarian anticommunist movement. By November 8, after several days of fierce fighting, all public unrest was crushed. The death toll was high: Close to thirty thousand Hungarians and several thousand Soviet troops were killed. In addition, over two hundred thousand Hungarians fled into neutral Austria. Many ended up in the United States. The Soviets arrested and later executed Nagy. With Soviet approval, János Kádár (1912–1989) assumed the Hungarian leadership, the beginning of his more than thirty years in power.

The Hungarian revolt and resulting massive Soviet response caused major repercussions. The incident weakened Khrushchev's standing at home. Soviet communist hardliners blamed Khrushchev's anti-Stalin speech for the turmoil in Eastern Europe. Khrushchev pulled back his support for reform, or political change, and instead increased Soviet economic aid to Eastern Europe, hoping to avoid more unrest and further use of military force. By June 1957, Khrushchev had prevailed over the internal political challenge, and for the time being, he turned his attention to the skies.

The missile race

Early in the morning of October 4, 1957, the Soviet Union launched the world's first Earth-orbiting satellite, *Sputnik I*. (*Sputnik* means "fellow traveler," a phrase often used by Soviet communists to refer to each other. A satellite is an constructed object that orbits, in this case, the Earth.) On November 3, the Soviets launched a satellite carrying a dog named Laika, who lived for ten days, proving that a living creature could survive in space for a period of time. These launches were a start for space exploration, but they were perhaps more important as propaganda (information spread to further one's own cause) victories for Khrushchev and the Soviet Union. The American public was shocked by the rapid technological advances the Soviets had made, though the United States was not too far behind, launching its first successful satellite on February 1, 1958.

Riding a wave of reversed popularity in the Communist Party following the crisis in Hungary, Khrushchev re-

placed Nikolay Bulganin (1895–1975) as Soviet premier in March 1958. Khrushchev was the secretary general of the Soviet Communist Party, the real office of power within the Soviet Union, and Bulganin had served as the Soviet premier. Now Khrushchev claimed both titles.

The U.S. scientific community and U.S. officials worried about the Soviets' intercontinental ballistic missile capabilities: Was the United States now vulnerable to nuclear missile attacks? Reports stated that the United States was falling behind in both missile technology and the number of long-range bombers; the threat of massive retaliation by the United States might no longer be an effective deterrent to hostile actions. Fears of a Soviet nuclear missile advantage rose in the American public. With substantial public support, Congress passed the National Defense Education Act in 1958, providing $5 billion for higher education to increase U.S. technological capabilities. An emphasis was placed on science, mathematics, engineering, and foreign languages. Funding increased for additional Strategic Air Command bombers and nuclear weapons. The United States also poured more funding into its space program. The National Aeronautics and Space Administration (NASA) was established in October 1958 to guide U.S. space program development.

On July 4, 1956, long before the Soviets launched their first satellite, the United States had begun to make se-

National Aeronautics and Space Administration (NASA)

The Soviet Union launched *Sputnik I* on October 4, 1957. It was the first artificial satellite to orbit Earth. The event stunned the American public and U.S. officials, who had thought the United States had a significant technological advantage over the Soviets. At that time, rocket and upper atmospheric research in the United States was primarily conducted by the Department of Defense (DOD). The DOD had been working on Project Vanguard. The goal of the project was to orbit a U.S. satellite by 1957, but the project had fallen behind schedule. Following the successful Soviet launch, the DOD launched its first satellite on February 1, 1958. However, the United States remained alarmed because of the rapid advances in the Soviet space program. Soon, Congress created the National Aeronautics and Space Administration (NASA), which began operations on Oc-

tober 1, 1958. NASA received a $100 million annual budget. The "space race" became a key feature of the Cold War rivalry between the two superpowers.

NASA tackled several avenues of research, including manned and unmanned spaceflight, information-gathering satellites, and aircraft safety research. Landmark successes came quickly: On May 5, 1961, Project Mercury launched the first American in space, Alan B. Shepard Jr. (1923–1998). On February 20, 1962, John H. Glenn Jr. (1921–) was the first U.S. astronaut to orbit Earth. However, continued Soviet advances in the "space race" had led President John F. Kennedy (1917–1963; served 1961–63) to proclaim on May 25, 1961, that a key goal of the United States was to be the first to land a man on the

cret espionage, or spy, flights over the Soviet Union, using high-altitude U-2 planes. Flying 12 miles high, they could photograph 750-mile-wide (1,200-kilometer) corridors. Through the U-2 photography, Eisenhower learned more about Soviet missile capabilities, Soviet nuclear testing, and the Soviet space program. The secret surveillance flights and other intelligence-gathering showed that the Soviets had no technological advantage; there was no reason to fear. The Soviets had not deployed intercontinental missiles.

However, Eisenhower could not let the public know that the United States had the advantage over the Soviet Union. Publicizing information about Soviet missile capabilities would reveal the extent of the secret U.S. spy program. As a result, public pressure forced Eisenhower to increase funding for the U.S. missile program, and the existing U.S. advan-

One of NASA's crowning achievements: Neil Armstrong is the first man to step on the Moon, July 20, 1969.

Moon; the goal date was the end of the 1960s. NASA would spend more than $25 billion during the rest of the decade on Project Apollo. On July 20, 1969, U.S. astronaut Neil A. Armstrong (1930–) became the first man to step on the Moon, fulfilling Kennedy's challenge.

Cooperation with the Soviets began in 1975 while the Cold War still persisted. A test rendezvous (linking up) and docking in space between separately launched American- and Soviet-manned space capsules proved successful. Shortly after the end of the Cold War, in 1993, the Soviet Union and the United States began a joint program to establish the International Space Station. By the late 1990s, American and Soviet astronauts were routinely sharing space quarters for long periods of time.

tage grew. Between 1957 and 1960, the United States would triple its stash of nuclear weapons, going from six hundred to eighteen hundred, including Polaris nuclear submarines. Intermediate-range ballistic missiles were sent to the North Atlantic Treaty Organization (NATO) countries in Europe to be shared among the Western European nations, including West Germany. NATO is a peacetime alliance of the United States and eleven other nations.

Back-and-forth test-ban proposals

Earlier, the Soviets had found U.S. test-ban proposals unacceptable because the proposals included on-site inspection requirements. The Soviets were unwilling to provide the United States with maps of their military installations. How-

Prominent world scientists gather in Geneva, Switzerland, in 1955 to discuss the prospects of a nuclear test ban. *Reproduced by permission of the Corbis Corporation.*

ever, in December 1957, aware of the U.S. buildup, Khrushchev began pressing for a ban on nuclear weapons testing. This time Eisenhower was not interested.

In March 1958, the Soviets proposed a nuclear-free zone in Central Europe, including West Germany, Poland, Czechoslovakia, and East Germany. The proposal suggested that the manufacture and deployment of nuclear weapons within this zone be banned. Again the United States and its NATO allies rejected the proposal, claiming West Germany might be left vulnerable to attack by Soviet conventional forces.

Unhappy with NATO's response, Khrushchev decided to put pressure again on West Berlin. By 1958, West Berlin had received $600 million in economic aid from the United States and had become a showcase of democratic capitalism. Close to three million East Germans, many of them young professionals, had moved to the West Berlin zone. Khrushchev believed the rearming of West Germany was in clear violation of post-war treaties. He threatened to end Soviet occupation of East Berlin and give the East German government control over access to West Berlin if the Western allies did not leave West Berlin. The Western allies did not want East Germany to gain the status of an independent nation. Not only would formal recognition of East Germany establish yet another communist nation, but it would potentially greatly hinder future reunification with West Germany into one Germany again. To appease Khrushchev and avoid further problems in Berlin, the United States and Britain agreed to the Soviet test-ban proposal in October 1958. The suspension of nuclear testing would last three years. From May 11 to August 5, 1959, representatives from the four main powers—the United States, the Soviet Union, France, and Britain—met in Geneva to determine the fate of Berlin. Though few agreements were reached, the crisis was averted, and tensions over Berlin declined for the next few years.

Spirit of Camp David

Khrushchev traveled to the United States in September 1959 to meet with Eisenhower. After touring an Iowa corn farm and being turned away from Disneyland because the United States feared for his safety, Khrushchev met with Eisenhower at Camp David, the presidential retreat in Maryland, 70 miles from Washington, D.C. Though they made little firm progress, they did agree to keep Berlin as it was for the time being and to meet again in Europe the following spring. The relationship of the two superpower leaders seemed to be on much stronger footing. The improved relations were referred to as "the spirit of Camp David."

The Middle East erupts

The Middle East is a large region that includes parts of southwestern Asia, southeastern Europe, and northern Africa. It extends from Turkey in the north to Sudan in the south and stretches to Iran in the east. It includes Egypt, Iraq, Saudi Arabia, Israel, Syria, Jordan, Yemen, Lebanon, Cyprus, Oman, Bahrain, Qatar, and the United Arab Emirates. The region was critically important to the United States and Western Europe because of its vast oil reserves and its long boundary with the Soviet Union. The boundary could be used to block potential expansion of Soviet influence toward the Persian Gulf. For these reasons, Eisenhower decided to forge an anti-Soviet alliance among Arab states. Britain had long been the dominant colonial power in the region, but its control had declined after World War II (1939–45). (Colonialism refers to a political and economic relationship in which a powerful country maintains control over the people of a poorer or weaker country. Most often the term is used in reference to Western European nations that historically controlled various underdeveloped countries.) Because of its close association with the new nation of Israel, the United States had a problem in filling the regional power void left by Britain. (The United States, through its strong pro-Israel lobby within the United States itself, provided substantial economic support of the new nation.) Attempting to pursue a more neutral approach to the Israel-Arab dispute, the United States helped arrange a defense treaty among willing Middle East nations. (Israel's violent displacement of Palestinian Arab populations in creating the new nation created lasting animosity.) Established in February 1955 and known as the Baghdad Pact, the treaty included Turkey, Iran, Pakistan, and Iraq, as well as Great Britain. The United States trusted that this group of nations would serve as a solid barrier to Soviet expansion in the Middle East. However, Egypt would soon prove this wrong.

Gamal Abdel Nasser (1918–1970) was the leader of Egypt. He had overthrown King Farouk (1920–1965) to capture control of the country in July 1952. At first, Eisenhower saw Nasser as a positive influence on Arab stability and signed a treaty with him in 1954. Under the treaty, Britain would withdraw all of its troops from Egypt. However, Nasser desired much more. He wanted to lead a pan-Arab nationalist movement, an alliance of all Arab nations to rid the region of outside political influences. The movement sought to eliminate Israel from the region to regain lost lands and to create a Palestinian state in its place. In 1955, Nasser declined to join the Baghdad Pact. Instead he asked for assistance from the Soviets to attack Israel. By September 1955, Egypt was receiving arms from Czechoslovakia at the request of the Soviets. In April 1956, Egypt formed a military alliance with

Saudi Arabia, Syria, and Yemen. In May, Nasser extended formal recognition to communist China. Nasser was becoming a hero to the Arab world in his drive to destroy Israel.

On July 19, 1956, Eisenhower responded to Nasser's actions by announcing that the United States would no longer offer financial assistance for the construction of the Aswan High Dam, a key project designed to greatly improve agriculture in Egypt through inexpensive hydroelectric power. On July 26, Nasser responded by nationalizing the Suez Canal, the main shipping link between the Mediterranean Sea and the Indian Ocean. This meant Nasser now controlled the movement of oil shipments from the Middle East to Western Europe. Britain, France, and Israel combined forces to take back the canal: On October 29, Israel launched an attack against Egypt. Two days later, French and British forces attacked with warplanes and paratroopers. Nasser responded by sinking ships in the canal, closing it to shipments. An oil crisis loomed for Europe. Highly upset by the French and British military action, Eisenhower introduced a United Nations (UN) resolution calling for a cease-fire in the region. The resolution was also supported by the Soviets, but Eisenhower feared the attack by Western forces would drive Egypt ever closer to the Soviets. By December 22, Britain and France had withdrawn their troops from Egypt.

Britain's *Empire Ken* sails into Port Said, Egypt, carrying reinforcements during the Suez Crisis of 1956. *Reproduced by permission of the Corbis Corporation.*

Though Egypt's forces had been overwhelmed in the Suez War, Nasser emerged from the conflict with greater prestige. The Western nations, on the other hand, were left divided. Stung by the UN resolution and threats from the Soviet Union, France would leave NATO by 1966 and pursue its own nuclear development program. The last bit of British influence in the Middle East had disappeared as well. As the Soviets passed more weapons to Nasser, Eisenhower went to

Egyptian president Gamal Abdel Nasser. *Reproduced by permission of the United Nations.*

Congress in January 1957 for expanded presidential powers in the region. As a result, the Eisenhower Doctrine was established: The president was granted the right to use force in the Middle East against any form of communist aggression. The doctrine made the United States the dominant foreign power in the region.

Inspired by Nasser's leadership in Egypt, nationalist movements erupted in various Arab countries. In February 1958, Nasser formed the United Arab Republic (UAR) alliance with Syria and Yemen. On July 14, 1958, the pro-Western government of Iraq fell to General Abdul Karim Kassem (1914–1963), who wanted Iraq to join the UAR. That same day, Camille N. Chamoun (1900–1987), the president of the pro-Western Lebanon government, requested U.S. aid to combat an attempted coup d'état, an illegal or forceful change of government, there as well. Eisenhower immediately sent fourteen thousand U.S. troops to Lebanon; he also sent air support for three thousand British troops who were defending Jordan's King Hussein (1935–1999). By placing eleven hundred Strategic Air Command aircraft on alert, Eisenhower warned the Soviets not to get involved in Lebanon.

By October 1958, stability had been restored in Lebanon and Jordan. In addition, Iraq's Kassem dropped his effort to join the UAR and ensured the security of Western oil company property in Iraq. Nevertheless, Iraq did withdraw from the U.S.-inspired Baghdad Pact in 1958. The name of the Baghdad Pact was changed to Central Treaty Organization (CENTO).

By 1961, Nasser's effort at uniting the Arab world was falling apart. Syria withdrew from the UAR, and Egypt became enemies with Syria and Iraq. The Soviet influence in the Middle East was challenged by U.S. influence. After the Suez War, the United States had replaced Britain and France as the most influential Western power in the region. The pro-U.S. governments of Lebanon, Jordan, and Saudi Arabia welcomed the Eisenhower Doctrine. Egypt, Syria, and Iraq looked to the Soviets for military and economic aid. However, the superpowers had trouble making the Middle East countries into dependent states; efforts to resolve the Israel-Palestine dispute would also prove futile. The oil reserves in the region gave these countries a degree of political and economic independence found in few other places. The value of the reserves allowed these countries to be nationalists.

Second Taiwan Strait crisis

In August 1958, the communist People's Republic of China (PRC), also known as Mainland China, had once again begun bombarding the offshore islands controlled by the Republic of China (ROC). Leaders of the ROC had established themselves on the island of Taiwan after being driven from the mainland by Chinese communists. The communists who led the PRC sought to force acceptance of their government as the official representative government of all Chinese people; they wanted diplomatic recognition of the ROC to stop. Khrushchev sent a note to Eisenhower threatening global nuclear war if the United States supported an attack against the Chinese mainland. Ignoring the threat, Eisenhower sent the U.S. Seventh Fleet back to the Taiwan Strait to escort ROC supply ships. The PRC artillery was careful not to hit the U.S. ships, and the United States showed no inclination to become further involved militarily. On October 6, 1958, a cease-fire went into effect when the United States offered the PRC a resolution that involved reduction of ROC forces on the smaller islands being bombarded. ROC president Chiang Kai-shek (1887–1975) consented to the U.S. proposal, and the second crisis in the Taiwan Strait quickly came to an end.

Despite Khrushchev's seemingly strong support of the PRC, Chinese communists in that government viewed his actions with great suspicion. They believed Khrushchev knew full well that the United States had no intention of going to war with the Soviet Union; and they seriously doubted that the Soviets would risk nuclear war on behalf of the PRC. In fact, the break between the PRC and the Soviet Union was widening. The Soviets were becoming increasingly fearful of the belligerent PRC leader, Mao Zedong (1893–1976), and his possible lack of restraint in the future use of nuclear weapons. The Soviets had been providing some assistance to PRC in the development of nuclear capabilities but stopped the assistance in 1959—they feared the PRC might turn its nuclear weapons on the Soviet Union. They also pressed PRC for repayment of a $2.4 billion debt from the Korean War (1950–53), despite the fact that the PRC was struggling economically. In 1958, Mao had introduced a massive economic program to transform the PRC's largely agricultural economy into a major industrial society. The program, called the Great Leap Forward, was a disaster and made the PRC even more reliant on Soviet economic assistance. From the Soviets' perspective, there were now enemies to the east and west: The PRC was a growing threat on the eastern border, and West Germany, supplied with nuclear missiles from the United States, menaced the western Soviet boundary.

Africa

For centuries, Britain, France, and Portugal had carved up sub-Saharan Africa into various colonial holdings. (Sub-Saharan Africa refers to the part of the continent that lies south of the Sahara, a region of deserts that extends across northern Africa. It includes all the countries south of Egypt, Libya, and Algeria; most of them are Third World nations, or poor underdeveloped or developing nations whose economies are primarily based on agriculture.) The Europeans who colonized Africa sought access to slaves and natural resources. A well-established region of European influence, the area stayed stable following World War II, remaining quite distant from the superpower rivalry through much of the 1950s. Though the United States generally opposed colonialism, it was evident that the colonial holdings of such Western European allies as Great Britain, France, Portugal, and Belgium had kept Africa relatively safe from communist expansion; the United States and the Soviet Union, therefore, focused on the oil-rich Middle East and other regions. However, by the late 1950s, the process of decolonization gained momentum in Africa. During decolonization, a

country ruled by a foreign power seeks to overturn that rule and gain national independence.

In the summer of 1960, the ongoing conflict between the superpowers shifted to sub-Saharan Africa, at least temporarily. On June 30, 1960, Belgium announced it was granting independence to Congo (from 1971 to 1997 known as Zaire; as of 1997 known as the Democratic Republic of Congo). On July 5, the Congolese army mutinied and attacked its white officers and a number of settlers. Congo's prime minister, Patrice Lumumba (1925–1961), was unable to maintain control as Belgian forces arrived to restore order. In reaction to the presence of the Belgian troops, a separatist movement rose up in the Congolese province of Katanga. (Separatists seek to gain political independence for their region of a country.) With the conflict widening, Lumumba asked for help from the United Nations (UN). A UN resolution called for replacement of the Belgian forces with an interna-

On July 1, 1960, Congolese troops march in celebration of their country's independence from Belgium a day earlier. The festivities were short-lived, however, as major conflicts began on July 5. *Reproduced by permission of the Corbis Corporation.*

tional military force on July 15. However, the UN military was unwilling to take on the Katanga separatist movement. Discouraged, Lumumba turned to the United States for assistance but was refused. He was considered too unreliable for long-term relations. Lumumba then approached the Soviets, who immediately responded with equipment and personnel. The United States saw the Soviets' aid as a violation of the UN resolution. Because Lumumba accepted Soviet assistance, U.S. officials considered him a communist and a threat to the region. CIA director Allen Dulles (1893–1969) put a plan in motion to overthrow Lumumba. Relying on pro-U.S. Congolese leaders, the plan led to Lumumba's overthrow in September and his assassination on January 17, 1961.

A Cuban revolution

Cuba was another Third World country that became the focus of Cold War rivalries. From 1934 through 1958, Cuba was ruled by dictator Fulgencio Batista y Zaldívar (1901–1973). Maintaining strong ties with the United States, Batista allowed U.S. corporations to dominate the economy of the island, including the sugar industry and oil production. The arrangement led to severe economic problems among the Cuban population. Unemployment and illiteracy were high, and disease was widespread. Because of U.S. corporate involvement in Cuba, only a small percent of the population accounted for most of Cuba's wealth. Young activist Fidel Castro Ruz (1926–) found the situation ripe for a revolt against the dictatorship. Leading the revolution, Castro seized power on January 1, 1959. He proposed to introduce major social and economic reforms. He also promised to reduce illiteracy, improve housing and health care, and combat organized crime. He wanted to end American economic domination. Like President Jacobo Arbenz Guzmán (1913–1971) in Guatemala, Castro proposed land reform, the breakup of large estates into smaller parcels for common citizens to own and farm. Alarmed by Castro's plans, U.S. businesses sought help from the Eisenhower administration.

Castro drew the ire of U.S. officials by rounding up hundreds of Batista supporters and executing them, with minimal legal process. Although the United States extended

Revolutionary leader Fidel Castro waves to the crowd after seizing power of the Cuban government on January 1, 1959. *Reproduced by permission of the Corbis Corporation.*

diplomatic recognition to Castro's government, Eisenhower refused to meet with Castro when Castro made a visit to the United States in April 1959. Castro sought financial aid from the United States to support his reforms, but the United States refused to give such aid. By late 1959, Castro's Cuba nationalized, or took control and ownership of, private businesses and foreign holdings on the island, including American banks.

Eisenhower concluded that Castro was a communist, although Castro was actually a nationalist, not a communist, at the time. Eisenhower saw the new Cuban leader as a threat to Latin America. Unable to obtain American aid, Castro signed a trade agreement with the Soviet Union in February 1960. Eisenhower then decided to initiate a CIA plan to overthrow Castro; the U.S. government would train Cuban refugees to carry out the plan. Upon hearing of the secret plot, Castro turned more fully to the Soviets for help and protection. The Soviet Union responded with economic aid. Castro also signed arms agreements with Eastern European countries. By the summer of 1960, Cuba had become part of the Soviet sphere of influence. Eisenhower responded decisively by reducing and then cutting U.S. imports of Cuban sugar. While Castro was nationalizing foreign land holdings, the United States made it clear that it would never allow the Guantánamo naval base, located on the eastern tip of Cuba, to be seized. Castro responded by nationalizing all other American interests. On September 26, 1960, Castro strongly denounced U.S. policies in a speech before the United Nations (UN) General Assembly. In October, Eisenhower placed an embargo, or trade stoppage, on most U.S. exports to Cuba, and by January 1961 Eisenhower had severed diplomatic ties with Cuba, leaving the island an outpost of Soviet influence in the Western Hemisphere.

Other major changes were brewing as well in the broader Third World arena. In September 1960, the UN General Assembly met at its headquarters in New York City. Seventeen new nations, sixteen of which were former Western colonies in Africa, were accepted as UN members. The UN was becoming an international organization of largely Third World nations, quite different from its original fifty members in 1945, which were mainly European nations. Seizing on the opportunity, on September 24 Khrushchev made a speech to the General Assembly in which he sought to align the Soviet Union with the Third World in opposition to Western colonialism. It was clear that the United States would no longer dominate UN activities.

Darkening skies

Following the meeting of Khrushchev and Eisenhower at Camp David in September 1959, the two superpowers had worked toward a summit meeting through early 1960. Key issues were a new U.S. proposal for a test-ban agreement and the Berlin occupation. By late March, in preparation for the summit meeting, the United States, Great Britain, and the Soviet Union had worked out the basic elements of a comprehensive nuclear test ban. The summit meeting was then scheduled for May in Paris. Hope was running high for greater cooperation between the two superpowers.

However, just as a major breakthrough in U.S.-Soviet relations seemed a certainty, shocking news halted diplo-

matic progress. On May 7, 1960, Khrushchev announced that on May 1 an American U-2 spy plane had been shot down deep inside the Soviet Union. Since July 1956, over two hundred U-2 missions had been flown. Though he had orders to commit suicide rather than be captured, the American pilot, Francis Gary Powers (1929–1977), was securely in Soviet hands. At first, Khrushchev tried to quietly resolve the matter by giving Eisenhower an opportunity to claim that he personally knew nothing of the spy flights and that any future flights would be stopped. Eisenhower refused to claim personal innocence. Next, Khrushchev, angry that the United States was spying during a period when the superpowers were working on a thawing of relations, asked for an apology. Not wanting to give in to a Khrushchev demand, Eisenhower angrily refused. The Paris summit meeting began as scheduled on May 19, 1960, but with Khrushchev's refusal to participate, little hope of progress existed; the U-2 spy controversy had chilled the diplomatic atmosphere. Eisen-

An angry Nikita Khrushchev pounds his fist at a United Nations session in October 1960. *Reproduced by permission of AP/Wide World Photos.*

hower returned to Washington, D.C., two days later. The test-ban agreement was left uncompleted and the future of Berlin unresolved.

For More Information

Alexander, Charles C. *Holding the Line: The Eisenhower Era, 1952–1961.* Bloomington: Indiana University Press, 1975.

Brands, H. W., Jr. *The Specter of Neutralism: The United States and the Emergence of the Third World, 1947–1960.* New York: Columbia University Press, 1989.

Divine, Robert A. *The Sputnik Challenge.* New York: Oxford University Press, 1993.

Dockrill, Michael. *The Cold War, 1945–1963.* London: Macmillan, 1988.

Kalb, Madeleine G. *The Congo Cables: The Cold War in Africa—From Eisenhower to Kennedy.* New York: Macmillan, 1982.

Kaufman, Burton I. *Trade and Aid: Eisenhower's Foreign Economic Policy, 1953–1961.* Baltimore, MD: Johns Hopkins University Press, 1982.

Khrushchev, Nikita S. *Khrushchev Remembers.* Edited by Strobe Talbott. Boston: Little, Brown, 1970.

Khrushchev, Nikita S. *Khrushchev Remembers: The Last Testament.* Edited by Strobe Talbott. Boston: Little, Brown, 1974.

Linden, Carl A. *Khrushchev and the Soviet Leadership.* Baltimore, MD: Johns Hopkins University Press, 1990.

Van Oudenaren, John. *Detente in Europe: The Soviet Union and the West Since 1953.* Durham, NC: Duke University Press, 1991.

Cuban Missile Crisis

9

In November 1960, U.S. senator John F. Kennedy (1917– 1963) of Massachusetts defeated Vice President Richard M. Nixon (1913–1994) in the presidential election. Kennedy was taking on a difficult job: U.S. relations with the Soviet Union were declining, and the world seemed to be proceeding deeper into crisis and conflict. A prime example of this was displayed on the evening of October 22, 1962, when Kennedy addressed the nation via television. The president had undisputable evidence that Soviet-built nuclear missiles capable of reaching the United States and many Latin American countries were in place in Cuba, 90 miles (145 kilometers) from the U.S. shoreline.

As noted in the *Public Papers of the Presidents of the United States,* in his televised address, Kennedy said, "Should these offensive military preparations continue ... further action will be justified. I have directed the Armed Forces to prepare for any eventualities [possible action].... It shall be the policy of this Nation to regard any nuclear missile launched from Cuba against any nation in the Western Hemisphere as an attack by the Soviet Union on the United States, requiring a full retaliatory response upon the Soviet Union.... No one can foresee precisely

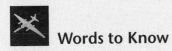

Words to Know

Bay of Pigs: Failed U.S.-backed invasion of Cuba at the Bay of Pigs by fifteen hundred Cuban exiles opposed to Fidel Castro, on April 17, 1961.

Capitalism: An economic system in which property and businesses are privately owned. Prices, production, and distribution of goods are determined by competition in a market relatively free of government intervention.

Communism: A system of government in which the nation's leaders are selected by a single political party that controls all aspects of society. Private ownership of property is eliminated and government directs all economic production. The goods produced and accumulated wealth are, in theory, shared relatively equally by all. All religious practices are banned.

Cuban Missile Crisis: A showdown in October 1962 that brought the Soviet Union and the United States close to war over the existence of Soviet nuclear missiles in Cuba.

Democracy: A system of government that allows multiple political parties. Their members are elected to various government offices by popular vote of the people.

National Security Agency (NSA): The United States' premier organization assigned to protect U.S. information systems and listen in on and analyze foreign intelligence information.

Quarantine: A blockade; during the Cuban Missile Crisis, the United States installed a buildup of naval ships around Cuba, with the intent of preventing any additional Soviet ships and their military cargo from reaching Cuba. Because blockades were against international law, the term "quarantine" was used instead.

what course it [the retaliation] will take or what costs or casualties will be incurred." In the following decades, especially during the 1990s as Soviet documents became available, records revealed that in late October 1962, the world was indeed at the brink of a nuclear holocaust. The intersection of the careers of a U.S. president and a newly established leader of a small nearby island, Fidel Castro Ruz (1926–), would keep the world's population on the edge of their seats for many days.

A young Fidel Castro

Born in Mayarí, Cuba, in 1926, Castro grew up in a solidly middle-class home. He graduated from the University of Havana in 1950 with a law degree. During most of Castro's early years, Fulgencio Batista y Zaldívar (1901–1973), an oppressive dictator (a leader who uses force and terror to maintain control), ruled Cuba. Batista had been in complete control of the island since 1933, either directly or through other presidents. Batista's economic policies helped establish light industries, such as canneries, and allowed foreign companies, many from the United States, to build their businesses in Cuba. U.S. corporations dominated the sugar industry, oil production, and other key aspects of the island's economy. Most of Cuba's wealth was owned by a tiny percentage of the population; most Cuban citizens lived in dire poverty. Under these circumstances, Cuba was ripe for revolution, and Castro, the handsome, intense young lawyer, proved to be a charismatic leader.

 People to Know

Fulgencio Batista y Zaldívar (1901–1973): Cuban dictatorial leader, 1933–44, 1952–59.

Anatoly Dobrynin (1919–): Soviet ambassador to the United States, 1962–86.

Fidel Castro Ruz (1926–): Cuban premier/president, 1959–.

Dwight D. Eisenhower (1890–1969): Thirty-fourth U.S. president, 1953–61.

John F. Kennedy (1917–1963): Thirty-fifth U.S. president, 1961–63.

Robert F. Kennedy (1925–1968): U.S. attorney general, 1961–64.

Nikita S. Khrushchev (1894–1971): Soviet premier, 1958–64.

In 1953, Castro attempted to overthrow Batista and was sent to prison. After his release in 1955, Castro went to Mexico and immediately gathered rebels together. In December 1956, Castro and his men landed in Cuba and carried on guerrilla, or irregular and independent, attacks against Batista's army for the next few years. The people of Cuba, especially the many who lived in poverty, increasingly supported the young revolutionaries, or those seeking radical change. On January 1, 1959, Batista fled Cuba. Within weeks, Castro established himself as premier.

Initially, the United States supported Castro, who was not a communist at the time. Communists believe that the best economic system is one that eliminates private ownership of property. Under this system, the goods produced and the wealth accumulated are, in theory, shared equally by all. A single party, the Communist Party, controls government and almost all other aspects of society. Communism is in direct contrast with the values of democratic, capitalist countries such as

A young Fidel Castro (seated). *Courtesy of the Library of Congress.*

the United States. A democratic government system requires government leaders and others who hold public office to be elected by the citizens in general elections. Candidates represent different political parties—and ultimately, all the people who vote for them. Capitalist economic systems allow private ownership of property and businesses. Competition in a free, or open, market determines prices, production, and distribution of goods.

The American media, including *Life* and *Reader's Digest* magazines, hailed Castro as an educated, daring, determined soldier. Castro wanted to lift Cubans out of poverty. He cut rents, proposed improved education and health care, and instituted farming reform, or dramatic change. He broke up large estates into smaller parcels for common citizens to farm. He also sought to end America's domination of the Cuban economy. However, Castro made no movement toward setting up free elections, which he had earlier promised to do. Appalled at Castro's actions, many middle-class and wealthy Cubans fled to the United States. From there, they began an anti-Castro campaign aimed at influencing the Cubans who stayed behind. To Castro's dismay, the United States did nothing to stop the anti-Castro effort. When Castro sought aid for his reforms from the United States, he was refused. During 1960, Cuba's relations with the United States rapidly slid downhill. The Soviet Union was ready and able to step in, signing a trade agreement with Castro in February 1960.

Moving toward communism

During mid-1960, Castro nationalized, or took control and ownership of, a billion dollars' worth of U.S. businesses in Cuba, including American oil refineries and banks. In response, U.S. president Dwight D. Eisenhower (1890–1969;

served 1953–61) halted U.S. importation of Cuban sugar, but the Soviet Union quickly agreed to buy the surplus. The Soviets also agreed to supply petroleum products to Cuba. In September 1960, Castro met Soviet premier Nikita Khrushchev (1894–1971) at the United Nations in New York City. Khrushchev warmly received Castro and privately gloated that communism had its first toehold in the Americas. Castro publicly aligned his country with the communist Soviet Union. On January 3, 1961, the United States and Cuba broke all diplomatic ties. For the most part, the American populace of the early 1960s believed that no leader would voluntarily turn toward communism; they figured that the Soviets must have been behind Castro all along. They overwhelmingly supported a hard-line anti-Castro policy.

President Eisenhower had early on suspected that Castro would take Cuba down the communist path, so in March 1960 he had secretly authorized the use of $13 million to train Cuban exiles, the people who had fled Cuba, to carry out an invasion of Cuba and oust Castro. Approximately fifteen hundred exiles volunteered to be trained for this job by the U.S. Central Intelligence Agency (CIA). The top-secret training took place in the Central American countries of Guatemala and Nicaragua.

The Bay of Pigs fiasco

When President Kennedy took office, he inherited the Cuban problem. He had been briefed by Eisenhower's administration about the plans to remove Castro. Surprised, Kennedy nevertheless allowed the CIA and the Cuban exiles to proceed. However, knowing that it would look bad for a powerful nation to invade a tiny island, he refused to involve the American military; U.S. military aircraft would not be allowed to provide cover for the invasion. Kennedy hoped it would appear that the United States had played no part. The CIA and the fifteen hundred exiles, sure that the Cuban people would rise up and aid their effort against Castro, went ahead with their invasion on April 17, 1961, at a swampy beach area known as the Bay of Pigs.

Castro had gotten word of the planned invasion through informants who knew some of the exiles and had

Anti-Castro forces captured during the failed Bay of Pigs invasion are marched off to prison on April 21, 1961.
Reproduced by permission of the Corbis Corporation.

his army ready with Soviet-made tanks. The defeat of the invading exiles was swift and complete. It was clear the failed invasion was backed by the United States, because the band of exiles could have never become so organized or bold otherwise. Kennedy was publicly embarrassed by the failure. He vowed that in the future he would consider more carefully the advice of those surrounding him.

The Cuban people had not risen up to overthrow Castro as expected. Instead, the Bay of Pigs invasion seemed to increase their support of Castro. Now firmly in the communist camp, Castro railed against American imperialism. (Imperialism is the practice of taking over other countries by force for economic or political gain.)

By this time, the Castro that Americans constantly saw on television was an eccentric-looking character: He always dressed in a military uniform, he had a scruffy beard, and his cigar seemed to be permanently attached to his mouth. Convinced that Castro was a serious threat to the

United States, President Kennedy ordered Operation Mongoose, a top-secret plan to oust Castro. Operation Mongoose encompassed various plots, from placing hallucinatory drugs in Castro's drinking water to assassinating him. However, Operation Mongoose never materialized.

Communism on the march

Khrushchev was eager to maintain the forward progress of communism in the Western Hemisphere. By the spring of 1962, he had already sent many advisors and arms to Cuba. The Soviet investment in the island was substantial. Cuba's locale was a logistic dream for Khrushchev and a nightmare for the United States. Khrushchev fumed over the fact that U.S. missiles with nuclear warheads were openly located in Turkey, Italy, and the United Kingdom, within easy striking distance of the Soviet Union. Khrushchev admitted that those warheads scared the Soviets. The Soviets had never placed nuclear weapons outside their country's boundaries, because the weapons positioned inside the Soviet Union had the capability of annihilating Western Europe and reaching the United States. Nevertheless, Khrushchev knew that if he stationed nuclear weapons in Cuba, only 90 miles from the U.S. coastline, it would cause Americans a great deal of anxiety.

When approached with the idea, Castro was not convinced that he wanted his island to be an outpost of Soviet nuclear weapons. But he soon agreed, and sent his brother Raúl and a Cuban military delegation to Moscow to work out the details. Castro wanted the missiles openly placed on Cuba, with the full knowledge of the international community. He hoped this would raise his status among Latin American leaders. But Khrushchev insisted on secrecy; he believed that once the missiles were in place, the United States could not act without the possibility of provoking war. So in secrecy the Soviets planned to install forty missile launchers in Cuba. Of the forty, twenty-four would be SS-5 medium-range ballistic missile (MRBM) launchers, each armed with two missiles. Each missile, armed with a nuclear warhead, had an explosive power equal to 1 million tons (907,000 metric tons) of TNT. At the end of World War II (1939–45), the city of Hiroshima, Japan, had been leveled in minutes by the equivalent of 13,000 tons (11,791 metric tons) of TNT. The MRBMs had a

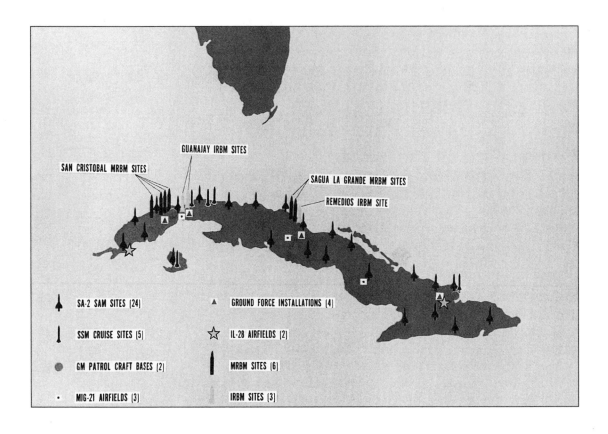

A map of Cuba in 1962 showing Soviet missile sites and the types of installations at each.
Reproduced by permission of the Corbis Corporation.

range of 1,100 miles (1,270 kilometers), so Washington, D.C.; Dallas, Texas; and all the southeastern states were at risk. The other sixteen missile launchers would be long-range, capable of sending missiles northward to Canada and south into Latin America. Calculations showed that the only major U.S. city they could not reach was Seattle, Washington.

In July 1962, Soviet ships sailed toward Cuba with their cargo of missile equipment. Also headed for Cuba was the latest Soviet military equipment plus over forty thousand Soviet troops. Soviet fighter planes known as MiG's, some bombers to be assembled in Cuba, and surface-to-air missiles (SAMs) to protect the nuclear missile sites all moved across the Atlantic Ocean to Cuba. The size of the undertaking was enormous. All the while, the Soviet government consistently assured the United States that the arms buildup in Cuba was purely defensive in nature—that the Soviet Union had no need to station missiles outside its own territory. These assurances would soon prove to be lies.

Revelations of October 14, 1962

Alarming intelligence reports from the National Security Agency (NSA) began late in 1960 and continued in 1961. The NSA was America's prime intelligence organization that listened to and analyzed foreign communications. Through intercepted messages, the NSA determined that Cuba was significantly building up its weapons, with the Soviet Union's help.

Additionally, the NSA heard Spanish being spoken on a surveillance tape from Czechoslovakia, an Eastern European nation under Soviet control; it turned out that Cuban fighter pilots were being trained in Czechoslovakia by the Soviet military. The NSA also intercepted messages that indicated that Soviet ships headed for Havana, Cuba, had no cargo listed—a quiet method of concealing the equipment they carried. The NSA reported on construction of SAM sites and new radar installations of air defense systems in Cuba. They also spotted Cubans training on Russian military equipment. U.S. officials in Washington, D.C., grew increasingly worried. Nevertheless, all these systems could be categorized as defensive systems, and Soviet authorities continued to insist that everything they provided to Cuba was purely defensive. U-2 reconnaissance aircraft, secret planes that gathered information, flew at high altitudes over Cuba, and the pictures they brought back did not indicate any offensive weapons sites in Cuba.

Then on October 14, 1962, a U-2 mission returned with chilling photographs. Processed and analyzed on October 15, the photos showed the first clear evidence of medium-range ballistic missiles at construction sites in an area known as San Cristóbal. The photographs arrived on the desk of the president's national security advisor, McGeorge Bundy (1919–1996), on the evening of October 15. The MRBM installation appeared almost complete; the longer-range equipment looked as if it would not be ready until the end of the year. Knowing that sleep would be hard to come by for a while, a grim Bundy decided to let the president sleep that night.

At 9 A.M. the next morning, Bundy showed and explained the photographs to President Kennedy. Kennedy immediately called together a small group of senior cabinet members, security officials, and military leaders to assess the situation and advise him. The group became known as Ex-Comm, short for Executive Committee of the National Secu-

Kennedy's Favorite Spy Photograph

Mounted on a wall in President Kennedy's office was a photograph of a Cuban launch site for Soviet SAMs, surface-to-air missiles. The picture clearly shows roads in a six-pointed star pattern connecting the launch sites. The picture was taken at an altitude of less than 500 feet (152 meters), at 713 miles (1,147 kilometers) per hour, by a U.S. Air Force RF-101C. Kennedy liked the photograph because of the clarity of the geometric design of the missile installations.

rity Council; it stayed almost continuously in session for the next two weeks. (The National Security Council is part of the executive branch of the U.S. government. The council advises the president on matters of foreign policy and defense.) With an eye cast toward historical documentation, Kennedy secretly had all the brainstorming discussions of Ex-Comm tape-recorded.

The following days brought the United States and the Soviet Union to the brink of nuclear war. When the Ex-Comm tapes became available in the 1990s at the close of the Cold War, they confirmed that there were several moments when one more command or one slight move on either country's part could have unleashed a nuclear holocaust. On October 16, 17, and 18 Ex-Comm discussions included a variety of proposals, from doing nothing, at least not immediately, to staging an invasion of Cuba. Members of the committee divided into two camps: hawks and doves. Hawks favored immediate military strikes to take out the missiles and Castro's communist government. Key hawks were General Maxwell Taylor (1901–1987), chairman of the Joint Chiefs of Staff, and other military leaders at the Pentagon. Doves, fearing massive casualties, favored a strategy of diplomacy and less aggressive tactics. Key doves were Secretary of State Dean Rusk (1909–1994) and Secretary of Defense Robert McNamara (1916–). At the outset, Attorney General Robert F. Kennedy (1925–1968), the president's brother, joined the Joint Chiefs of Staff in supporting an invasion or a surprise air strike. However, after further discussions, he decided an air strike was not in the best interests of the United States. In fact, many Ex-Comm members changed their minds—supporting one position, then another—as ideas were discussed.

All Ex-Comm members agreed from the start on one objective: The missiles must be removed from Cuba one way or another. President Kennedy and Ex-Comm could not permit this armed Soviet intrusion into the Americas, within

LAUNCH POSITION

MISSILE-READY TENTS

MISSILE ERECTORS

easy reach of North, Central, and South America. If the United States did not respond, the committee reasoned, Khrushchev would push for more communist influence in the region; this would undermine U.S. leadership in the Western Hemisphere and cause a massive negative reaction among the American public. Kennedy's political future would be in doubt, and fear of eventually being surrounded by Soviet-controlled communist states would increase.

Aerial reconnaissance photo shows a Soviet missile site in San Cristóbal, Cuba, on November 3, 1962. *Reproduced by permission of the Corbis Corporation.*

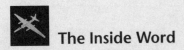

The Inside Word

The response of the U.S. intelligence system during the Cuban Missile Crisis helped President John F. Kennedy navigate the ominous days of late October 1962. Three groups played key roles in providing information from surveillance and reconnaissance missions. (Surveillance and reconnaissance refer to examination and survey of enemy territory and activities.) The groups included the Signals Intelligence, the Strategic Air Command, and the Tactical Air Command.

Signals Intelligence, or SIGINT, is part of the National Security Agency (NSA). NSA is America's premier organization assigned to protect U.S. information systems and listen in on and analyze foreign intelligence information. NSA is the largest employer of mathematicians in the United States; NSA employees are often referred to as the "codemakers and codebreakers." SIGINT has a long and fabled history: In World War II (1939–45) SIGINT broke the codes of the Japanese military, helping bring an end to the war. SIGINT monitored the Soviet arms buildup in Cuba at its earliest stages, in mid-1960. SIGINT listened in on and analyzed Soviet communications discussing the operation to supply Cuba with weapons; they also heard messages from Soviet ships headed for Havana. Then they intercepted Cuban discussions about the arrival of "Russian equipment" at the unloading docks.

By May 1961, SIGINT listened to radio chatter from Cuba about special ship cargo—defensive radar systems associated with antiaircraft weapons. Then in August and September 1962, SIGINT picked up information that SAMs, surface-to-air missiles, had arrived on the island. Subsequently it reported that fifteen SAMs were operational, most likely in position to protect secret operations. In other words, the SAMs were in position to shoot down U.S. Air Force reconnaissance flights.

President Kennedy addresses the American people

On Thursday, October 18, intelligence reports given to Ex-Comm indicated that medium-range missiles were almost ready, capable of being launched from Cuba in about eighteen hours. That afternoon, Soviet foreign minister Andrey Gromyko (1909–1989), in the United States for a United Nations meeting, met with President Kennedy at the White House. Kennedy did not reveal his proof of the missiles. Gromyko still insisted that Soviet military assistance for

The Strategic Air Command (SAC) of the U.S. Air Force operated the high-flying U-2 aircraft that photographed various portions of Cuba. In October 1962, photographs taken on U-2 missions revealed definite construction of bases for intermediate-range ballistic missiles only 90 miles (145 kilometers) from the U.S. coastline.

While U-2s continued their high-altitude photography, the Tactical Air Command (TAC), also part of the U.S. Air Force, used the RF-101C aircraft to take low-level photographs of Cuban missile sites and of the docks where Soviet ships brought their cargo. The crews of the RF-101Cs directed photography on daring flights that traveled at 700 to 1,000 miles (1,126 to 1,609 kilometers) per hour, often at treetop level. U-2 and RF-101C aircraft continued making reconnaissance flights throughout the Cuban Missile Crisis. On October 27, one U-2 was lost over Cuba when it was shot down by a SAM.

SIGINT provided round-the-clock information to senior military and political leaders. The SIGINT command center was under the direction of Juanita Moody, who had served as a cryptanalyst (codebreaker) during World War II. She and Lieutenant General Gordon Blake took the responsibility of overseeing the staff of the command center and getting information to the White House. It was SIGINT, through interception of radio messages from Soviet vessels, that first notified President Kennedy on October 24 that the "quarantine" appeared to be working. Mapping the location of the Soviet vessels, SIGINT confirmed that the ships appeared to be stopped in the water outside the ring of American ships.

SIGINT, along with U-2 and RF-101C aircraft, continued surveillance and reconnaissance as the Cuban missiles were dismantled and shipped back to the Soviet Union.

Cuba was only defensive. Late that night, Ex-Comm decided against immediate invasion of Cuba and settled tentatively on a more cautious plan—a naval blockade around Cuba that would prevent any additional Soviet ships and their military cargo from reaching Cuba.

President Kennedy did not want to announce the grave situation to the American public until a plan of action was decided upon, so he continued his planned schedule of campaign appearances as if nothing was amiss (the purpose of these appearances was to support various candidates for the upcoming November midterm elections). As plans favoring the blockade firmed up, he cancelled the rest of his campaign appearances. Kennedy thought the blockade most likely would not trigger immediate war. While demonstrating that the United States would not tolerate the missiles, the U.S. response still gave Khrushchev a way out and time to withdraw from the situation. Because blockades were against international law, the term "quarantine" was used instead.

Once the decision for a quarantine was made, Kennedy requested that the television networks clear out a prime-time evening slot on Monday, October 22, for an urgent address to the nation. Anatoly Dobrynin (1919–), the Soviet ambassador to the United States, who knew nothing of the offensive missiles, was handed the text of Kennedy's speech shortly before airtime. Dumbfounded, he quietly went back and sat in his embassy office, attempting to gather himself before relaying Kennedy's message to Moscow's leaders.

Addressing the American people, President Kennedy explained the situation fully. As noted in the *Public Papers of the Presidents of the United States,* Kennedy announced that the quarantine was scheduled to begin the morning of October 24, that the U.S. military was on full alert and prepared for any scenario, and that any nuclear missile launched would require a "full retaliatory response." Kennedy called for immediate meetings of the Organization of American States (OAS) and the United Nations Security Council. (All the nations of North, Central, and South America make up the OAS, which was created to ensure mutual protection and cooperation in the Western Hemisphere.) Kennedy called "upon Chairman Khrushchev to halt and eliminate this clandestine [secret], reckless, and provocative threat to world peace and to stabilize relations between our two nations." Kennedy called on Khrushchev "to move the world back from the abyss [pit or depth] of destruction." As Kennedy spoke, the Joint Chiefs of Staff put the level of U.S. military alert worldwide at DEFCON 3, heightened state of preparedness for nuclear war. DEFCON, short for Defense Condition, is a rating system describing progressive alert levels used within the military; DEFCON 5 is normal peacetime readiness, while DEFCON 1 is maximum force readiness (for instance, an enemy's missiles are in the air and a nuclear war is imminent). For the first time in history, all planes of the U.S.

An editorial cartoon depicting a western-style showdown between cowboys: on the left, U.S. president John F. Kennedy; on the right, Cuban president Fidel Castro (riding donkey) and Soviet leader Nikita Khrushchev (riding horse). *Illustration by Leslie Gilbert Illingworth,* Daily Mail *(London). Courtesy of the Library of Congress.*

air defense system were armed with nuclear weapons. U.S. nuclear submarines took up assigned positions, and nuclear missiles located in the United States were readied for firing.

To the brink of nuclear war

On October 23, Khrushchev denounced the quarantine as a violation of international law. Khrushchev vowed that his ships would continue on course, that any American ship trying to stop them would be fired on by Soviet submarines stationed around Cuba. Those Soviet submarines had each been armed with a nuclear warhead, and their crew members had orders to fire if provoked. It appeared Moscow would push to the brink of nuclear war. The secretary general of the United Nations issued a plea to the United States and the Soviet Union, asking them not to push the world into war.

On the morning of October 24, the U.S. quarantine went into place, and the U.S. military went to DEFCON 2, the last level before nuclear war. This alert level was reached at no other time in history. Then U.S. intelligence reported an amazing development: It appeared that the Soviet ships had halted in the ocean. Secretary of State Rusk made his famous statement, "We're eyeball to eyeball and I think the other fellow just blinked," as noted in Dino A. Brugioni's *Eyeball to Eyeball: The Inside Story of the Cuban Missile Crisis.* Yet Khrushchev did not back down entirely. He relayed a message to President Kennedy calling the quarantine an aggressive act, and the missiles already in Cuba remained. However, on October 25, the Soviet vessels carrying military equipment turned around. Those with no military equipment proceeded; they were searched and then allowed to go on to Havana.

Meantime, at President Kennedy's request, Robert Kennedy was having secret "backdoor" meetings with Soviet ambassador Dobrynin. On the evening of October 26, a long emotional letter from Khrushchev offered to remove the missiles from Cuba if the United States vowed not to invade Cuba. Dobrynin and Robert Kennedy met, and Dobrynin brought up the offensive U.S. missiles located in Turkey. The next morning, October 27, before President Kennedy could respond to Khrushchev's first letter, a second, more demanding letter insisted that the United States agree to remove the missiles in Turkey if the Soviets agreed to remove the missiles in Cuba. Events that Saturday—known as Black Saturday because many felt it was the day the world came closest to annihilation—turned even uglier. A U.S. U-2 flight over Alaska drifted into Soviet airspace, and the Soviets regarded it as a test of their defense system. The U-2 simply drifted out of Soviet airspace without incident, but it caused much tension among Soviet leaders. Then in Cuba, another American U-2 was spotted and brought down with a surface-to-air missile. The pilot was killed. Amid the worsening situation, the U.S. military command was clamoring for a fight. In their book *Cold War: An Illustrated History, 1945–1991,* Jeremy Isaacs and Taylor Downing report that Secretary of Defense McNamara walked out of the White House that evening into the open air and thought he would never live to see another Saturday.

Robert Kennedy advised the president to simply ignore Khrushchev's demands in the second letter and accept the terms of the first letter. President Kennedy agreed. Robert Kennedy then met with Dobrynin and informed him that the United States would halt the quarantine and not invade Cuba if the Soviets would pull out the missiles. When Dobrynin asked about the missiles in Turkey, Kennedy assured him that those missiles would be removed after the crisis was over. However, Kennedy insisted that this agreement be kept secret, because the United States could not appear to withdraw protection for Western Europe for its own purposes. Dobrynin relayed this information to Moscow. Soviet leaders did not realize that the United States considered the missiles in Turkey outdated and had intended to remove them soon anyway. The next morning, October 28, Khrushchev agreed to remove the missiles from Cuba. Immediately both sides breathed easier. DEFCON was reset at alert level 5, the lowest concern level. Khrushchev proceeded to bring the Soviet missiles back to the Soviet Union.

Both Khrushchev and President Kennedy could claim their diplomacy halted the crisis when it appeared to be spiraling out of control. Castro, on the other hand, gained no advantage from their agreement; he was outraged over the missiles being removed, angered because he was totally left out of the negotiations by Krushchev and not even consulted about their removal, but he could do nothing about it. Despite the appearance of defeat, Khrushchev's main goal was to keep Cuba communist, and in the early twenty-first century, Cuba remained a communist country.

By the spring of 1963, the United States had removed all its missiles from Turkey. Press reports never mentioned that their removal had anything to do with the Cuban Mis-

Attorney General Robert F. Kennedy (left) consults with President John F. Kennedy on October 1, 1962, during the Cuban Missile Crisis. *Reproduced by permission of the Corbis Corporation.*

President John F. Kennedy looks relieved after a news conference in November 1962, following the end of the Cuban Missile Crisis. *Reproduced by permission of the Corbis Corporation.*

sile Crisis. Few people knew that the missiles in Turkey had been replaced by much more effective missiles on a Polaris submarine.

The world had been to the brink of nuclear war, but at that point, having scared themselves mightily, the superpowers compromised. Sobered leaders in Washington, D.C., and Moscow began serious talks to start the process of bringing nuclear weapons under control with a test-ban treaty. In June 1963, a direct hot line was set up between Washington, D.C., and Moscow to help reduce the chance of nuclear war occurring because of miscalculation or misunderstanding.

For More Information

Books

Allison, Graham T., and Philip Zelikow. *Essence of Decision: Explaining the Cuban Missile Crisis.* 2nd ed. New York: Longman, 1999.

Brubaker, Paul E. *The Cuban Missile Crisis in American History.* Berkeley Heights, NJ: Enslow, 2001.

Brugioni, Dino A. *Eyeball to Eyeball: The Inside Story of the Cuban Missile Crisis.* New York: Random House, 1991.

Chang, Laurence, and Peter Kornbluh, eds. *The Cuban Missile Crisis, 1962: A National Security Archive Documents Reader.* New York: New Press, 1998.

Chrisp, Peter. *Cuban Missile Crisis.* Milwaukee, WI: World Almanac Library, 2002.

Finkelstein, Norman H. *Thirteen Days/Ninety Miles: The Cuban Missile Crisis.* New York: J. Messner, 1994.

Fursenko, Aleksandr, and Timothy Naftali. *"One Hell of a Gamble": Khrushchev, Castro, and Kennedy, 1958–1964.* New York: W. W. Norton, 2000.

Huchthausen, Peter A., and Alexander Hoyt. *October Fury.* Hoboken, NJ: Wiley, 2002.

Isaacs, Jeremy, and Taylor Downing. *Cold War: An Illustrated History, 1945–1991.* Boston: Little, Brown, 1998.

Kennedy, John F. *Public Papers of the Presidents of the United States: John F. Kennedy, Containing the Public Messages, Speeches, and Statements of the President, 1963.* Washington, DC: U.S. Government Printing Office, 1963.

Kennedy, Robert F., and Arthur Schlesinger. *Thirteen Days: A Memoir of the Cuban Missile Crisis.* W. W. Norton, 1999.

Lynch, Grayston L. *Decision for Disaster: Betrayal at the Bay of Pigs.* 2nd ed. Washington, DC: Brassey's, 2000.

May, Ernest R., and Philip D. Zelikow, eds. *The Kennedy Tapes: Inside the White House during the Cuban Missile Crisis.* New York: W. W. Norton, 2002.

Medina, Loreta M., ed. *Cuban Missile Crisis.* San Diego: Greenhaven Press, 2002.

Thompson, Robert S. *The Missiles of October: The Declassified Story of John F. Kennedy and the Cuban Missile Crisis.* New York: Simon and Schuster, 1992.

Triay, Victor Andres. *Bay of Pigs: An Oral History of Brigade 2506.* Gainesville: University Press of Florida, 2001.

Web Sites

George Washington University. "The Cuban Missile Crisis, 1962: The 40th Anniversary." *National Security Archive.* http://www.gwu.edu/~nsarchiv/nsa/cuba_mis_cri/ (accessed on August 4, 2003).

National Security Agency. *NSA and the Cuban Missile Crisis.* http://www.nsa.gov/docs/cuba (accessed on August 4, 2003).

U.S. Air Force. "Cold War History: 1949–1989." *USAF Museum.* http://www.wpafb.af.mil/museum/history/coldwar/cw.htm (accessed on August 4, 2003).

Washington Post. "Reliving the World's Most Dangerous Days." *Cuban Missile Crisis*. http://www.washingtonpost.com/wp-srv/world/digital archive/index.html (accessed on August 4, 2003).

Other Sources

Kenny, Charles, ed. *John F. Kennedy: The Presidential Portfolio—History as Told through the John F. Kennedy Library and Museum*. Compact disc (audio). New York: PublicAffairs, 2000.

Mutual Assured Destruction

10

Andrey Sakharov (1921–1989), father of the Soviet Union's first true hydrogen bomb, witnessed the test of that bomb on November 22, 1955. He was distressed by what he saw and disturbed by the results of his work. As noted on the Public Broadcasting Service's *Race for the Superbomb* Web site, Sakharov wrote, "When you see all of this yourself, something in you changes. When you see the burned birds who are withering on the scorched steppe [land], when you see how the shock wave blows away buildings like houses of cards, when you feel the reek [smoke] of splintered bricks, when you sense melted glass, you immediately think of times of war ... All of this triggers an irrational yet very strong emotional impact."

Between 1945 and 1991, the Cold War dominated global affairs. The Cold War was a war of ideological differences between the United States and the Soviet Union, the countries that emerged as superpowers after World War II (1939–45). The Cold War came about because of differences in political, economic, and cultural systems, but ultimately what defined the Cold War was nuclear weapons. By the late 1960s, both superpowers had spent and were continuing to

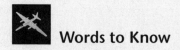

Words to Know

Cold War: A prolonged conflict for world dominance from 1945 to 1991 between the two superpowers, the democratic, capitalist United States and the communist Soviet Union. The weapons of conflict were commonly words of propaganda and threats.

Communism: A system of government in which the nation's leaders are selected by a single political party that controls all aspects of society. Private ownership of property is eliminated and government directs all economic production. The goods produced and accumulated wealth are, in theory, shared relatively equally by all. All religious practices are banned.

Limited Test-Ban Treaty of 1963: An agreement between the United States, the Soviet Union, and Great Britain that banned nuclear bomb testing in the atmosphere, in outer space, or underwater. They could continue underground testing as long as radioactive fallout did not reach outside the country doing the testing.

Mutual assured destruction (MAD): A military strategy in which the threat of catastrophic damages by a nuclear counterstrike would deter any launch of a first-strike attack.

Strategic Air Command (SAC): A unit established by the U.S. military with the goal of identifying targets in the Soviet Union and being ready to deliver nuclear weapons to those targets.

Strategic arms: Military weapons key to the strategy of making the enemy incapable of conducting war; generally refers to long-ranging weapons.

Strategic Triad: The United States' trio of weapons aimed at the Soviet Union; the arsenal consisted of long- and intermediate-range missiles fitted with nuclear warheads, long-range bombers carrying nuclear weapons, and nuclear-powered submarines with onboard nuclear-tipped missiles.

Tactical arms: Military weapons that allow flexibility and skillful maneuverability in combat; generally referring to short-range weapons.

spend billions of dollars every day to develop and deploy nuclear weapons. Neither country wanted to use these weapons, but both wanted the dubious security of knowing they could annihilate the other side if the other side were to attack. If each could destroy the other, then starting a war meant assured self-destruction. Ironically, the buildup of nuclear weapons deterred the superpowers from starting a war with each other. "Assured destruction," a term first used about

1964, bluntly describes the end result of a nuclear war. The term soon evolved into "mutual assured destruction," appropriately abbreviated MAD.

Scientists and government leaders from both countries hoped that the threat of catastrophic damages by a nuclear counterstrike would deter the other side from launching a first-strike attack. At the same time, they continued to try to outwit the other side, building up their arsenals, or collections of weapons, with new arms and defense systems. This policy of deterrence, an attempt to discourage another nation from initiating hostile activity by threatening severe retaliation such as nuclear war, led the United States to develop the "Strategic Triad." The triad, or trio, of weapons, all aimed at the Soviet Union, included long- and intermediate-range missiles fitted with nuclear warheads, long-range bombers carrying nuclear weapons, and nuclear-powered submarines with onboard nuclear-tipped missiles. The Soviet Union responded by developing and deploying, or strategically distributing, the same types of weapons, all aimed at the United States. From the late 1950s and into the 1960s, the nuclear arms race was on.

Beginning to build nuclear stockpiles

In 1951, the U.S. Air Force began the Atlas missile project, the development of the first intercontinental ballistic missiles (ICBMs). It also concentrated on developing its attack force of long-range bombers. Both the missiles and bombers would carry nuclear warheads over thousands of miles to the Soviet Union. These long-range missiles and bombers were known as "strategic" weapons. Some political and military strategy experts began to worry that the United States would have to react to even a small conflict in Europe with an all-out nuclear assault. Because of the emphasis on long-range weapons that carry large payloads, weapons of lesser capability for responding with more limited means were neglected as part of the arsenal. So short-range, or "tactical," weapons were designed. These included rockets with ranges of about 100 miles (161 kilometers) and small artillery, both armed with nuclear warheads that could target advancing troops or other specific military sites rather than annihilate whole regions. The United States built both strategic and tactical weapons for its nuclear stockpiles.

Dr. Strangelove, or How I Learned to Stop Worrying and Love the Bomb

The movie *Dr. Strangelove, or How I Learned to Stop Worrying and Love the Bomb* arrived in theaters in 1964, only two years after the October 1962 Cuban Missile Crisis. The crisis took the world's superpowers, the United States and the Soviet Union, to the brink of nuclear war. The ruling military strategy of the 1960s was deterrence, or "mutual assured destruction" (MAD): If one superpower launched a first strike, it would kill millions and destroy the country being attacked. However, before this happened, the attacked country would launch a counterattack, thus assuring the mutual destruction of both countries. With MAD as the end result, neither superpower wanted to launch a first strike. Under these circumstances, it seemed that only a horrendous mistake or a madman controlling the command center would initiate a nuclear war.

Dr. Strangelove, directed by Stanley Kubrick (1928–1999), explores the madman scenario. In the early 1960s, the madman character, Jack D. Ripper, an insane U.S. Air Force general, orders a long-range bomber equipped with nuclear warheads to attack the Soviet Union. He is the only one who knows the code to call the bomber back but quickly seals off all communication channels. Dr. Strangelove, played by come-

Peter Sellers as Dr. Strangelove. *Reproduced by permission of the Kobal Collection.*

dic actor Peter Sellers (1925–1980), and President Muffley, also played by Sellers, try desperately but unsuccessfully to return the bombers to the United States. The Dr. Strangelove character is a German scientist who was brought to the United States after World War II to work on the U.S. missile projects. Considerable comic exaggeration is used throughout the movie. For example, the pilot of the bomber, played by Slim Pickens (1919–1983), straddles the nuclear bomb as it drops over the Soviet Union, slapping the bomb with his Stetson hat and yelling "Yahoo!" as if he's riding a bronco in a rodeo.

By the mid-1950s, the Soviet Union had successfully tested the hydrogen bomb and was developing ICBMs. Although the United States still had a greater number of nu-

clear weapons, the Soviets were making great strides in building up their country's nuclear arsenals. In response, the U.S. military services accelerated development of missile delivery systems—the ICBMs, intermediate-range ballistic missiles (IRBMs), and a new class of submarines. The United States spared no expense to make the systems operational as quickly as possible.

The Atlas ICBM missile, which could deliver a nuclear warhead 6,500 miles (10,459 kilometers) from the launch site, became the air force's number one priority. Two more ICBMs, Titan II and the Minuteman, were in development. Becoming operational in 1958, the Thor was the first U.S. IRBM; its range was 1,725 miles (2,776 kilometers). Meanwhile, the U.S. Navy designed and tested a new class of nuclear-powered submarine. The first nuclear-powered submarine, the USS *Nautilus,* went to sea in January 1955.

During the same period, U.S. Air Force general Curtis LeMay (1906–1990), who was in charge of the Strategic Air

Two U.S. B-47 bombers fly in formation in August 1953. *Reproduced by permission of the Corbis Corporation.*

Command (SAC), convinced Congress to fund more strategic and tactical nuclear weapons, as well as long-range bombers to carry the weapons. By the late 1950s, the air force had taken delivery of over two thousand B-47 Stratojet aircraft, including bombers, reconnaissance planes, and aircraft designed for training purposes. The B-47 could refuel in midair. Built by Boeing Aircraft, the B-47 would be the design prototype of the new Boeing 707 commercial jet airliner, which provided the basic design for airliners that followed. SAC also had roughly five hundred of the enormous, long-range B-52 bombers. Both the B-47s and B-52s could deliver nuclear bombs to the Soviet Union.

The Strategic Triad

To discourage an enemy attack, both the United States and the Soviet Union depended on the credible threat of retaliation. They had accumulated sufficient means to utterly destroy any foe, thus giving any potential enemy a second thought about taking offensive hostile action. The three nuclear deterrent systems developed in the 1950s in the United States became known as the Strategic Triad. The Triad included long-range bombers carrying nuclear weapons, land-based ICBMs, and nuclear-powered submarines. Each system was independent of the other, and each carried enough force to destroy the enemy. The enemy could not hope to destroy all three systems at the same time in a first strike, so the Strategic Triad seemed invincible. Each part of the Triad was operational by the early 1960s.

SAC kept a minimum of twelve long-range B-52 bombers airborne around the clock; each one carried three or four nuclear bombs. Refueled in midair, the B-52s traveled over North America and over the Mediterranean Sea. To back them up, half of the B-52 attack force on the ground stayed on alert and could be airborne in fifteen minutes.

Operational by 1959, the Atlas ICBMs were housed in underground missile silos in the central United States; a few resided on the West Coast and in New York State. The underground silos were for protection from enemy attack. An elevator raised the missile to the surface, because Atlas could only be fired from above ground.

Fifty-four technically advanced Titan II missiles were deployed in underground concrete sites by December 31, 1963; they were located near Tucson, Arizona; Jacksonville, Arkansas; and Wichita, Kansas. Quicker-reacting than the Atlas, the 150-ton (136-metric-ton) Titan IIs could be launched within one minute of an order. These missiles remained on alert into the early 1980s. The smaller (40-ton, or 36-metric ton) Minuteman, with the same long range of more than 6,000 miles (9,654 kilometers), was still in development. SAC deployed Thor IRBMs at sites in England in 1959, where they were maintained—ready to fire—by the Royal Air Force. During the Cuban Missile Crisis in October 1962, approximately 182 ICBMs were readied for immediate launch.

The third component of the Strategic Triad was ballistic missile submarines, referred to as SSBNs. These submarines were easily maneuverable and could hide for long periods in the depths of the ocean. Between 1960 and 1966, the U.S. Navy launched forty-one SSBNs (or "boomers," as

A Ballistic Missile Early Warning System tracking site in Clear, Alaska.
Reproduced by permission of the Corbis Corporation.

they were nicknamed). Each carried sixteen Polaris nuclear missiles. The submarines lay undetectable on the bottom of every ocean, on twenty-four-hour alert.

In addition to the offensive weapons, early-warning radar systems were essential. Operational by 1962, the Ballistic Missile Early Warning System (BMEWS) maintained three tracking sites: the first in Thule, Greenland; the second in Clear, Alaska; and the third on England's east coast at Fylingdales Moor. With radar trained on the Soviet Union, these sites could track any incoming missile. Information automatically went to the North American Air Defense Command, known as NORAD, located underground near Colorado Springs, Colorado. In turn, NORAD immediately alerted SAC, under the command of General Thomas Power (1905–1970), in Omaha, Nebraska. SAC served as the command center, the place where orders to fire nuclear weapons would originate. However, if SAC were destroyed, local commanders could give orders to fire nuclear weapons if they believed the United States to be under nuclear attack.

Although at the time exact figures were not available, the Soviet Union was believed to have nuclear capabilities similar to those of the United States. The Soviets had fewer weapons, but their nuclear warhead stockpile was considerable. Soviet ICBMs, aimed at U.S. cities, were housed in underground silos, just as the U.S. missiles were. A large Soviet SSBN force patrolled the depths of the oceans.

Keeping tensions high

Several occurrences greatly heightened tensions in the early 1960s. First, in May 1960, a U.S. Air Force U-2 reconnaissance (spy) flight flying high in the sky over the Soviet Union was brought down by new Soviet antiaircraft weapons. U.S. president Dwight Eisenhower (1890–1969; served 1953–61) refused to apologize to the Soviets; he also refused to promise that the spying would stop. Furious, Soviet leader Nikita Khrushchev (1894–1971) refused to participate in a scheduled summit meeting of world powers that month in Paris.

Next, on October 30, 1961, over the remote northwestern Soviet island of Novaya Zemlya, the Soviets tested what became known as the Soviet superbomb. The nuclear bomb had a force equal to 50 million tons (45 million metric tons) of TNT. (In comparison, the bomb that destroyed Hiroshima, Japan, in 1945 had a force equal to 13,000 tons of TNT.) The superbomb was the largest explosion on earth up to that date, but Khrushchev promised future bombs double its size. This promise was never turned into action, and in the early twenty-first century, the bomb of October 30, 1961, remained the largest bomb ever exploded.

The closest the superpowers came to initiating a worldwide nuclear holocaust was October 1962 during the Cuban Missile Crisis. The level of U.S. military alert worldwide was at DEFCON 2 alert, the last level before nuclear war and the first time in history that this alert level was reached. DEFCON, short for Defense Condition, is a rating system describing progressive alert levels used within the military; DEFCON 5 is normal peacetime readiness, while DEFCON 1 is maximum force readiness (for instance, an enemy's missiles are in the air and a nuclear war is imminent). The ICBMs in their silos and the SSBNs in the ocean were prepared for firing. It took high-level diplomacy and some luck to prevent an actual nuclear war (see Chapter 9, Cuban Missile Crisis).

Scared silly

Despite the nuclear arms race, as early as 1953 President Eisenhower, in his "Atoms for Peace" speech to the General Assembly of the United Nations, had proposed using nuclear power for peaceful purposes such as electrical power generation. The proposal was brushed aside. However, Khrushchev kept alive the notion of negotiating on constructive nuclear research and development. In 1956 at the Twentieth Congress of the Communist Party, he stated that war between the United States and the Soviet Union was not inevitable. Yet it took the Cuban Missile Crisis, when the superpowers took the world to the brink of nuclear war, to convert talk into action.

Scared silly by the crisis, U.S. and Soviet leaders set up a direct line of communication, a hot line between the White House and the Kremlin, or Soviet government, in Moscow. Going into effect on June 20, 1963, the Hot Line Agreement was designed to reduce the risk of a nuclear war being caused by misunderstanding, miscalculation, or accident. The hot line utilized transatlantic cables and radiotelegraph circuits

Nuclear Accidents

A number of chilling accidents involving B-52s carrying thermonuclear bombs occurred in the 1960s. The bombs ride in the B-52s in an unarmed state and must be armed by special procedures that would take a crew member a few minutes to execute. The bombs are equipped with safety devices designed to keep an unarmed bomb from detonating even if it falls to the earth because of an accident. Although there have been a number of close calls, a thermonuclear explosion has miraculously never occurred as a result of an accident. Recently, the opening of military archives revealed a considerable number of near misses. Two of the most famous are the Palomares Incident and the Thule Accident.

One near miss occurred on January 17, 1966. Known as the Palomares Incident, a U.S. Air Force B-52 bomber based in North Carolina was on routine patrol over the southeastern coast of Spain. The B-52 carried four unarmed B-28 hydrogen bombs. Attempting to refuel in midair at 30,000 feet (9,144 meters), the B-52 collided with the fueling boom (the instrument through which the fuel enters the plane needing refueling) of the KC-135 tanker jet. The resulting explosion released the four bombs; three fell to the ground around Palomares, a farming community near the coastal highway, and the fourth fell 5 miles (8 kilometers) offshore in the Mediterranean Sea. Immediately, the United States announced there was no public health danger.

The bomb that fell into the Mediterranean Sea spurred an intensive underwater search. The search involved thirty-three naval vessels and took eighty-one days. Eventually, the bomb was located by a submersible at 2,500 feet (762 meters). Fortunately, the bomb was intact and apparently had leaked no radiation.

Of the three bombs that landed near Palomares, one landed in a dry riverbed, relatively intact. Although safety devices in all three prevented the thermonuclear devices from exploding, the high explosives in two of the bombs detonated, spreading radioactive particles over approximately 650 acres of farmland, more than 1 square mile (2.6 square kilometers). Winds then spread the plutonium dust and made it impossible to determine how far the dust was spread. For the next three months, seventeen hundred U.S. military personnel and Spanish civil guards moved an estimated 1,750 tons (1,587 metric tons) of plutonium-contaminated soil and vegetation, primarily tomatoes, from around Palomares. It was shipped to the United States for disposal. The U.S. personnel wore protective clothing, but the Spanish workers were not well protected. After the initial cleanup effort, the U.S. Atomic Energy Commission (AEC) and Spain's Junta de Energía Nuclear (JEN) began a program to monitor the health of those living in the area. AEC provided funds, and JEN performed the monitoring programs. By the

Submarine crewmen recover a B-28 hydrogen bomb that had been missing for 81 days, since it fell into the sea after an accident over Palomares, Spain. *Reproduced by permission of the Corbis Corporation.*

mid-1980s, costs for the cleanup, the monitoring programs, and the five hundred medical claims filed by villagers from Palomares added up to more than $120 million.

Another incident, the Thule Accident, occurred on January 21, 1968. A B-52 bomber carrying four unarmed B-28 hydrogen bombs was on an early-warning patrol mission. It was flying high above the early-warning radar towers on the U.S. air base in Thule, Greenland (at that time, a province of Denmark). Suddenly, a fire broke out on the aircraft. Minutes later, smoke filled the B-52, and electrical power was lost. Six of the seven crew members ejected safely. The aircraft crashed 7 miles (11 kilometers) from the base onto ice-covered North Star Bay at a speed of 560 miles (900 kilometers) per hour. As at Palomares, the thermonuclear devices did not detonate even in the inferno of the crash. However, the high explosives within the bombs surrounding the thermonuclear devices did explode (just as they had at Palomares). Radioactive materials spread over the ice. A massive cleanup followed. In the next eight months, seven hundred U.S. military personnel and Danish civilians at Thule collected 10,500 tons (9,524 metric tons) of snow, ice, and debris in barrels. The barrels were sent to the Savannah, Georgia, River Plant for disposal. Aircraft debris went to Oak Ridge, Tennessee, for disposal. The cleanup cost approximately $9.4 million. Years later, studies of Danish workers who were involved in the cleanup reported high incidences of cancer. U.S. Air Force personnel who participated in the cleanup were not monitored.

The Palomares Incident and the Thule Accident provoked protests from the international community. Neutral, nuclear-free countries wanted U.S. aircraft carrying nuclear weapons to stop flying over their countries. By the late 1960s the Strategic Air Command (SAC) suspended airborne patrol missions. Instead, SAC depended on land-based early-warning radar systems and on the speed and efficiency of the U.S. Air Force in getting B-52s airborne.

for constant communication readiness. In 1963, the United States, the Soviet Union, and Great Britain, which was also processing nuclear weapons, negotiated a three-way agreement that banned nuclear bomb testing in the atmosphere, in outer space, or underwater. They could continue underground testing as long as radioactive fallout did not reach outside the country doing the testing. This agreement was known as the Limited Test-Ban Treaty of 1963.

Despite the encouraging agreements, the Soviets put forth an all-out effort after the Cuban Missile Crisis to match U.S. weapons production. The Soviet SS-9 Scarp ICBM missiles became operational and could target sites 7,000 miles (11,263 kilometers) away. By the late 1960s, the Soviet Union surpassed the United States in its ICBM count. The Soviets also introduced advanced SSBNs of the "Yankee" class, each capable of carrying sixteen nuclear missiles. The United States likewise kept its strategic and tactical nuclear weapons production in high gear and its Strategic Triad primed and ready. Both superpowers now had the means to annihilate the world many times over.

Opposing the bomb

Nuclear technology has stirred conflict and controversy from its earliest days. The awesome power of nuclear test bombs caused widespread fear among the general public. Many people opposed the nuclear arms race, some for moral reasons and some because of environmental concerns. Even scientists who understood the technology deplored the way it was being used. Albert Einstein (1879–1955), America's most famous physicist, openly agonized a few years later that his 1939 letter to U.S. president Franklin D. Roosevelt (1882–1945; served 1933–45), which stressed the urgency of the atomic bomb situation, helped spawn the development of the bomb. J. Robert Oppenheimer (1904–1967), director of the Manhattan Project, which produced two types of atomic bombs by 1945, vehemently opposed U.S. development of the hydrogen bomb. Likewise, Igor Kurchatov (1903–1960), the scientist who headed the Soviet Union's nuclear program, became increasingly alarmed about the destructive power of nuclear weapons. After observing the 1955 test of the first true Soviet hydrogen bomb, Kurchatov and Andrey Sakharov regretted the consequences of their accomplishments. From then until his death in 1960, Kurchatov stressed the use of nuclear power for the good of humankind.

The first mass public outcry against nuclear weapons happened in Great Britain. The Campaign for Nuclear Disarmament (CND) formed in London in spring 1958. One of the founders was British mathematician and philosopher Bertrand Russell (1872–1970). Russell feared that humankind would not long survive if the superpowers became involved in a sort of nuclear game. CND organized a protest march at Easter from London to Aldermaston, where British nuclear weapons were researched and produced. It was in this march that the logo for nuclear disarmament, soon to become the worldwide symbol for peace, first appeared—on round, lollipop-shaped cardboard signs.

Soviet nuclear physicist Andrey Sakharov.
Reproduced by permission of the Corbis Corporation.

At Easter the next year, the Ban the Bomb march, which became an annual event, again proceeded down the same path to Aldermaston. Ban the Bomb protests and marches spread to West Germany, Holland, and Sweden. By late 1960, the militant Committee of 100 had formed. It was an organization in favor of nuclear disarmament that was dedicated to inciting civil disobedience, or willfully disobeying the law for a common cause. Its members planned protests at Holy Loch in Scotland, where a U.S. nuclear submarine carrying Polaris missiles had docked. The eighty-nine-year-old Russell, the committee's president, was arrested and sent to prison for inciting civil disobedience. Although he was released after one week, his imprisonment sparked worldwide outrage. The CND's march to Aldermaston and the Committee of 100 protests began what would become an international peace movement. The citizens of Western Europe and the United States were keenly aware of the stakes of the nuclear arms race. However, people in the Soviet Union

The peace symbol used extensively through most of the second half of the twentieth century originated in London, England, in the spring of 1958. Gerald Holton, a commercial artist in London, designed the symbol for banners for the first antinuclear protest march. The people involved in the march, which was organized by the Campaign for Nuclear Disarmament (CND), held lollipop-shaped signs bearing the peace symbol as they marched from London to Aldermaston on Easter weekend. Aldermaston was a British site for research and production of nuclear weapons.

Holton's first banner featured a white circle drawn on a purple square; inside the circle was a symbol that looked like a cross with its arms drooping downward. Holton used semaphore, a visual signaling system involving flags and arm movements, to create the symbol. He chose the letters N and D (for "nuclear disarmament") for his design. The semaphore code for D is a man holding flags with one arm straight up and

Gerald Holton's peace symbol is shown on an American flag. *Photograph by Wally McNamee. Reproduced by permission of the Corbis Corporation.*

one straight down so as to make a straight line. The N semaphore code is a man holding flags with both arms pointed down and away from his sides. By layering one code letter over the other, Holton made the now famous peace symbol.

and Eastern Europe rarely had access to news of what was going on. But concern over nuclear weapons was growing, and even U.S. president John F. Kennedy (1917–1963; served 1961–63) remarked at a commencement speech in June 1963 that the money used for developing nuclear weapons could be better spent improving the lives of people.

More bombs, more treaties

China detonated its first hydrogen bomb on October 16, 1964. Five nations now had nuclear weapons: the United

Duck and Cover

During the 1950s, schoolchildren throughout the United States were taught the "duck and cover" drill. For a bomb drill, a school commonly rang its bell in a pattern of short—long—short—long—short—long and so on. This pattern was in contrast to the fire drill bell of three long rings. Upon hearing the bell rings for the bomb drill, children moved to a central hall, or under their desks, sat down on the floor with knees tucked under, and covered their ducked heads with their hands. Whether principals and teachers really thought children would be safer in this position during a nuclear attack is debatable. However, it made everyone feel better to at least have a plan.

Schoolchildren in 1944 participate in a "duck and cover" drill. *Reproduced by permission of the Corbis Corporation.*

States, the Soviet Union, Great Britain, China, and France. The 1963 Limited Test-Ban Treaty had been a small step forward, but neither China nor France had signed it. By the mid-1960s, both superpowers, with rapidly advancing nuclear research, were building systems or shields to protect themselves from ICBM attack. These were called antiballistic missiles (ABMs). Although it was unlikely that such systems could provide anywhere near complete protection in a nuclear attack, both countries spent billions of dollars developing them. In 1967, U.S. president Lyndon B. Johnson (1908–1973; served 1961–69) approached the new Soviet prime minister, Aleksey Kosygin (1904–1980), about curtailing ABM deployment, due to the overwhelmingly high cost of development and the unreliable performance. Kosygin only spoke of reducing the total number of strategic missiles, so ABM development continued.

Meanwhile, several nuclear treaties were signed and ratified (passed by the individual governments involved) in

1967 and 1968. In 1967, the United States, the Soviet Union, and Great Britain signed and ratified the Outer Space Treaty, which banned putting nuclear weapons in orbit around the Earth and using the Moon or other celestial bodies for installation or testing of nuclear weapons. Also in 1967, twenty-four Latin American countries banned the "manufacture, acquisition, testing, deployment, or other use of nuclear weapons" in their countries. The treaty was called the Latin American Nuclear-Free Zone Treaty. Cuba did not sign the treaty. Most important, the United States, the Soviet Union, and Great Britain were the first three countries to sign and ratify the Nuclear Nonproliferation Treaty in 1968. They also agreed to not share nuclear weapon technology with those countries that did not have such technology already. Under this agreement, nations without nuclear weapons agreed not to acquire them, and nations with nuclear arms would negotiate for disarmament. Over the next few years, over one hundred more countries signed the treaty. Progress continued in November 1969 with the Strategic Arms Limitation Talks (SALT) in Helsinki, Finland.

For More Information

Books

Frankel, Benjamin, ed. *The Cold War, 1945–1991*. Vol. 3. Detroit: Gale, 1992.

Freedman, Lawrence. *Kennedy's Wars: Berlin, Cuba, Laos, and Vietnam.* New York: Oxford University Press, 2000.

Isaacs, Jeremy, and Taylor Downing. *Cold War: An Illustrated History, 1945–1991*. Boston: Little, Brown, 1998.

Maier, Pauline, Merritt R. Smith, Alexander Keyssar, and Daniel J. Kevles. *Inventing America: A History of the United States*. New York: W. W. Norton, 2003.

Rhodes, Richard. *Dark Sun: The Making of the Hydrogen Bomb*. New York: Simon and Schuster, 1995.

Sagan, Scott D. *The Limits of Safety: Organizations, Accidents, and Nuclear Weapons*. Princeton, NJ: Princeton University Press, 1993.

Web Sites

"Arms Control Treaties." *Atomic Archive*. http://www.atomicarchive.com/Treaties/index.shtml (accessed on August 5, 2003).

"Ballistic Missile Submarines (SSBNs)." *United States Strategic Command.* www.stratcom.af.mil/factsheetshtml/submarines.htm (accessed on August 5, 2003).

"A History of the CND Logo." *Campaign for Nuclear Disarmament.* http://www.cnduk.org/INFORM~1/symbol.htm (accessed on August 5, 2003).

Titan Missile Museum. http://www.pimaair.org/titan_01.htm (accessed on August 5, 2003).

United States Air Force Museum. http://www.wpafb.af.mil/museum/index.htm (accessed on August 5, 2003).

U.S. Navy, Office of Information. *United States Navy Fact File: Fleet Ballistic Missile Submarines—SSBN.* http://chinfo.navy.mil/navpalib/factfile/ships/ship-ssn.html (accessed on August 5, 2003).

The World Wide Web Virtual Library: Naval and Maritime: Submarines. http://www.iit.edu/~vlnavmar/subs.html (accessed on August 5, 2005).

An Unsettled World ▌11

Communism was a central theme during the 1960 presidential election between the Democratic candidate, U.S. senator John F. Kennedy (1917–1963) of Massachusetts, and the Republican candidate, Vice President Richard M. Nixon (1913–1994). Since the late 1940s, Nixon had a strong record of fighting the threat of communism in the United States. Communism is a system of government in which a single political party—the Communist Party—selects government leaders and controls nearly all other aspects of society. Private ownership of property is prohibited, and the government directs all economic production. The goods produced and the accumulated wealth are, in theory, shared relatively equally by all.

During the presidential campaign, Kennedy took a tough stance against communism to match Nixon's record, and he ended up winning in a very close race. When Kennedy took office in January 1961, Soviet premier Nikita Khrushchev (1894–1971) released two U.S. Air Force officers being held by the Soviets. The officers had been shot down the previous July while flying in Soviet airspace on a recon-

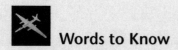

Words to Know

Alliance for Progress: A program designed to block the spread of communism by improving the overall quality of life for Latin Americans. The Alliance attempted to reduce disease, increase literacy, and ease poverty throughout the region.

Bay of Pigs: Failed U.S.-backed invasion of Cuba at the Bay of Pigs by fifteen hundred Cuban exiles opposed to Fidel Castro, on April 17, 1961.

Berlin Wall: A wall dividing the Soviet-controlled sector of Berlin from the three Western-controlled zones, built in an attempt to stem the tide of refugees seeking asylum in the West.

Cold War: A prolonged conflict for world dominance from 1945 to 1991 between the two superpowers, the democratic, capitalist United States and the communist Soviet Union. The weapons of conflict were commonly words of propaganda and threats.

Communism: A system of government in which the nation's leaders are selected by a single political party that controls all aspects of society. Private ownership of property is eliminated and government directs all economic production. The goods produced and accumulated wealth are, in theory, shared relatively equally by all. All religious practices are banned.

Cuban Missile Crisis: A showdown in October 1962 that brought the Soviet Union and the United States close to war over the existence of Soviet nuclear missiles in Cuba.

Imperialism: The process of expanding the authority of one government over other nations and groups of people.

Peace Corps: A U.S. program designed to promote world peace and friendship by going abroad and assisting developing nations.

Prague Spring: A brief thaw in Cold War communist policies when in 1968 Czechoslovakia's Communist Party leader, Alexander Dubcek, sought to modernize communism with certain democratic reforms, including greater freedom of the press.

Third World: Poor underdeveloped or developing nations in Africa, Asia, and Latin America; most Third World countries have economies primarily based on agriculture, with few other industries.

Vietcong: Vietnamese communists engaged in warfare against the government and people of South Vietnam.

naissance mission. Kennedy recognized Khrushchev's act as a goodwill gesture and responded by removing importation restrictions on certain Soviet food and offering to increase scientific and cultural exchanges between the two countries.

Despite this hopeful beginning, relations between the two superpowers would soon dramatically deteriorate. Kennedy's pledge to be tough on communism, along with his inexperience in foreign affairs, made him very cautious about improving relations with the Soviets, regardless of Khrushchev's offers. Yet Kennedy was determined to demonstrate his leadership capabilities, and he wanted the lead role in developing foreign policy. He appointed Dean Rusk (1909–1994), a little-known former Truman administration State Department official, as his secretary of state. Unlike previous secretaries of state, Rusk would serve as an advisor, not a policy maker. In addition to Rusk, Kennedy relied on a small inner circle of advisors, including Secretary of Defense Robert S. McNamara (1916–). Historians believe the small number led to some poor decisions in the early 1960s, when the United States had to respond to serious Soviet challenges.

While Kennedy was hesitant to cooperate, Khrushchev was inconsistent in his actions. Rejecting the inflexible policies and brutal style of the previous Soviet leader, Joseph Stalin (1879–1953), Khrushchev truly desired to change the direction of the Soviet Union and improve the lives of Soviet citizens. To reach this goal, he felt he needed to ease tensions with the West. But under pressure from communist hard-liners, Khrushchev would routinely switch between being friendly and challenging the West. De-

People to Know

Leonid Brezhnev (1906–1982): Leader of the Soviet Union Communist Party, 1964–82.

Fidel Castro Ruz (1926–): Cuban premier/president, 1959–.

Alexander Dubcek (1921–1992): Czechoslovakian Communist Party leader, 1968.

Lyndon B. Johnson (1908–1973): Thirty-sixth U.S. president, 1963–69.

John F. Kennedy (1917–1963): Thirty-fifth U.S. president, 1961–63.

Nikita S. Khrushchev (1894–1971): Soviet premier, 1958–64.

Robert S. McNamara (1916–): U.S. secretary of defense, 1961–68.

Ngo Dinh Diem (1901–1963): Republic of Vietnam president, 1954–63.

Richard M. Nixon (1913–1994): Republican vice president, 1953–61; Republican candidate for U.S. president, 1960; thirty-seventh U.S. president, 1969–74.

Dean Rusk (1909–1994): U.S. secretary of state, 1961–69.

spite his personal gestures to Kennedy, Khrushchev would talk tough in public. For example, to potentially expand Soviet influence, he would openly encourage revolutionary independence movements in Third World countries. (Third World countries are poor underdeveloped or developing nations in Africa, Asia, and Latin America. Most Third World countries have economies primarily based on agriculture, with few other industries. In the 1960s, many of these countries were still under the political control of other countries, mostly Western European nations.) As a result of the U.S.-Soviet rivalry, the Third World would serve as a major stage of conflict during the 1960s. The two superpowers competed over the allegiance of various nations. They either supported existing governments or tried to install new ones friendly to either democracy or communism. The tough talk and sometimes poor decision-making of the two superpower leaders nearly made the Cold War into a nuclear war. The Cuban Missile Crisis, especially, nearly led to war. This incident was a showdown in October 1962 that brought the Soviet Union and the United States close to war over the existence of Soviet nuclear missiles in Cuba. (See Chapter 9, Cuban Missile Crisis.)

On November 22, 1963, President Kennedy was shot and killed in Dallas, Texas, allegedly by Lee Harvey Oswald (1939–1963), while on a campaign trip. Vice President Lyndon B. Johnson (1908–1973) immediately took office, showing the Soviets that the U.S. power structure remained intact despite the president's sudden death. Like Kennedy, Johnson had a strong interest in domestic affairs but little foreign policy experience. He forged ahead with a sweeping social reform program, which he called the "Great Society." Under Johnson's leadership, many landmark pieces of legislation were passed, including the Civil Rights Act of 1964, which outlawed all discrimination on the basis of race, religion, or ethnic origin, covering employment, education, housing, and public accommodations, and the Voting Rights Act of 1965, which ensured full political voting rights for all adults. However, Cold War confrontations consumed much of Johnson's time and energy and eventually contributed to his decision to not seek another term after just over five years in office.

Almost eleven months after Kennedy's death, Khrushchev fell from power in the Soviet Union. Having backed down in confrontations with Kennedy in Berlin and

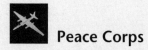

Peace Corps

On October 14, 1960, after a long day of campaigning for the upcoming presidential election, the Democratic candidate, U.S. senator John F. Kennedy of Massachusetts, arrived at the University of Michigan campus in Ann Arbor. It was 2 A.M., and Kennedy was ready to get some rest before another active day. However, ten thousand students turned out to greet the candidate at that late hour. In a spontaneous address before the crowd, Kennedy proposed an international volunteer organization. He challenged the youthful crowd to serve their country, to represent the United States by going abroad to assist developing nations. Three months later, the newly elected Kennedy mentioned the program again in his inaugural address on January 20, 1961. On March 1, he signed an order establishing the Peace Corps. Kennedy appointed his brother-in-law, R. Sargent Shriver (1915–), to be the first Peace Corps director. Congress passed legislation on September 22 of that year making the Peace Corps a permanent program.

The overarching goal of the Peace Corps as stated in the legislation is to "promote world peace and friendship." To accomplish this goal, the agency recruited volunteers skilled in education, agriculture, health care, and public works. Volunteers worked two-year terms and learned to speak the language of the country they were assigned to; their living conditions were similar to the living conditions of the people they assisted. Another key objective of the program is to create a better understanding of Americans among the Third World populations. One of the first groups of volunteers in the summer of 1961 was sent to the African nation of Ghana. Upon arrival at the airport, the fifty-one American volunteers quickly impressed their host country by singing the national anthem of Ghana in the local native language.

In the first year, the Peace Corps sent five hundred volunteers to eight developing countries. By 1963, seven thousand volunteers were working in forty-four countries, and in 1966, over fifteen thousand volunteers were working in fifty-two countries. As the Cold War neared its end in 1991, the Peace Corps expanded to Eastern Europe, going to Poland and Hungary in June 1990 and to the former Soviet states of Estonia, Latvia, and Lithuania in 1992. In 1993, Peace Corps volunteers began serving in the People's Republic of China. The Peace Corps is one of the most successful programs created during Kennedy's administration.

Cuba, Khrushchev was removed from office on October 15, 1964, in a bloodless coup. Leonid Brezhnev (1906–1982), a Communist Party hard-liner, replaced Khrushchev as leader of the party, and Aleksey N. Kosygin (1904–1980) became the head of the Soviet government. Through the 1960s, Brezhnev would increasingly dominate Soviet affairs, overshadowing Kosygin. Brezhnev would become the longest-serving Soviet leader during the Cold War.

Second-strike strategies

During his first few months in office in early 1961, Kennedy reassessed U.S. Cold War strategies. He did not favor the brinkmanship policy of his predecessor, Dwight D. Eisenhower (1890–1969; served 1953–61), which emphasized the threat of nuclear weapons as a deterrent to any hostile action by the Soviets. Kennedy believed that the potential for global annihilation was too great with this policy in place. He wanted other means to retaliate against hostile actions, something substantially less destructive than nuclear weapons. He sought a new strategy that would give him greater flexibility in responding to various levels of hostile actions and threats. In addition to nuclear weapons, Kennedy's new strategy included greater use of covert, or secret, operations and antiguerrilla forces (small groups of soldiers specializing in surprise attacks) and more emphasis on conventional (nonnuclear) air, ground, and naval forces.

To support this new strategy, military spending increased dramatically from $43 billion in 1961 to $56 billion by 1963. The number of naval ships doubled, and the army expanded from eleven to sixteen divisions. The number of tactical air squadrons grew from sixteen to twenty-three. For antiguerrilla operations, Kennedy created a counterinsurgency force called the Green Berets, a name Kennedy personally chose. (Counterinsurgency is organized military action designed to combat guerrilla forces, or insurgents, that are attempting to overthrow an established government.) The U.S. Army's Special Forces School at Fort Bragg, North Carolina, trained 114,000 U.S. soldiers and 7,000 foreign military officers by June 1963. The Special Forces were specifically trained to perform in Latin America and Southeast Asia.

The nuclear arsenal, or weapons stockpile, also grew under Kennedy's new plan. Kennedy's goal was second-strike capability—a nuclear arsenal large enough to ensure that some U.S. missiles would survive a Soviet first strike; the sur-

Airmen refuel a missile carrying a nuclear warhead in 1964. *Reproduced by permission of the Corbis Corporation.*

viving missiles would destroy the Soviet Union in an automatic second strike. This differed from earlier strategies that focused on firing off as many missiles as possible before the enemy's missiles struck. Second-strike capability meant that even in the event of a surprise attack, massive retaliation was possible. To prepare for this scenario, the United States installed solid-fuel Minuteman missiles in underground silos; submarines were equipped with Polaris missiles. By the end of the decade, the United States would have over a thousand intercontinental ballistic missiles (ICBMs), seven hundred missiles for submarine launch, and more than five hundred long-range B-52 bombers capable of carrying nuclear weapons. All missiles carried nuclear warheads.

The Soviets did not stand still while the United States pursued its new military defense strategy. In early 1965, Brezhnev announced a massive increase in Soviet nuclear arms development. He sought to reach the level of nuclear capability that the United States had achieved and maintain superiority over the People's Republic of China (PRC), which now had its own nuclear weapons. By the late 1960s, new missile technologies, including the antiballistic missile (ABM) defense system and multiple-warhead missiles, were being developed by both superpowers. They would be very costly for both countries to produce. Because of the cost, President Johnson and Brezhnev agreed to consider new proposals for limiting the future growth of nuclear arsenals and restricting the spread of nuclear weapons to other nations. Though progress was slow, Johnson did sign three arms agreements. One pact, the 1967 Latin American Nuclear-Free Zone Treaty, banned the spread of nuclear weapons to Latin America; another, the Outer Space Treaty, prohibited the use and deployment of nuclear weapons in space or on the Moon. The most important treaty was the 1968 Nuclear Nonproliferation Treaty (NPT), which banned the spread of nuclear weapon capabilities to nonnuclear countries worldwide.

The Berlin and Cuba crises

Two major Cold War crises came quickly for Kennedy. Soon after taking office, Kennedy personally approved a plan to invade Cuba—against Secretary of State Rusk's advice. About four years before Kennedy became president, Fidel Castro Ruz (1926–) had led a revolution in Cuba to overthrow Fulgencio Batista y Zaldívar (1901–1973), a dictator the United States worked with because he was not communist. Castro did not begin his regime as a communist, but he began to lean toward the Soviet Union for support when the United States showed hostility toward his economic reform programs. The Eisenhower administration had come up with a plan to oust Castro, and following Kennedy's approval of the

plan, some fifteen hundred Cuban exiles, trained in Guatemala by the U.S. Central Intelligence Agency (CIA), made an amphibious (water) landing at the Bay of Pigs in Cuba on April 17, 1961. However, just before the invasion, CIA bombers failed to hit their targets in an initial air strike. Fearing impending doom for the operation, Kennedy cancelled a second strike. He ordered that the U.S. personnel not take any further active role. Without the expected air support, almost twelve hundred of the exiles were easily captured after three days of fighting. (The captured invaders were later freed in December 1962 in exchange for $53 million worth of tractors and other equipment.) The operation proved a disaster and placed the United States and President Kennedy in a very bad public light (see Chapter 9, Cuban Missile Crisis).

Shortly after the failed invasion of Cuba, Berlin once again became the focus of Cold War tension. In early June 1961, Kennedy and Khrushchev met in Vienna, Austria. The Soviet leader pressed Kennedy for a German peace treaty that

Soviet leader Nikita Khrushchev (left) talks with U.S. president John F. Kennedy at their summit in Vienna, Austria, in June 1961. Soviet foreign minister Andrey Gromyko (center, without glasses) looks on. *Reproduced by permission of AP/Wide World Photos.*

would recognize the existing boundaries of Eastern Europe, where Soviet influence had become well established. Because of the rapidly escalating post–World War II (1939–45) tensions in the late 1940s between the Soviet Union and the Western allies, a peace treaty officially ending the war and resolving the future of Germany had never been signed. Khrushchev also demanded that Western military forces leave Berlin, a German city that was jointly controlled by the Western allies and the Soviets. Kennedy rejected Khrushchev's demands.

In response, on August 13, the East Germans began building a wall through the middle of Berlin. The Soviets wanted to stop the flow of approximately one thousand people a day leaving East Berlin for West Berlin. The decrease in population was hurting the East German economy. As a result of the creation of the wall, the United States and the Soviet Union resumed nuclear weapons testing, ending a three-year break. Kennedy sent an additional fifteen hundred U.S. soldiers to Germany and began preparing for a nuclear showdown. Seeing Kennedy's strong response, Khrushchev backed off his demands (see Chapter 3, Germany and Berlin).

Khrushchev faced increasing criticism from Soviet Communist Party leaders. He had backed down on his demands for a Berlin settlement in late 1961, and even though the U.S. invasion of Cuba failed, the threat of a future invasion lingered. In an effort to strengthen his leadership position, Khrushchev decided early in 1962 to deploy nuclear missiles in Cuba, only 90 miles (145 kilometers) from the U.S. coastline. Months later, on October 14, 1962, a high-altitude U.S. spy plane spotted Soviet missile bases under construction in Cuba. Two extremely tense weeks followed, during which the United States blockaded Soviet cargo ships carrying missiles to Cuba. On October 28, Khrushchev announced that he would remove the missiles in Cuba. In return, Kennedy agreed not to invade Cuba and secretly promised to remove medium-range Jupiter missiles from Turkey. Kennedy won widespread praise for his handling of the crisis and for averting military engagements. Khrushchev's defeat in Cuba was another blow to his image at home in the Soviet Union. It would cost him his leadership position less than two years later (see Chapter 9, Cuban Missile Crisis).

After experiencing firsthand a nuclear near miss in Cuba, both Kennedy and Khrushchev were ready to begin

arms control talks. Although the two superpowers could not agree on a broad test-ban treaty, they did agree to ban nuclear testing in the atmosphere, in outer space, and beneath the ocean surface. The Limited Test-Ban Treaty went into effect on October 11, 1963. This treaty provided an important foundation for future arms control talks.

U.S. president John F. Kennedy prepares to sign the Limited Test-Ban Treaty in 1963; cabinet officials, senators, and Vice President Lyndon B. Johnson (far right) look on. *Reproduced by permission of the Corbis Corporation.*

Latin American challenges

Castro's increasingly pro-Soviet position would lead to further Cold War challenges for the United States in Latin America in the 1960s. Latin America encompasses all of the Western Hemisphere south of the United States. It consists of all nations in Central and South America as well as Mexico and the islands of the West Indies.

During the 1960s, all conflicts in Latin America were thrust into a Cold War framework of communist influence

Alliance for Progress

Just as preparation for the ill-fated U.S.-supported invasion of communist Cuba was in its last stages, U.S. president John F. Kennedy introduced a new aid program for all other Latin American countries. On March 13, 1961, the president announced the Alliance for Progress. The program was designed to block the spread of communism by improving the overall quality of life for Latin Americans. The Alliance would attempt to reduce disease, increase literacy, and ease poverty throughout the region. Kennedy believed that if these conditions could be improved, radical political movements such as communism would look less attractive to the poor. In August, the United States and twenty-two other countries agreed on a charter, or set of rules. Kennedy pledged $10 billion of U.S. money over the next ten years to match $10 billion contributed by other nations that supported the program.

The Inter-American Committee was established to guide funds from contributing nations to the appropriate Latin American programs and countries. Through the next few years, the highly ambitious program encouraged agricultural reform, health and sanitation improvements, housing projects, reading programs, better wages, and stabler prices of goods. Kennedy expressed hopes that the program would not only block communist expansion, but encourage growth of democracies. At the time, military dictatorships governed most Latin American countries.

Despite grand hopes, the Alliance for Progress was a major failure. High pop-

versus American influence. Americans viewed troubles in Latin American countries as communist-inspired; the Soviets saw U.S. intervention in Latin America as imperialism. Imperialism is the policy of expanding the rule of one nation over foreign countries.

In Panama, a Central American country, nationalists began protesting U.S. control of the Panama Canal Zone located within their country. (Nationalists have a strong loyalty to their own nation and favor independence from other nations.) The canal was built in 1903 by the United States to improve transportation between the east and west coasts of the United States. The United States had retained control over the canal and an area surrounding it known as the Canal Zone. The protests led to anti-American riots in January 1964. Four ulation growth rates in Latin America prevented the program from making meaningful headway. In fact, during the 1960s, unemployment rose and agricultural production declined. Though some new schools, hospitals, and other facilities were built, the improvements in sanitation, housing, literacy, and health care could not keep up with the population growth, so relatively few people were served. Democracies also lost ground as popularly elected presidents in Argentina, Peru, Guatemala, Ecuador, the Dominican Republic, and Honduras were overthrown by their militaries. Wealthy people in Latin America viewed the Alliance for Progress as a greater threat to them than communism. They believed the Alliance would improve the condition of the general population and better enable them to challenge the influence of the wealthy through such things as land reform. Tensions between Latin America and the United States actually increased.

Combating the potential spread of communism quickly took priority over improving the social, political, and economic conditions in Latin America. U.S. military assistance to Latin American dictators increased steadily during the 1960s, especially under President Lyndon Johnson, who took office after Kennedy was assassinated. The United States found that dictatorships could prevent the spread of communism better than weak democracies. With new priorities and not much progress to show for the program, Johnson and Congress significantly reduced funding for the Alliance for Progress in 1965 and 1966.

U.S. soldiers and twenty-four Panamanians were killed during four days of rioting. The Panamanian government suspended diplomatic relations with the United States. Because of his distrust of Castro, President Johnson suspected that the Cuban leader was somehow behind the unrest. Though order was soon restored, the issue remained unresolved, and agreement over the future control of the Canal Zone would not be reached until 1977, when U.S. president Jimmy Carter (1924–; served 1977–81) signed a treaty giving Panama control over the zone beginning on December 31, 1999.

The United States also became involved in other parts of Latin America. In 1964, President Johnson offered the support of a U.S. naval force to help the Brazilian military overthrow leftist (politically radical or liberal) civilian president

Anti-American demonstrations take place in Panama City in November 1964. Later riots resulted in thirteen injuries.
Reproduced by permission of the Corbis Corporation.

João Belchior Marques Goulart (1918–1976), but the Brazilian forces successfully overthrew the government without U.S. military assistance. In Chile, the Johnson administration secretly spent at least $3 million to help elect an anticommunist president, Eduardo Frei Montalva (1911–1982).

In the Dominican Republic, civil war broke out in early 1965. The country's military had overthrown the elected government in 1963 and promised elections the following year. However, the elections were postponed because the military feared the same leaders would be elected again by the people. A group of military officers who supported the ousted leaders rebelled violently, resulting in a growing civil war. Fearing that Castro may have influenced the rebels, resulting in communist influence, President Johnson sent twenty-two thousand U.S. troops to protect the military leadership in April 1965.

Though U.S. involvement had successfully ended the revolt in the Dominican Republic, demonstrations in protest of U.S. intervention broke out throughout Latin America. The U.S. military intervention violated the Good Neighbor policy established in the 1930s by President Franklin D. Roosevelt (1882–1945; served 1933–45). The policy promised that the United States would not militarily intervene in the internal politics of Latin American countries. In addition, Johnson had acted without the approval of Congress or the Organization of American States (OAS), an organization of Western Hemisphere nations established in 1948 to maintain political stability in the region by providing a forum for resolving disputes. To ease the situation in the Dominican Republic, the OAS sent a multinational military force to replace U.S. troops in September 1966. A pro-U.S. civil government, led by Joaquín Balaguer (1907–2002), was elected later that year. The mood of the population had changed enough by then to elect a right-wing pro-U.S. government.

In 1967, arms control talks turned to Latin America. The United States, the Soviet Union, Great Britain, France, and the People's Republic of China (PRC) signed a treaty prohibiting the use of nuclear weapons in Latin America. All Latin American countries except for Cuba and Guyana later signed the treaty. Despite the widespread disturbances in Latin America during the 1960s, no further communist expansion occurred in the region.

Upheaval in communist China

The Far East is the easternmost part of Asia, including the communist People's Republic of China (PRC), Japan, Korea, and the democratic Republic of China (ROC) on Taiwan. Although the PRC had a communist government, it did not have a good relationship with the Soviet Union in the early 1960s. PRC leader Mao Zedong (1893–1976) did not approve when Khrushchev denounced the policies of former Soviet leader Joseph Stalin. Khrushchev's statements against Stalin were part of an effort called de-Stalinization, a plan to introduce reforms to the Soviet Union. These reforms included allowing greater personal freedoms for Soviet citizens, lessening the powers of the secret police, closing concentration and hard-labor camps, and restoring certain legal processes. The PRC leadership thought Khrushchev's policies weakened the original principles of communism. The PRC also resented the Soviets' lack of support during the Taiwan Strait crisis of 1958, Soviet backing of India in a border dispute with PRC, and withdrawal of Soviet nuclear technical assistance from the PRC in 1959. Furthermore, PRC did not trust the new limited test-ban treaty between the Soviet Union and the United States.

On the other hand, the PRC showed interest during this time in improving relations with the United States and easing trade restrictions. President Kennedy expressed interest as well. Having no formal diplomatic relations, the two countries communicated through the U.S. ambassador in Poland and the PRC's Warsaw representative. But a major hurdle soon arose: The PRC stated that in order to have good relations with the PRC, the United States would have to end its support of the ROC, the democratic Chinese government in Taiwan. In reaction, Congress instead passed resolutions reaffirming U.S. support for the ROC. Further, the United States opposed recognition of the PRC and its admission into the United Nations, an international peacekeeping organization. Kennedy dropped all further discussions. In October 1964, the PRC exploded its first nuclear device. Even more ominously, in June 1967, PRC exploded its first hydrogen bomb.

In an effort to maintain his position of power during the late 1960s, Mao introduced the Cultural Revolution in the PRC. It would last a year and nearly result in civil war. The Cultural Revolution included the purge of tens of thousands of technical experts and government workers who Mao claimed did not loyally support the communist government. Mao wanted to restore a radical edge to the communist movement within China; he felt it was getting too conservative with too many people of influence wanting to improve relations with the United States and the Soviet Union. Perhaps five hundred thousand Chinese people were killed, including many teachers and intellectuals. Mao closed universities and sent students to work in the fields. He also organized the Red Guards—students, peasants, and workers from around the country—to help carry out the purge. The purge consisted of murders and sending thousands of educators and leaders to remote rural regions to perform peasant labor. Red Guard activities significantly heightened anti-American and anti-Soviet sentiments in the PRC; many of

those who favored improved relations with these countries were purged or afraid to speak out any longer.

The Prague Spring: More communist upheaval

In 1966, the economy in Czechoslovakia was struggling, so the country's communist leaders began to shift control of industry from the central government to local organizations, hoping to improve the situation. However, the reform progressed too slowly, and public unrest, including student riots, increased. In January 1968, Alexander Dubcek (1921–1992) was appointed the new Czechoslovakian Communist Party leader. Dubcek wanted to modernize communism with certain democratic reforms, including greater freedom of the press. Communist leaders in other Eastern European countries and in Moscow feared that the reforms would undermine communist control, first in Czechoslovakia and then in their own countries.

In July 1968, Soviet leader Leonid Brezhnev demanded that Dubcek back off from these democratic reforms. When Dubcek continued his efforts, Brezhnev sent Warsaw Pact troops and tanks into Czechoslovakia to overthrow him. (The Warsaw Pact was a mutual military alliance between the Soviet Union and the Eastern European nations under Soviet influence.) Dubcek was arrested, taken to Moscow, and eventually ousted from the Communist Party. Hard-line Communist Party leaders took the place of Dubcek and other Czech government officials.

Dubcek's short period of leadership is known as the Prague Spring because it represented a brief thaw in Cold War communist policies. (Prague was the capital of Czechoslovakia.) Western countries protested the heavy-handed Soviet response but did not intervene to save Dubcek. Because the Soviets used force to suppress Dubcek's reforms, their relations with the United States chilled again. The Soviet invasion of Czechoslovakia subdued political and economic reform movements within the Eastern bloc for over twenty years. The Eastern Bloc was a group of nations composed of the Soviet Union and its allies and satellite governments in Eastern Europe, the Caribbean, Asia, and Africa.

War in Indochina

In 1968, the United States was experiencing its own violent public unrest. Racial inequalities in the U.S. social system led to race riots in the nation's cities. In addition, outside the Chicago hotel where the Democratic National Convention was being held, police used clubs and tear gas on protesters demonstrating against the Vietnam War (1954–75). Indochina—and Vietnam in particular—proved to be the region that would consume most of America's resources and energies during the 1960s, particularly after 1964. Indochina is a peninsula in Southeast Asia that extends from the southern border of the PRC into the South China Sea. It includes, among other countries, Vietnam, Cambodia, and Laos. These three countries had valuable natural resources, especially rubber and rice, and as a result, they were colonized by the French in the nineteenth century. However, following World War II, a communist revolutionary named Ho Chi Minh (1890–1969) led the communist Vietminh army in a war against French troops to regain Vietnam's independence. By 1954, an agreement was reached dividing Vietnam into two regions. North Vietnam would be communist, ruled by Ho Chi Minh; South Vietnam would have a pro-West, anticommunist government. However, communist forces continued waging guerrilla warfare in South Vietnam, and U.S. assistance gradually replaced the French influence.

Immediately after the failure of the 1961 Bay of Pigs invasion in Cuba, Kennedy turned to Indochina, hoping to regain public confidence in his efforts to contain communism. As a senator, Kennedy had opposed U.S. involvement in Vietnam in the early 1950s, but on May 25, 1961, Kennedy went to Congress for additional defense funds to increase military aid to South Vietnam. South Vietnam did not serve any vital interests of the United States. However, Kennedy had become a believer in the "domino effect" theory, which maintained that if one country fell to communist influence, others would follow. If South Vietnam fell to the communists, Laos and Cambodia could be next—and perhaps other countries after that. In addition, Kennedy did not want to be considered soft on communism.

The situation in Vietnam continued to deteriorate despite increased U.S. financial aid. In October 1961, South Vietnam president Ngo Dinh Diem (1901–1963) requested U.S. combat troops. South Vietnamese communist rebels, called the Vietcong, controlled about 80 percent of South Vietnam's villages. While in control, the Vietcong pursued land reforms, taking land from the wealthy landlords and distributing it among the peasants to farm. President Kennedy was determined to fight the Vietcong's guerrilla warfare tactics with Green Beret counterinsurgency strategies (antiguerrilla warfare). He also planned to improve the South Vietnamese army: By late 1963, the number of U.S. military advisors in South Vietnam increased from 700 to 16,700. The advisors took an active role in combat and covert operations in North Vietnam as well. Kennedy approved a CIA plan to overthrow Ngo, who was declining in popularity, inhibiting the fight against the communists, and not making meaningful reforms. Ngo was assassinated less than three weeks before President Kennedy's assassination.

In August 1964, North Vietnam staged a small-scale attack on two U.S. destroyers in the Gulf of Tonkin. In response, Congress passed the Gulf of Tonkin Resolution. The resolution gave President Johnson sweeping powers to commit U.S. forces to the region, though he refrained from increasing U.S. military involvement until after the presidential election in November. During his campaign, Johnson portrayed his Republican challenger, U.S. senator Barry Goldwater (1909–1998) of Arizona, as one who was eager to start a nuclear war. Johnson asserted that he would not send U.S. combat troops to Vietnam, and he won the election in a landslide victory. Despite his campaign pledges, President Johnson would soon dramatically escalate U.S. involvement in Vietnam.

On February 7, 1965, the United States began a bombing campaign called Operation Rolling Thunder—authorized by President Johnson—just inside North Vietnam's boundary. The operation began one day after eight American advisors were killed and over one hundred wounded by a Vietcong attack. The following month, Johnson sent in U.S. Marine ground troops to defend newly established U.S. air bases. Still, the Vietcong were gaining momentum, capturing more areas of South Vietnam in skirmishes against the U.S.-backed South Vietnamese army. In July 1965, Johnson approved the use of fifty thousand U.S. ground troops in South Vietnam. By now, Johnson had transformed the U.S. policy on Vietnam: Instead of limited assistance, the South Vietnamese government now had a major military commitment from the United States. Johnson was determined not to have South Vietnam fall to the communists. By December 1965, two hundred thousand U.S. troops were in Vietnam; by 1968, over five hundred thousand U.S. troops were there. The American soldiers found conditions in Vietnam deplorable. They suffered from stifling heat, tropical humidity, biting insects, and tropical diseases and lived with the constant threat of sniper fire and booby traps.

With $2 billion in military aid and economic assistance from both the Soviets and the PRC between 1965 and 1968, North Vietnam was able to match the continuing escalation of U.S. involvement. The PRC also sent three hundred

thousand troops into North Vietnam to help operate antiaircraft and communications facilities. Their presence served to deter a U.S. invasion of North Vietnam. The United States did not want to draw the PRC into a larger combat role as it had in Korea in 1950 (see Chapter 2, Conflict Builds). The U.S. strategy at this point was to try to contain the battle and outlast North Vietnam. U.S. military leaders kept coming to Johnson saying that with a few more planes and troops the war could be won. But with each increase, victory seemed no closer.

By late 1967, 13,500 Americans had been killed in Vietnam combat. Public opinion was turning against Johnson and his steady escalation of U.S. war efforts. In 1967, three hundred thousand war protesters marched in New York City. Thousands of demonstrators surrounded the Pentagon in Washington, D.C. In November 1967, General William C. Westmoreland (1914–) assured Johnson that victory was close at hand. Then, on January 31, 1968, to the surprise of everyone (including U.S. intelligence), the Vietcong and the

North Vietnamese launched a massive offensive throughout
South Vietnam. They attacked more than one hundred towns
and villages. Intense fighting erupted in the streets of Saigon,
the capital city, and extended into the U.S. embassy, where
several Americans were killed. This attack is known as the Tet
Offensive, named for the Vietnamese Lunar New Year celebration called Tet. U.S. forces repelled the North Vietnamese
after several weeks, and the Vietcong suffered heavy losses.
However, the American public saw this massive attack as evidence that the United States was nowhere near victory. Public protests, first seen on college campuses, spread across the
nation. Johnson's domestic agenda came to a standstill as
members of Congress became disillusioned with what many
were now calling "Johnson's War." As a result, Johnson's
Great Society plan became another casualty of Vietnam.
Chanting antiwar slogans, protesters constantly encircled the
White House, and Johnson could not go anywhere without
facing hostile crowds.

Johnson's approval rating dropped to 30 percent in early 1968, meaning only 30 percent of Americans approved of Johnson's performance. American casualties in Vietnam were mounting, and the cost of the war undermined the nation's economy. Secretary of Defense Robert S. McNamara resigned in opposition to continuing the war effort; he was replaced by Clark Clifford (1906–1998). On March 31, 1968, Johnson announced in a television address that he would stop the bombing of North Vietnam in order to get peace talks going. He then stunned the nation by adding that he would not run for reelection in November. Peace talks began in Paris on May 13, but no progress was made. Meanwhile, fighting intensified in South Vietnam and would continue for years.

During the Kennedy-Johnson years of 1961 to 1969, the U.S. goal of containing communism around the globe suffered two major setbacks: Soviet relations with Cuba strengthened, and the Vietnam War proved unwinnable for the United States. The period was marked by dramatic, tense, and often bloody events associated with the Cold War rivalry. Despite these events, arms control discussions between the two superpowers gained momentum, and several treaties were signed. The Republican candidate, former Vice President Richard M. Nixon, defeated the Democratic candidate, Vice President Hubert Humphrey (1911–1978), in the November 1968 presidential election by pledging to end U.S. involvement in Vietnam. Though that war did not end for several more years, Nixon and Brezhnev would adopt a policy known as détente, a mutual agreement to relax or ease tensions between the United States and the Soviet Union.

For More Information

Books

Cohen, Warren I., and Nancy B. Tucker, eds. *Lyndon Johnson Confronts the World: American Foreign Policy, 1963–1968.* Cambridge, MA: Cambridge University Press, 1994.

Divine, Robert A., ed. *The Johnson Years.* Lawrence: University Press of Kansas, 1987.

Edmonds, Robin. *Soviet Foreign Policy: The Brezhnev Years.* Oxford: Oxford University Press, 1983.

FitzSimons, Louise. *The Kennedy Doctrine.* New York: Random House, 1972.

Gelb, Norman. *The Berlin Wall: Kennedy, Khrushchev, and a Showdown in the Heart of Europe.* New York: Times Books, 1986.

Gelman, Harry. *The Brezhnev Politburo and the Decline of Detente.* Ithaca, NY: Cornell University Press, 1984.

Higgins, Trumbull. *The Perfect Failure: Kennedy, Eisenhower, and the CIA at the Bay of Pigs.* New York: Norton, 1987.

Paterson, Thomas G., ed. *Kennedy's Quest for Victory: American Foreign Policy, 1961–1963.* New York: Random House, 1995.

Seaborg, Glenn T. *Stemming the Tide: Arms Control and the Johnson Years.* Lexington, MA: Lexington Books, 1987.

Slusser, Robert M. *The Berlin Crisis of 1961: Soviet-American Relations and the Struggle for Power in the Kremlin, June–November 1961.* Baltimore, MD: Johns Hopkins University Press, 1973.

Web Sites

John F. Kennedy Library and Museum. http://www.cs.umb.edu/jfklibrary/index.htm (accessed on August 6, 2003).

Lyndon Baines Johnson Library and Museum. http://www.lbjlib.utexas.edu (accessed on August 6, 2003).

PBS Online. "Vietnam Online." *American Experience.* http://www.pbs.org/wgbh/amex/vietnam (accessed on August 6, 2003).

Woodrow Wilson International Center for Scholars. *The Cold War International History Project.* http://www.wilsoncenter.org/index.cfm?fuseaction=topics.home&topic_id=1409 (accessed on August 6, 2003).

Home Front Turmoil: The 1960s

12

The 1960s decade was a period of severe Cold War tension between the United States and the Soviet Union. The technological capabilities of both countries dramatically increased. Nuclear weapons stockpiles grew, and spy satellites, or constructed orbiting objects, circled Earth. Both the Soviet and the U.S. government spent vast amounts on defense to keep up with or go ahead of the other. By 1960, military-industrial complexes—the partnership of military, defense, and industry—had brought economic growth to America and a good living to a small population of workers in the Soviet Union. But the new decade would bring turbulent times to the superpowers.

For American citizens and many other people around the world, the United States represented freedom and hope: The U.S. government was democratic and designed to protect the people's right to life, liberty, and the pursuit of happiness. Yet the United States regularly contradicted these principles by its treatment of African Americans. And although freedom of speech was a keystone of the democratic system, the country's reaction to Vietnam War (1954–75) protesters

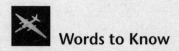

Words to Know

Black Power: The right of African Americans to define and organize themselves as they saw fit and to protect themselves from racial violence, as defined by civil rights leader Stokely Carmichael.

Cold War: A prolonged conflict for world dominance from 1945 to 1991 between the two superpowers, the democratic, capitalist United States and the communist Soviet Union. The weapons of conflict were commonly words of propaganda and threats.

Communism: A system of government in which the nation's leaders are selected by a single political party that controls all aspects of society. Private ownership of property is eliminated and government directs all economic production. The goods produced and accumulated wealth are, in theory, shared relatively equally by all. All religious practices are banned.

Counterculture: Those people who rejected the dominant values and behavior of U.S. society.

Cultural Revolution: Chinese program ordered by leader Mao Zedong (1893–1976) designed to keep all Chinese people loyal to the ideas of communism.

Democracy: A system of government that allows multiple political parties. Their members are elected to various government offices by popular vote of the people.

Military-industrial complex: The partnership of military, defense, and industry.

Racism: Discrimination based on skin color.

Silent Majority: Term coined by President Richard Nixon to characterize the public who were not politically vocal to justify the continuation of the Vietnam War.

Vietcong: Vietnamese communists engaged in warfare against the government and people of South Vietnam.

suggested that this freedom was not entirely guaranteed. Race riots over the inequalities that African Americans endured broke out in large U.S. cities and throughout the South. White Americans joined with blacks in marches and demonstrations. The Soviets used racism in America as propaganda, information spread to further one's own cause, questioning the U.S. commitment to freedom and justice for all. Many Americans, particularly college students, looked with horror at television footage of the war in Vietnam. They took to the streets, protesting U.S. actions in Vietnam, but police fought them with tear gas, clubs, even gunfire. The Soviet government continually pointed to the unrest in America as an example to their people that the U.S. system of government had failed.

In the Soviet Union, families who lived and worked in "secret cities" prospered. The secret cities were technological hubs where the latest top secret military equipment and weapons were developed. To keep up with American militarism, the Soviets spent billions on research and industrial facilities. Yet the communist system was not working well for most Soviet citizens. Most of them lived a drab existence. Housing was terribly overcrowded, and food was scarce. Communist rule in Eastern European countries survived only because of ruthless oppression ordered by the communist leaders in Moscow. The communist People's Republic of China (PRC), by this time more commonly referred to simply as China, was undergoing the Cultural Revolution. Ordered by China's leader, Mao Zedong (1893–1976), this so-called revolution was designed to keep all Chinese people loyal to the ideas of communism.

People to Know

Lyndon B. Johnson (1908–1973): Thirty-sixth U.S. president, 1963–69.

Nikita S. Khrushchev (1894–1971): Soviet premier, 1958–64.

Martin Luther King (1929–1968): African American civil rights leader.

Mao Zedong (1893–1976): Chairman of the People's Republic of China and its Communist Party, 1949–76.

Richard M. Nixon (1913–1994): Thirty-seventh U.S. president, 1969–74.

Military-industrial complexes

By 1960, half of all U.S. federal government expenditures, or spending, went to the military and to the development of the latest military technology, including new aircraft, radar, ships, weapons, and electronic and telecommunication systems. The goal was to stay ahead of the Soviet Union in military might. Together, the U.S. military and the Department of Defense employed approximately 2.5 million people. The government contracted with large aerospace technology corporations, including Lockheed in Georgia and the San Francisco, California, area; Ling-Temco-Vaught (LTV) in Dallas–Fort Worth, Texas; Boeing in Seattle, Washington; and McDonnell-Douglas and Hughes in southern California. These corporations employed tens of thousands of Americans. The partnership of military, defense, and industry came to be known as the military-industrial complex. This grouping reached out into a multitude of regions, touching a great number of American families. Large and small businesses subcontracted to provide materials needed by the military and aerospace industry. Universities throughout the nation received government contracts for technological research. The salaries people earned by this work allowed them to buy consumer goods, which in turn kept other companies, such as auto manufacturers, growing rapidly. But some Americans were left out of the good living generated by the military-industrial complex. For example, most African Americans lived in poverty, enduring discrimination, low wages, and unemployment.

In Soviet society, the military-industrial complex was hidden in secret cities where industry and research facilities coexisted, often in a setting much like a university campus. The scientists and other employees were well paid, well fed, and well housed. In contrast, the majority of Soviets struggled just to feed their families. Two of the best known secret cities were Arzamas-16, where the Soviet atomic bomb was developed, and Akademgorodok, a flourishing science city of sixty thousand in western Siberia. The Soviet military-industrial complex brought prosperity to only a small number of Soviets.

Racial strife in the United States

During the 1950s, Americans lived in a segregated society; generally, blacks and whites did not mix. This was especially true in the South, where racism, or discrimination based on skin color, had long been a part of everyday life. Whites and blacks ate at separate restaurants, attended different schools, and could not even drink from the same water fountains. By the mid-1950s, people began to protest against the inequalities that black Americans had to face on a daily basis. In May 1954, the U.S. Supreme Court ruled in *Brown v. Board of Education of Topeka* that schools for black students were inferior to schools for white students. The Court ordered that all states with segregated school systems integrate their schools immediately—that is, allow blacks and whites to attend the same schools together. This decision sparked social unrest

throughout the remainder of the 1950s, and by the 1960s the unrest exploded into widespread demonstrations.

In the 1950s, a young black Baptist minister, Dr. Martin Luther King Jr. (1929–1968), began preaching nonviolent civil disobedience, the use of peaceful protests to demonstrate against injustice, to African Americans. King led black Americans and supportive white Americans in boycotts (for example, refusing to use segregated stores or restaurants), sit-ins (occupying tables and counters at restaurants and refusing to leave), and peaceful marches. The peaceful demonstrations frequently were met by police who used their clubs to beat the protesters. Police also used police dogs, cattle prods, and fire hoses on marchers, resulting in a number of serious injuries. King was arrested numerous times for participating in such events as sit-ins and demonstrations.

In August 1963, King led 250,000 people in the March on Washington. There, as noted in *Turbulent Years: The 60s,* he delivered his famous "I Have a Dream" speech, call-

Demonstrators hold hands to build force against water being sprayed by riot police in Birmingham, Alabama, during a protest of segregation practices. *Reproduced by permission of the Corbis Corporation.*

An aerial shot of the March on Washington, a civil rights demonstration in the nation's capital. *Courtesy of the National Archives and Records Administration.*

ing for equal opportunities for black Americans: "I have a dream that my four little children will one day live in a nation where they will be judged not by the color of their skin but by the content of their character." In 1965, King led a march from Selma to Montgomery, Alabama, to protest the fact that very few blacks had been able to register to vote. Hundreds of marchers were attacked and beaten by whites and by state and local law officials along the way until the

National Guard, the military reserve unit for each state, was called in to protect them.

Just as in the South, blacks in large northern cities lived in poverty. After a white policeman shot and killed a black teen in New York City in July 1964, five days of rioting broke out in Harlem and Brooklyn, two neighborhoods with large black populations. Despite King's call for nonviolent protests, tension ran high in the cities, and violence erupted. Rioting in the Watts section of Los Angeles, California, in the summer of 1965 lasted six days and left thirty-four dead. The riots, sometimes referred to as black rage, spread to cities throughout the United States in the summers of 1966 and 1967, including in Detroit, Michigan, where, in 1967, forty-three people lost their lives and property losses cost millions. Between 1964 and 1968, two hundred people died during riots, and several hundred million dollars' worth of property was destroyed.

Many northern blacks gave up on nonviolent methods of solving America's discrimination problems. They preferred the message of Malcolm X (1925–1965), a member of the Black Muslims, a group that promoted separation of the races. This separatist movement differed from the anti-segregation movement. Separatism, endorsed by Malcolm X, wanted to create a separate black society from mainstream white society; on the other hand, civil rights leaders such as King wanted to end separation of the races and merge blacks into mainstream white society. Malcolm X rejected nonviolence and stressed that black men must defend themselves from what he called the "white devil" any way they thought necessary. Malcolm X was assassinated in 1965, but he left behind his *Autobiography,* which became like a Bible for young blacks searching for their identity. In 1966, another black leader, Stokely Carmichael (1941–1998), advocated separation from whites and Black Power, which he defined as the right of African Americans to define and organize themselves as they saw fit and to protect themselves from racial violence. He hoped to instill racial pride in black Americans. Huey Newton (1942–1989) and Bobby Seale (1936–) formed the Black Panther Party in 1967 in Oakland, California. Eldridge Cleaver (1935–1998) became a famous Panther leader. The Panthers never appeared in public without their guns. Although they organized free meals for hungry black children, they also were

Civil rights leader Martin Luther King Jr. *Reproduced by permission of Getty Images.*

involved in violent shootouts with police. The Black Power movement brought some black Americans greater pride in their identity. However, the majority of black Americans still favored King's nonviolent approach as the best way to expand opportunities for blacks in the United States.

King was a strong supporter of the Great Society social reform programs of President Lyndon B. Johnson (1908–1973; served 1963–69). These programs included Job Corps (to train unemployed workers), Head Start (to aid in early education of poor children), and Medicare (to provide health care for seniors). Construction of respectable low-rent housing for the poor was another part of the Great Society plan. Johnson signed the Civil Rights Act of 1964, which outlawed all discrimination on the basis of race, religion, or ethnic origin, covering employment, education, housing, and public accommodations, and the Voting Rights Act of 1965, which ensured full political voting rights for all adults. But by 1968, Johnson's efforts had been slowed by the cost of the Vietnam War. King became a critic of the war because he thought the vast sums being spent on it should be used to help fund Johnson's domestic programs, which were designed to end poverty and hunger in America. On April 4, 1968, as King stood on the balcony of his motel room in Memphis, Tennessee, he was assassinated by white ex-convict James Earl Ray (1928–1998), though evidence that more than one gunman was involved remained.

Soviet leaders decried the racism and violence in America. How, they asked, could America be devoted to democracy and justice and at the same time condone racism? This was a legitimate question, but it was also part of the Soviets' Cold War strategy: Like the United States, Soviet leaders wanted to win the arms race, but perhaps even more, they wanted to win over the minds of their citizens. Their strong criticism of racism was an effective propaganda tool, encouraging Soviet citizens to see the flaws in Western society. Outside the Cold War framework, even nations friendly to the United States were beginning to doubt America's devotion to liberty and justice for all.

The Vietnam War and antiwar protests

Vietnam is a country in Southeast Asia. In the late 1940s and early 1950s, a communist revolutionary named Ho Chi Minh (1890–1969) led a Vietnamese army in battles against French troops who were trying to maintain French colonial rule in Vietnam. Ho Chi Minh and his army beat the French, but not everyone in Vietnam wanted Ho Chi Minh as their ruler, especially those in the southern part of the country. So in 1954, President Dwight D. Eisenhower (1890–1969; served 1953–61) sent U.S. military advisors to support the anticommunist army in southern Vietnam. In May, a peace settlement officially divided Vietnam into North Vietnam, where Ho Chi Minh became president, and South Vietnam, where Ngo Dinh Diem (1901–1963) became president. But soon fighting resumed, this time between the South Vietnamese army and the Vietcong, a group of communist-trained rebels within South Vietnam. U.S. president John F. Kennedy (1917–1963; served 1961–63) sent troops to South Vietnam during his time in office; his successor, Johnson, was reluctant to send any more troops, but the communists were rapidly gaining the upper hand. Johnson feared that if the United States abandoned Vietnam, the international community would no longer believe U.S. promises to defend against communism. The United States would potentially lose credibility and prestige. Therefore, Johnson decided to commit more troops. About 200,000 U.S. troops were fighting in Vietnam by the end of 1965. Ultimately, 540,000 troops would be in Vietnam by 1967. By 1968, the United States had dropped more bombs on Vietnam than it dropped during the time it was involved in World War II (1939–45).

The United States also dropped tons of chemicals on Vietnam. One was Agent Orange, used to kill jungle foliage where enemy troops hid. Another chemical, napalm, was a fiery gasoline-like gel substance that not only burned plants but stuck to and burned human flesh. U.S. soldiers were ordered to "search and destroy" villages where Vietcong might hide. Civilians—men, women, and children—were also killed by U.S. and South Vietnamese forces who were in a difficult situation to determine who were Vietcong sympathizers and who were not.

The Vietnam War became the first prime-time television war. The daily tragedies of Vietnam were shown every night on network news broadcasts. A daily death toll was generally announced. These televised war reports changed many Americans' views toward the war. By 1965, university students and faculty were leading "teach-ins" about the war. Teach-ins were marathon lecture and debate meetings that were meant to educate people about the Vietnam War. Critics of the war said the old "domino theory" had little meaning in Vietnam. The domino theory maintained that if one country fell to communism, other countries in the region would similarly fall, like dominoes. Critics asserted that Vietnam was fighting a civil war, in which citizens of the same country fight against each other. Therefore, critics said, the United States had no business interfering. They objected to the loss of lives, the financial cost of the war, and the destruction of property and land in the Vietnam countryside. Nevertheless, the U.S. presence in Vietnam continued to expand.

A Vietnamese mother carries her severely burned child after being caught in a napalm attack during the Vietnam War in 1972.
Photograph by Nick Ut. Reproduced by permission of AP/Wide World Photos.

In order to commit such large numbers of troops, the United States had to increase its draft call, in which all eighteen-year-old U.S. men had to register to enter the military. During the Vietnam War, if they were not in high school or college, they would be drafted and quickly enrolled in the

U.S. military. This meant the draft took a disproportionate number of young black men as well as young men from other minority groups because these groups tended to include large numbers of poorer Americans who could not afford college tuition. Twenty-five percent of the U.S. troops in action were drafted, as opposed to those who willingly signed up to be in the military, but these draftees made up 50 to 70 percent of those killed in action. This was because many of the enlisted men had become officers while draftees served as combat infantry. To avoid the draft, some young men stayed in school as long as they could or joined the National Guard. Some illegally evaded the draft by packing up and moving to Canada, where they stayed for many years.

Students watched in horror as nightly news broadcasts showed the misery and death of Vietnamese villagers and soldiers from both Vietnam and the United States. On university campuses, more and more students attended the teach-ins. Soon the gatherings evolved into organized groups that stormed university buildings and demanded that schools cut ties with the U.S. Defense Department, which funded many university research projects. Students also organized demonstrations against companies that manufactured war materials. In addition, they organized demonstrations against military recruitment on campus. Buildings housing the Reserve Officers' Training Corps (ROTC), a student-oriented military training corps, were trashed; some of them were burned. Over the next few years, protests spread out from the universities across the nation and onto the streets of cities and small towns. In 1967, thousands marched in New York City

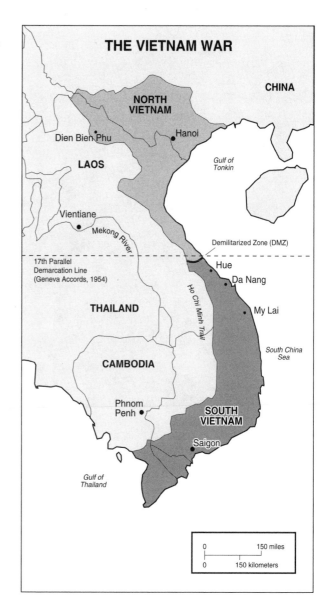

A map of the regions of the Vietnam War. *Map by Christine O'Bryan. Reproduced by permission of the Gale Group.*

Thousands of antiwar protesters demonstrate against the Vietnam War at the United Nations Plaza in New York City in 1967.
Reproduced by permission of AP/Wide World Photos.

and on the Pentagon in Arlington, Virginia. In 1968 and 1969, huge marches were held nationwide so people all across the country would be marching on the same day. Protesters burned their draft cards and the American flag, declaring that the war was immoral and had no purpose except making money for the military-industrial complex.

The counterculture

Many of the war protesters were part of the baby boom generation. Following World War II, as soldiers returned home, young couples started families. Between 1946 and 1964, the U.S. birthrate increased significantly, causing a "baby boom." The first baby boomers were college age in the mid-1960s, and if they were not fighting in Vietnam, they could be found protesting the war on campuses and in the streets. During the 1960s and early 1970s, baby boomers between eighteen and twenty-four years of age made up roughly 20 percent of the

U.S. population. They distrusted "old" Americans—anyone over thirty—who seemed intent on sending them to a war with no clear purpose and no end. Although some parents joined with their children to protest the war in Vietnam, many did not. The "generation gap" developed between parents and their children: Young people rejected the beliefs and values of the older generations, and older people found the lifestyle of the young disrespectful and amoral. The young questioned the materialism they had been surrounded by in the 1950s and 1960s. Their parents had fought patriotically in World War II, then came home to earn a good living and acquire the latest consumer items. Young people, seeing the horrors of war on television each night, questioned the values of the older generation and searched for deeper meanings to life. In their youthful exuberance, they turned to rock music, "free love," or sexual freedoms, and psychedelic art; some experimented with marijuana and the psychedelic drug LSD. In some families, the deep rifts of the "generation gap" never healed.

Both young men and women wore their hair long; tie-dyed T-shirts, bell-bottom jeans, and sandals were popular. A new name for these young people, "hippies," was coined. Their youthful counterculture, or those people who rejected the dominant values and behavior of U.S. society, centered on music of popular rock groups. The Beatles, the Rolling Stones, the Grateful Dead, the Who, the Jefferson Airplane, the Doors, Jimi Hendrix (1942–1970), Janis Joplin (1943–1970), Bob Dylan (1941–), Arlo Guthrie (1947–), and Joni Mitchell (1943–) were just a few of the rock musicians who made vinyl record albums full of songs enjoyed by the counterculture youth.

San Francisco's Haight-Ashbury district became a central location for the counterculture. In the summer of 1967, thousands gathered there for what became known as the "summer of love." Young people handed out flowers to strangers as a symbol of peace and love. They hoped free love and drugs such as marijuana and LSD would expand their consciousness. The popular musical *Hair* combined all the major themes and conflicts of the day: love, sex, drugs, strong antiwar sentiments, and hair—long hair.

In August 1969, approximately five hundred thousand people descended on Max Yasgur's 600-acre dairy farm near Bethel in upstate New York for a rock music festival

✈ Counterculture Protest Song

Country Joe McDonald wrote the song "I-Feel-Like-I'm-Fixin'-to-Die Rag" for his band, Country Joe and the Fish, as a protest to the Vietnam War effort. It was widely played across the United States. The band also performed the song at the Woodstock music festival in August 1969. The following lyrics are Verse 2 and the refrain.

Well, come on generals, let's move fast;
Your big chance has come at last.
Gotta go out and get these reds—
The only good commie is the one who's dead
And you know that peace can only be won
When we've blown 'em all to kingdom come.

[Refrain]
And it's one, two, three,
What are we fighting for?
Don't ask me, I don't give a damn,
Next stop is Vietnam,
And it's five, six, seven,
Open up the pearly gates,
Well there ain't no time to wonder why,
Whoopee! We're all gonna die.

Country Joe McDonald, of the popular psychedelic rock band Country Joe and the Fish. *Photograph by Roger Ressmeyer. Reproduced by permission of the Corbis Corporation.*

called Woodstock. In three rain-soaked days, the crowd heard Joan Baez (1941–), Hendrix, Joplin, Guthrie, the Who, the Grateful Dead, the Jefferson Airplane, and other popular musicians. The three-day love-in, a public gathering held to profess mutual love and protest inhumane government policies, amid the music caught the attention of the nation. Older Americans had little understanding of the event and looked on it with contempt.

Backlash

Although many young people protested the war and participated in the counterculture, they were part of a minority in America. The "Silent Majority," as coined by President

Nixon, characterized the public who were not politically vocal to justify the continuation of the Vietnam War. These Middle Americans, that segment of U.S. society with average income and education and conventional values and conservative attitudes, were dismayed by the antiwar demonstrations and the hippies. Many Middle Americans, labor union members, and minorities had lost their sons in the Vietnam War and were proud of their sons' service to the country. They were outraged by the antiwar protests. Furthermore, they considered the rock music and sexual permissiveness of the counterculture excessive and an insult to the American way of life—allegiance to the national government and its economic system.

Although the Silent Majority supported the military in Vietnam and continued to hope for victory, the U.S. government overestimated citizens' support of the war effort and consistently underestimated the communists' will to continue fighting. The seemingly endless war led to President John-

Three young ladies protest the war in Vietnam in Boston, Massachusetts, on April 15, 1970. *Reproduced by permission of the Corbis Corporation.*

son's decision not to run for reelection in 1968. The victor in the election, former Republican vice president Richard M. Nixon (1913–1994), began withdrawing troops from Vietnam in 1969 but increased bombing in Cambodia to destroy enemy supply camps. (More protests followed; on May 4, 1970, four students at Kent State University in Kent, Ohio, were shot and killed by National Guardsmen during a war protest. Eleven more were injured.) After more rounds of bombing over North Vietnam in 1971 and 1972, the communists still hung on. The United States had military might to spare, but U.S. leaders did not want to escalate the war to such a point that a nuclear confrontation with China or the Soviet Union might result. Both China and the Soviet Union had remained involved by supplying the communists of North Vietnam with military materials.

In March 1973, the last U.S. troops left Vietnam. Approximately fifty-eight thousand U.S. soldiers had lost their lives. Huge areas of Vietnam's jungle and farmland were ruined for decades, poisoned by the chemicals U.S. planes had dropped. The war cost the United States roughly $150 billion. In the end, which did not come until April 30, 1975, South Vietnam surrendered to the communist North. Only the countries of Laos and Cambodia fulfilled the predictions of the domino theory by falling to the communists. Thailand, Burma (later renamed Myanmar), Malaysia, and other Asian nations did not.

Soviet citizens' struggles

While the United States struggled with racial tensions and the Vietnam War, the Soviet Union faced problems at home as well. Some Soviet families benefited from the military-industrial complex, but for most Soviet citizens, life in the 1960s was a dull sequence of low-skilled jobs and the daily task of endlessly waiting in lines everywhere for food and clothing. Housing was cheap because the government paid part of the cost, but overcrowding was common. One communal apartment might house several families and single people, all in the same space. The occupants made the best of the situation by celebrating holidays and special occasions together and playing games in the evening. The Soviet government provided free education, health care, and full

Kent State and Jackson State Universities

Elected in 1968, President Richard M. Nixon promised to begin to decrease the United States' involvement in the Vietnam War. In 1969, he began U.S. troop withdrawal but suddenly escalated the war in May 1970 by ordering the invasion of Cambodia, a country neighboring Vietnam. He argued that U.S. withdrawal could be speeded up if enemy supply bases in Cambodia were destroyed. Reaction on college campuses was swift; protests broke out across the country. As noted in *Cold War: An Illustrated History, 1945–1991,* Nixon further incited people when he called the antiwar protesters "bums."

Nixon sent National Guard troops to control the rioting of students. At Kent State University in Kent, Ohio, the troops opened fire, killing four students and injuring eleven. At Jackson State University in Jackson, Mississippi, police shot and killed two students. Several governors declared states of emergency on their university campuses. Throughout the nation, approximately five hundred campuses temporarily shut down. Many Americans still supported the war effort, and they clashed

A wounded African American man is escorted away from a riot area after demonstrations at Jackson State College in Jackson, Mississippi, turned violent on May 12, 1967. *Reproduced by permission of the Corbis Corporation.*

with and demonstrated against the antiwar protesters. Some Americans supported Nixon's actions, but others demanded his impeachment, a legislative proceeding charging a public official with misconduct. The country had not been so divided since the American Civil War (1861–65).

employment. But productivity was very low because there was little incentive to work hard. Highly skilled individuals often held unskilled jobs; jobs were guaranteed but there was little chance for promotion; and more money would not be as useful because there was nothing to buy but the few necessities due to a lack of consumer culture like in the West. People could not earn enough to buy the luxuries that appeared from time to time in state-owned department stores. As part of the communist way, the people had no freedom of speech or press, and all religious activities were banned.

The Soviet economy was run by the Central Government in Moscow. Five-year plans were drawn up, and middle managers in local areas assigned workers their tasks. The workers were encouraged to keep up with the United States, especially in agricultural production. But the Soviet system was inefficient and inflexible and could not respond to local needs; it was highly centralized and possessed very rigid decision-making. Its output, therefore, lagged far behind America's robust economy.

Soviet leader Nikita Khrushchev (1894–1971) was constantly urging collective farms, which would provide more local control, to set higher output goals. During Khrushchev's "meat campaign," the collectives, which strongly supported the idea of increased local control, eagerly set goals that they could never reach. They then set about butchering animals throughout the countryside to meet the one-year goal. The livestock herds were destroyed, and it took years to recover. Likewise, plans for huge grain harvests were unrealistic: About 90 million acres were plowed up and planted in wheat. For the first few years, the harvests were good, but overuse of the land soon decreased its production severely. The Soviets then had to buy grain from the United States—an embarrassment, but necessary to keep people from starving.

Khrushchev, who had denounced former Soviet premier Joseph Stalin (1879–1953) as a brutal leader, loosened some of the restrictions in Soviet society. Art galleries opened; Soviets began enjoying a variety of musical performances; and hundreds, even thousands, gathered for poetry readings. Poets were especially popular with the Soviet public. One of the most famous was Yevgeny Yevtushenko (1933–), who read with energy and passion, delighting his audiences. Young Soviets also began to pick up snatches of Western culture. Western clothing fashions such as blue jeans were prized, and radios brought Western rock and roll. Although Western music was forbidden, vinyl records were occasionally smuggled in and reproduced. Soviet teens idolized Elvis Presley (1935–1977) and the Beatles as much as Western teens did.

Conservative Soviet communists became concerned about the young people's craving for Western culture and

Yevgeny Yevtushenko

Born on July 18, 1933, in Zima, Siberia, Russia, poet Yevgeny Yevtushenko became a leader of Soviet youths who were daring to question communist authority in the late 1950s and early 1960s. Yevtushenko traveled widely in the West until 1963; his travel was curtailed after he published in English *A Precocious Autobiography,* an uncensored, frank discussion of what he perceived to be flaws in Soviet society. Yevtushenko demanded artistic freedom and was politically outspoken. He attacked the policies of the late Soviet leader Joseph Stalin with his poem "The Heirs of Stalinism" (1961) and criticized the Soviet government's anti-Jewish policies with "Babiy Yar" (1961).

Russian poet Yevgeny Yevtushenko. *Courtesy of the Library of Congress.*

In the 1970s, Yevtushenko continued to write. He was also involved in acting, directing films, and photography. He supported the Nobel Prize–winning Soviet author Aleksandr Solzhenitsyn (1918–) when Solzhenitsyn was exiled for his writings. In the late 1980s, when Soviet communist policies had relaxed somewhat, Yevtushenko published the journal *Ogonek,* which introduced Soviets to poets whom they had not been allowed to hear or study before.

goods. They also feared the creativity and freethinking of the fledgling Soviet art community. They urged Khrushchev to again crack down. Khrushchev agreed and began to caution young people to conform to communist doctrine, to reject all things Western, or find themselves in trouble with Soviet authorities. Protests in the Soviet Union and Soviet satellite countries led only to tighter control and repression of the people.

China's Cultural Revolution

Appalled at Khrushchev's tentative move away from the strict communist doctrine of the Stalin years, Mao Zedong, leader of the People's Republic of China, or more simply, China, instituted his Cultural Revolution in 1966. Mao's objective was to ensure that all Chinese people remained loyal to the philosophy of communism. He believed the only way to accomplish this goal was to purge, or eliminate, from Chinese society any trace of traditional Chinese culture and Western (that is, noncommunist) ideas or influence.

To carry out this massive purge, Mao enlisted a million young people from universities and militant youth groups in China. In every town and city, young men and women were organized as the Red Guards. Each Red Guard wore a red arm band and carried a little red book of Mao's "thoughts." Devoutly loyal to Mao, the Red Guards fanned out over China; their first targets were teachers and intellectuals, whom they accused of having deviant, dangerous ideas and opinions. Everyone in a place of authority—in government, factories, businesses, and local Communist Party committees—was subjected to the abuses of the Red Guards. Verbal abuse turned to physical violence as the Red Guards tortured and murdered thousands. Millions of Chinese people were arrested and sent to labor camps, accused of favoring improved relations with the United States and the Soviet Union and tending toward aspects of a market economy. Others committed suicide before the Red Guards could reach them.

Mao called the purge a fight against the "four olds": "old cultures," "old customs," "old habits," and "old thoughts." The "olds" extended to old paintings, old books, antiques, and museum exhibits, many of which were destroyed. Anyone or anything that might take attention or reverence away from Mao and communist doctrine was eliminated. Nearly four hundred thousand people were killed.

The Cultural Revolution severely damaged the framework of Chinese society. Most universities closed between 1966 and 1970. Industrial manufacturing capabilities decreased dramatically after management leaders were purged. Charging that local Communist Party leaders had moved away from pure communism, the Red Guards took over provincial and city governments and shredded the party's leadership structure. The Communist Party officials who lived through the purge remained apprehensive and barely functioned. A few brave moderates called for an end to the purge in 1967. Mao gave his answer by organizing a frenzied rally of a million Red Guards in Tiananmen Square in the center of the capital city of Beijing.

By the late 1960s, Mao was apparently satisfied that the Red Guards had successfully purged anyone not totally loyal to him. Mao ordered the Red Guards to take the purge to the countryside. Cities slowly began to regain some order, but farmers experienced the Red Guards' wrath. Accusing each other of not being idealistic enough, Red Guard members began to fight among themselves, forcing Mao to call out China's regular army later in 1967 to restore order. By 1969 and 1970, China's schools, government, and industries slowly began to function again. Any dissidents who happened to be left were silent, not daring to speak out again for decades.

For More Information

Books

Feinstein, Stephen. *The 1960s: From the Vietnam War to Flower Power*. Berkeley Heights, NJ: Enslow, 2000.

Isaacs, Jeremy, and Taylor Downing. *Cold War: An Illustrated History, 1945–1991*. Boston: Little, Brown, 1998.

Kallen, Stuart A. *A Cultural History of the United States through the Decades: The 1950s*. San Diego, CA: Lucent Books, 1999.

Maier, Pauline, Merritt R. Smith, Alexander Keyssar, and Daniel J. Kevles. *Inventing America: A History of the United States*. New York: W. W. Norton, 2003.

Stolley, Richard B., ed. *Time of Transition: The 70s*. Alexandria, VA: Time-Life Books, 1998.

Stolley, Richard B., ed. *Turbulent Years: The 60s*. Alexandria, VA: Time-Life Books, 1998.

Thousands of Red Guards celebrate China's Cultural Revolution in Tiananmen Square on May 1, 1969. *Reproduced by permission of the Corbis Corporation.*

Détente: A Lessening of Tensions

13

From 1969 through 1975, the United States and the Soviet Union, the world's two superpowers, established policies promoting détente between them. Détente, French for "lessening of tensions," marked a relaxing of tensions between the rival nations, exemplified by increased diplomatic, commercial, and cultural contact. Western and Eastern European countries also experienced a détente and better cooperation during this period. The Cold War entered a new phase during détente. Consistent contact and communication between the United States and the Soviet Union was perhaps the greatest single achievement of détente. The détente period is also significant because it marked the beginning of improved relations between the United States and China. Recognizing that China and the United States could become allies pushed the Soviets toward détente. These positive changes were bright spots in U.S. foreign affairs at a time when the United States seemed all but consumed by the challenge of extricating itself from the Vietnam War (1954–75).

The first treaty of the Strategic Arms Limitation Talks (SALT I), signed by the United States and the Soviet Union in

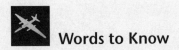

Words to Know

Brezhnev Doctrine: A Soviet act that proclaimed the right of the Soviet Union to intervene in the internal affairs of other communist states and to impose its particular communist principles on them.

Capitalism: An economic system in which property and businesses are privately owned. Prices, production, and distribution of goods are determined by competition in a market relatively free of government intervention.

Cold War: A prolonged conflict for world dominance from 1945 to 1991 between the two superpowers, the democratic, capitalist United States and the communist Soviet Union. The weapons of conflict were commonly words of propaganda and threats.

Communism: A system of government in which the nation's leaders are selected by a single political party that controls all aspects of society. Private ownership of property is eliminated and govern-

ment directs all economic production. The goods produced and accumulated wealth are, in theory, shared relatively equally by all. All religious practices are banned.

Democracy: A system of government in which several political parties compete.

Détente: A relaxing of tensions between rival nations, marked by increased diplomatic, commercial, and cultural contact.

Strategic Arms Limitation Talks (SALT): Discussions between the United States and the Soviet Union aimed at lessening the threat of nuclear war by bringing the arms race under control.

Watergate scandal: A scandal that began on June 17, 1972, when five men were caught burglarizing the offices of the Democratic National Committee in the Watergate complex in Washington, D.C. This led to a cover-up, criminal convictions, and, eventually, the resignation of President Richard Nixon.

May 1972, lessened the threat of nuclear war by bringing the arms race under control. The treaty represented the core of détente. The negotiations that led up to SALT I continued after it was signed and established a direct line of communication between the two superpowers.

Even with all the talk of cooperation, the United States and the Soviet Union continued their competitive Cold War struggle. Neither gave up a single offensive weapon already in development or production. Likewise, as governmental troubles occurred in nations around the world, neither country gave up opportunities to further its global influence, political philosophy, and economic goals in those afflicted areas. The Soviet Union promoted communism as the best system of government. In a communist government, a single political party controls almost all aspects of society. Communist economic theory includes a ban on private ownership of property and businesses so that goods produced and wealth accumulated can be shared equally by all. The United States supported democracy, a completely different political system, as the best choice for people around the globe. In a democracy, several political parties select candidates to run for election to various government offices; the people vote to elect one candidate for each office. In the United States, democracy is paired with capitalism, an economic system that allows property and businesses to be privately owned. Competition determines prices, and individuals who compete successfully in business can accumulate private wealth. The government is only minimally involved in controlling goods and production.

 People to Know

Willy Brandt (1913–1992): West German chancellor, 1969–74.

Leonid Brezhnev (1906–1982): Leader of the Soviet Union Communist Party, 1964–82.

Jimmy Carter (1924–): Thirty-ninth U.S. president, 1977–81.

Charles de Gaulle (1890–1970): French president, 1958–69.

Gerald R. Ford (1913–): Thirty-eighth U.S. president, 1974–77.

Henry Kissinger (1923–): U.S. national security advisor, 1969–75; secretary of state, 1973–77.

Mao Zedong (1893–1976): Chairman of the People's Republic of China and its Communist Party, 1949–76.

Richard M. Nixon (1913–1994): Thirty-seventh U.S. president, 1969–74.

The European détente began through the efforts of Charles de Gaulle (1890–1970), the president of France, and Willy Brandt (1913–1992), the West German chancellor who came to power in 1969. Both sought to open communications with the East, Eastern Europe, and the Soviet Union, and they achieved major improvements in East-West relations.

In August 1974, America's Watergate scandal, which stemmed from the burglarizing of the offices of the Democratic National Committee and the cover-up that followed, and the subsequent resignation of U.S. president Richard M. Nixon (1913–1994; served 1969–74) interrupted détente. Détente activities culminated in the Helsinki Accords, signed in the summer of 1975 by thirty-five nations, including the United States, now under the leadership of Gerald R. Ford (1913–; served 1974–77) . However, by the spring of 1976, détente had stalled; superpower relations would go into a freeze by the spring of 1977.

China opens to the United States

By early 1969, tensions between the People's Republic of China (PRC) and the Soviet Union were at an all-time high. The PRC was by this time simply called China. China's leaders, Mao Zedong (1893–1976) and Premier Zhou Enlai (1898–1976), had cast a wary eye toward Czechoslovakia, where the Soviets had stopped a revolt in 1968. The Brezhnev Doctrine (1968), named after Soviet leader Leonid Brezhnev (1906–1982), proclaimed the right of the Soviet Union to intervene in the internal affairs of other communist states and to impose its particular communist principles on them. Although the doctrine largely applied to the Soviet satellite nations of Eastern Europe, China's leaders feared that Soviet aggression would someday focus on China. They were also not happy that the Soviets treated them arrogantly when the Chinese tried to share industrial and military technology with the Soviets. China had managed to develop its own nuclear weapons during the 1960s but had done so without Soviet help. By 1969, the border between China and the Soviet Union, over 3,000 miles (4,827 kilometers), was guarded by an ever-expanding military buildup on both sides. Sporadic fighting broke out between Soviet and Chinese troops.

U.S. president Richard Nixon and his national security advisor, Henry Kissinger (1923–), decided to take advantage of the Soviet-Chinese rift. In early 1970, Kissinger began secretly traveling to Warsaw, Poland, where he met with Chinese officials. This secret type of negotiation is referred to as a back channel. China had long isolated itself from the rest of the world, and the small amount of information that leaked out about its brutal 1960s Cultural Revolution (see Chapter 12, Home Front Turmoil: The 1960s) convinced other nations that they wanted nothing to do with China anyway. But now the United States and China saw that the opening of relations between them could be advantageous, for a number of reasons. China could be an effective block to further Soviet aggression eastward. Fearful of Soviet aggression, China was eager to respond to the United States, a powerful potential ally. President Nixon was also trying to wind down the war in Vietnam. He believed China was supplying weapons to communist North Vietnam, the U.S. enemy in this conflict. He hoped that opening talks might halt this activity, thereby helping him pull U.S. troops out of Vietnam more quickly. Lastly, Nixon and Kissinger believed that if the Soviets thought the United States and China were becoming allies, the Soviets would push for better relations with the United States. The Soviets feared that China and the United States might form a partnership against the Soviet Union.

Secret back-channel talks with Kissinger progressed, and before long the United States eased trade and travel restrictions to China. In spring 1971, China invited the U.S. Ping-Pong team to play a tournament in Beijing, the capital city. The team traveled to China in April 1971, was warmly received, and set a positive tone for future exchanges. In July, Kissinger became the first U.S. government representative to visit China since the communist revolution in 1949. The talks between Kissinger, Mao, and Zhou were still secret and still cordial, and they paved the way for a visit by President Nixon. Nixon's plane touched down in China on February 21, 1972, beginning a very public visit. Live television covered Nixon and his wife, Pat, as they walked with Chinese officials along the Great Wall, a 1,500-mile (2,400 kilometers) wall that runs across northern China. A beaming Nixon toasted Mao and Zhou in the Great Hall of the People. Nixon agreed to begin withdrawing U.S. troops from Taiwan, a nation the United States had long supported and China had opposed. Nixon's only disappointment came when the Chinese did not agree to halt support for the North Vietnamese. Nevertheless, tensions were lessened over both Taiwan and Vietnam. Nixon's historic trip to China was a Cold War turning point. It paved the way for full diplomatic relations with China seven years later in 1979 during the administration of Jimmy Carter (1924– ; served 1977–81). It greatly strengthened America's position in the world. Overall, the trip served to put a great deal of pressure on the Soviet Union. A U.S.-China alignment was the Soviet Union's worst nightmare: The Soviets and Chinese already had strained relations; improved U.S.-Chinese relations would result in major rivals to

Ping-Pong Diplomacy

The U.S. table tennis team was one of the first groups of Westerners to travel to China after the Cultural Revolution ended (see Chapter 12, Home Front Turmoil: The 1960s). The team's opportunity to visit China originated by chance: The U.S. team was in Japan for the world Ping-Pong championships early in 1971, and a young American player stumbled onto the wrong team bus. He sat down and soon discovered he was surrounded by Chinese team players, none of whom would speak to him. It was forbidden for the young Chinese to talk to foreigners. Feeling the snub was uncalled for, the Chinese team captain spoke to the American. The next day. the American team leader approached the Chinese team captain. With youthful eagerness and in the spirit of international competition, he asked if the U.S. team might be allowed to visit Beijing for a tournament.

Although no Americans had been in China for years, the time was right, politically speaking, to allow such a visit. The request went all the way to Chinese leader Mao Zedong, because no one else in China could make such an important decision. Mao, who was in the midst of improving relations with the United States, saw Ping-Pong as a great opportunity for exchange between the two countries.

In April 1971, in packed arenas, the American players competed against the Chinese players, who were known to be some of the best in the world. The Chinese defeated the Americans easily, but the warm hospitality the young Americans received seemed genuine and very enthusiastic. Although the U.S. team lost its matches, it scored big points for foreign diplomacy: Shortly after the U.S. team visit, Secretary of State Henry Kissinger traveled secretly to China to speak directly with Mao and President Richard Nixon was invited to China for a summit in February 1972.

the east and west, which, the Soviets feared, could develop a growing anti-Soviet coalition.

Strategic Arms Limitation Talks (SALT I)

The Strategic Arms Limitation Talks (SALT I)—negotiations for limitation of offensive and defensive nuclear weapons in the Soviet Union and the United States—had begun in 1969. Fearing that China and the United States might form a partnership against the Soviet Union, Soviet leaders were eager to improve relations with the United States. After Nixon's trip to China, Kissinger quietly visited Moscow and paved the way for

the completion of SALT I. The negotiations revolved around offensive intercontinental ballistic missiles (ICBMs), multiple independently targetable reentry vehicles (MIRVs), and antiballistic missile (ABM) systems. ICBMs carried single nuclear warheads to a target thousands of miles away. MIRVs were offensive multiple warheads, each guided to a different target but installed atop a single missile. ABM systems were proposed defense systems to intercept incoming missiles. There was no assurance ABMs could really defend against all incoming missiles. But if one country had a working ABM, it could go on the offensive against the other and then protect against retaliation. Therefore, if the United States tried to develop an ABM, the Soviet Union would feel compelled to also develop an ABM, and vice versa. The cost of attempting to develop an ABM was billions of dollars. The United States was not eager to spend this money, and the Soviet Union, its economy struggling, was desperate not to spend that much.

Ultimately, SALT I capped the number of ICBMs for a five-year period; only ICBMs already manufactured or in the construction process would be allowed. No cap was put on MIRVs, so the race to build MIRVs continued. The only real progress came on the question of ABMs. Each country was allowed two ABM systems: one to protect its capital city and one to defend a field of offensive missiles. This ruling would significantly slow any ABM development, to the great relief of both countries.

President Nixon arrived in Moscow on May 22, 1972, for the signing of the treaty. He was the first American president to go to the Kremlin, the seat of the Soviet government in Moscow. Although the Soviets would have been much happier if Nixon had gone to Moscow before Beijing, SALT I was signed, and Brezhnev offered toasts all around. A few days later, Nixon and Brezhnev signed the Basic Principles of Relations between the United States and Soviet Union. The Soviets had proposed and prepared the Basic Principles, and they considered the document a major achievement in détente. It stated that neither superpower would take advantage of a situation at the expense of the other. It was a kind of charter, or set of rules and guiding principles, for détente. It spoke of peaceful coexistence, long a Soviet catchphrase. Each superpower was to strive to lessen the chance of military conflicts and nuclear war. Kissinger and Nixon did not consider the document as important as the Soviets did. As noted in *Cold War: An Illustrated History, 1945–1991*, it is likely Nixon had not even read the document when he signed it.

The meeting in Moscow established a working relationship between the United States and the Soviet Union. New lines of communication had been established and would eventually lead to discussions on trade and allow U.S. tourists to travel to the Soviet Union. While in Moscow, Nixon had offered to sell U.S. surplus wheat to the Soviets. Soon after Nixon's return to the United States, the Soviets agreed to buy four hundred million bushels of wheat for roughly $700 million and obtained U.S. loans to do so. Some U.S. officials chuckled that the Soviets were quite good at capitalist negotiations. Conservatives believed the United States had been outsmarted in the deal. Nevertheless, the Soviets would continue to buy U.S. grain for many years.

Despite all the arms control talk and the signing of the Basic Principles, both countries knew that détente rested on

the principle of strategic weapons parity, or equality, and mutual deterrence. Each side had the capability to destroy the other even if the other side struck first. Nixon and Kissinger knew this; Brezhnev knew it as well. Kissinger considered this relationship necessary for long-term coexistence between the two superpowers. Enforcing détente was merely a way to establish less tense relations and lessen the risk of anyone launching a nuclear war. As for arms control, the Soviet Union went right on with its buildup, uninterrupted, because they were behind the United States in the ICBM race. This was allowed because they had room to expand under their caps, whereas the United States did not; this was a major issue with some critics of the agreement. Soon, the Soviets had exceeded U.S. ICBM launchers by 50 percent. Both countries continued developing new MIRVs and new nuclear submarines.

U.S. president Richard Nixon (left) exchanges documents with Soviet premier Leonid Brezhnev following the signing of the SALT treaty. *Photograph by Wally McNamee. Reproduced by permission of the Corbis Corporation.*

Ostopolitik

Ostopolitik was a new policy instituted by West German chancellor Willy Brandt. Brandt took over leadership of

West Germany in October 1969. He replaced Konrad Adenauer (1876–1967), who had been adamant in his refusal to recognize East Germany as an independent nation. *Ostopolitik* recognized East Germany and territorial changes that occurred at the conclusion of World War II (1939–45), including the new boundaries of Poland. This new policy was a major force in the so-called European détente. Another major force was Charles de Gaulle, the president of France, who refused to let the United States position its nuclear weapons in France. De Gaulle also pulled out of the North Atlantic Treaty Organization (NATO), which was formed for the mutual protection of the United States and Western European nations. Both Brandt and de Gaulle were hoping for a more cooperative relationship with Eastern Europe, even though Eastern European countries were under the strong influence of the Soviet Union.

In December 1972, East and West Germany signed a mutual recognition treaty. Also, for the first time since Berlin was divided into four sectors (Soviet, British, American, and French; after World War II), West Germany officially recognized East Berlin as part of East Germany. In turn, East Germany recognized the role of the United States, Britain, and France in West Berlin and guaranteed access to West Berlin from West Germany (see Chapter 3, Germany and Berlin). This détente-influenced mutual political recognition marked a new beginning in East-West European cooperation. The U.S.-Soviet détente would ultimately collapse by 1976, but the European détente continued to flourish.

Influence of Cold War worldwide

The lines of communication established between the superpowers were pressed into active negotiations at the end

of 1972. A new round of talks began on extending the agreements of SALT I. In the summer of 1973, Brezhnev traveled to the United States for a summit. At this summit, a document called the Prevention of Nuclear War was signed. The document bound both countries to do everything possible to prevent nuclear war.

Both the United States and the Soviet Union proved that despite talks and treaties, neither country would stop trying to extend its influence in the world. The situation in Europe had stabilized, so there was little Cold War competition left there, but many countries in the Third World were very unstable. (The term *Third World* refers to poor underdeveloped or developing nations in Africa, Asia, and Latin America. Most Third World countries have economies primarily based on agriculture, with few other industries.) The Soviets supported revolutionary liberation movements within these countries whenever they erupted. They expected the revolutionaries to adopt communism and ally themselves

A large crane removes equipment from a Titan II missile silo, as part of the SALT agreements.
Photograph by Roger Ressmeyer. Reproduced by permission of the Corbis Corporation.

with the Soviet Union. The United States supported extremely conservative governments that were strongly anticommunist—but often run by brutal dictators. The Cold War would therefore continue, on a global scale.

Chile

In 1970, the communist-leaning Salvador Allende Gossens (1908–1973) was elected as Chile's new president. Many Chileans questioned his policies, and he might have lost power before long. Nevertheless, through the U.S. Central Intelligence Agency (CIA), Nixon and Kissinger engineered a military coup (short for coup d'état; an illegal or forceful change of government) in which Allende was killed. General Augusto Pinochet Ugarte (1915–1999) took control. Although he was a ruthless dictator, the United States was willing to officially recognize him as president of Chile because he was noncommunist.

Iran

Between 1972 and 1979, to combat a growing Soviet presence in the Middle East, the United States allowed Mohammad Reza Pahlavi (1919–1980), the shah, or ruler, of Iran, to buy approximately $20 billion worth of U.S. weapons. (The shah had been returned to power by a CIA coup in the 1950s. See Chapter 14, A Freeze in Relations.) The shah allowed no political freethinking and brutally punished anyone speaking out. Nevertheless, his pro-American stance kept Nixon pleased and communism at bay.

Angola

Long under Portuguese rule, the African country of Angola was given its independence in 1975. Civil war among various factions ensued. The United States, China, and South Africa supported one side of the guerrilla warfare, or irregular and independent attacks; the Soviets supported the other. Taking it a step higher, the United States engaged the CIA in covert, or secret, activities to support the guerrillas whose sentiments leaned toward America. In response, the Soviets sent ten thousand Cuban soldiers into Angola to help support the government for over a decade.

The October War—The Yom Kippur War

On October 6, 1973, the Jewish holiday of Yom Kippur, Egypt and Syria launched a surprise attack on Israel. Unprepared, Israel suffered territorial losses and pleaded for quick help from the United States. While Egypt and Syria were backed with Soviet materials, Israel received war planes and other supplies from the United States. Within ten days Israel was on the offensive, trapping Egypt's Third Army on the Sinai Peninsula. The Soviets threatened to intervene to save the Third Army; the Soviets did not want to see Egypt, a pro-Soviet country (though not solid) suffer another embarrassing defeat to Israel as in 1967. The United States put all its nuclear armed forces on alert but at the same time called on Israel to stop advancing. Israel complied, and both the United States and the Soviet Union backed off. The October War proved that the two superpowers had no intention of putting the new rules or guidelines of détente into practice. Through intelligence, the Soviets probably knew of

Israeli artillerymen hold their ears as they shoot their weapons on the Syrian border during the October War in 1973.
Reproduced by permission of the Corbis Corporation.

Egypt's plan to attack Israel but did not warn the United States ahead of time. The crisis eventually took the super-powers closer to nuclear war than they had been since the Cuban Missile Crisis in October 1962 (see Chapter 9, Cuban Missile Crisis).

Cuba, again

The only détente-era direct confrontation between the United States and the Soviet Union occurred in 1970. The Soviets began building a submarine base at the Bay of Cien-fuegos in Cuba. The base would supply Soviet nuclear sub-marines. After a U-2 spy aircraft flying over Cuba took a pho-tograph of the construction, the United States confronted the Soviets, arguing that agreements made at the end of the Cuban Missile Crisis prohibited such construction. The Sovi-ets quickly backed away, and the crisis blew over.

Watergate

The beginning of the end of détente actually oc-curred only a few months after Nixon's triumphant trip to China in February 1972. On June 17, 1972, a security guard at the Watergate building complex in Washington, D.C., caught five men breaking into the Democratic National Committee Headquarters office. One of the men, James W. McCord Jr. (1918–), worked for the Committee to Reelect the President (CREEP). The break-in eventually led directly to the White House—and to Nixon himself—and to presi-dential impeachment proceedings, a legislative process charging a public official with misconduct. With the prob-lems of Watergate at the forefront, détente became entan-gled in a web of domestic American politics. Détente had al-ways depended on the personalities of Kissinger, Nixon, and Brezhnev. But weakened by the Watergate scandal, Nixon could do little.

On August 9, 1974, Nixon became the first American president in history to resign. He was replaced by Vice Presi-dent Gerald Ford—who himself had replaced Spiro Agnew (1918–1996) a year earlier after Agnew was forced to resign due to an income tax evasion scandal—making him the first U.S. president who had never been popularly elected to ei-

ther the office of president or vice president. Ford would continue pursuing the policies of détente.

When Nixon left Washington, D.C., he left behind more than the break-in scandal. His legacy includes an improvement in U.S.-Chinese relations and many other notable foreign relations achievements. He, Kissinger, and Brezhnev had established détente essentially by themselves, and it had worked to lessen Cold War tensions between the two superpowers. By withdrawing from Vietnam, Nixon recognized that America had limits to its power. But he also showed communist-fearing Americans that the communist world outside the Soviet Union was not a monster ready to devour the United States. Instead it had many centers that were rarely even loosely joined to one another. Because Nixon understood this, he defined his Nixon Doctrine, announced in July 1969, as a shift in American foreign commitments. It was a shift away from immediately sending American troops wherever a communist rebel group threatened to gain control in a country.

Richard Nixon gives his farewell speech on August 9, the day he resigned from the U.S. presidency. His daughter, Tricia Cox, and son-in-law, Edward Cox, are behind him. *Courtesy of the Library of Congress.*

End of the Vietnam War

When Richard Nixon campaigned for the U.S. presidency in 1968, he claimed he would bring an honorable end to the Vietnam War if he was elected. Nixon won the election over his Democratic opponent, Vice President Hubert Humphrey (1911–1978), and entered the White House in January 1969. By March, Nixon unveiled a new policy for the war; the policy was called Vietnamization. It called for the South Vietnamese army, which the United States had been supporting, to take over responsibility for fighting the war. Meanwhile, American troops, numbering over five hundred thousand at the time, would be phased out. As this policy was put into action, Nixon's national security advisor, Henry Kissinger, entered secret negotiations with the communist North Vietnamese to bring an end to the war. However, the talks were not productive. The United States hoped that in the spirit of détente cooperation, the Soviet Union and China could help bring an end to the war by talking with their fellow communists in North Vietnam. But this did not occur. In reality, neither country had much influence over the North Vietnamese.

To give the South Vietnamese army a fighting chance after U.S. ground troops were to be withdrawn from the war as part of Vietnamization, Nixon decided to attack North Vietnamese base camps in neighboring countries to destroy their war supplies and their sanctuaries, or safe places normally protected from attack. Because of continued public protests against the war and an unsupportive Congress, Nixon ordered secret bombing of Cambodian targets and support of South Vietnamese raids into Laos, another neighbor of Vietnam.

Finally, the secret peace talks became more productive in October 1972. Both countries had a reason to talk: Nixon needed to show progress in ending the war to the American public to gain reelection, and North Vietnam was not making satisfactory progress in gaining control of South Vietnam. On October 26, days before the presidential election, Kissinger made a public announcement: "Peace is at hand." Nixon won easily, boosted by the good news. However, the South Vietnamese, who had been left out of the ne-

The United States would no longer act as the global police; it would rely more on other Western nations to take more responsibility with U.S. backing. Government leaders and the American public alike hoped this policy would help them avoid all future entanglements that resembled the one in Vietnam. Indeed, China took the Nixon Doctrine as a positive sign and opened the door for renewed relations.

President Richard Nixon is surrounded by U.S. soldiers during his visit to Saigon during the Vietnam War. *Reproduced by permission of AP/Wide World Photos.*

eleven days of intensive bombing in North Vietnam through late December; this was known as the "Christmas bombing." Public protests again erupted around the United States. Though highly unpopular, the bombings soon led to a cease-fire settlement, which went into effect on January 27, 1973. Two months later, Nixon proclaimed "peace with honor" as the last American soldiers left Vietnam on March 29. However, fighting in South Vietnam would continue for two more years. Finally in early 1975, a North Vietnamese offensive took control of South Vietnam and captured its capital, Saigon. The last Americans and some pro-American Vietnamese evacuated in overloaded helicopters from the U.S. embassy's rooftop.

The war had finally ended. For the first time, the United States was on the losing side of a war, and the costs were dramatic. The United States spent $155 billion fighting the Vietnam War, and approximately fifty-eight thousand U.S. soldiers and over two million Vietnamese soldiers and civilians were killed.

gotiations, rejected the settlement, believing it placed them in an impossible situation. They believed they were being sold out and would be left without outside assistance against a superior North Vietnamese army. Further talks broke down.

To bring North Vietnam back to the negotiating table, Nixon ordered

Helsinki Accords

The Final Act of the Conference on Security and Co-operation in Europe, more commonly known as the Helsinki Accords, was signed on August 1, 1975, in Helsinki, Finland. Signers included thirty-five nations, which included Canada, the United States, and the Soviet Union. Historians view this signing as the mountaintop of détente. The accords consisted of three parts or "baskets," as they were called. The first basket recognized all existing borders of European nations and called for cooperation and peaceful settlement of disputes with neighbors. The second basket called for cooperation of all the nations in trade, cultural exchanges, and scientific and industrial advances. The third basket involved human rights, calling for the free movement of people and free circulation of information and ideas. Human rights refers to certain economic and political freedoms that all people, simply by being human, deserve. Examples of human rights include freedom from oppression, freedom from unlawful imprisonment and execution, and freedom from torture, persecution, and exploitation.

The third basket caused Soviet leaders to pause. Its terms were not compatible with communism. However, in the spirit of détente, Brezhnev was able to persuade these leaders to overcome their doubts about basket three. He went to Helsinki to sign the accords. President Ford also went, to sign for the United States. At the same time, symbolizing a new era of cooperation, the American space program and the Soviet space program joined together—literally, by the linkage of each country's spacecraft—high above Earth and carried out joint experiments.

Détente stalled

In addition to the Helsinki Accords, President Ford reaffirmed the U.S. commitment to détente in a November 1974 summit meeting with Brezhnev in Vladivostok, located in the far eastern reaches of the Soviet Union. Ford also kept Henry Kissinger in his cabinet, or group of top advisors, as secretary of state. Despite all these efforts, détente had been partially derailed when Nixon left office. The Soviets could not understand why he was forced from office for what seemed in their view an insignificant act. With the key détente figure of Nixon now gone, the Soviets doubted that détente could go on without him.

Meanwhile, the 1976 U.S. presidential election loomed. One Democratic hopeful, U.S. senator Henry "Scoop" Jackson (1912–1983) of Washington, had already criticized the U.S. policy of détente. He saw no reason why the United States should cap its number of missiles. He opposed further trade with the Soviet Union unless the Soviets allowed Soviet Jews to emigrate to Israel. Russian Jews were persecuted for their religious beliefs in the Soviet Union; Soviet authorities began applying a tax on Jews emigrating out of the Soviet Union, which made it much more difficult for many. This was a pet issue with Jackson, who wanted the Soviets to ease up on their emigration policies toward the Jews.

Meanwhile, a Republican candidate, Ronald Reagan (1911–), the governor of California, was also forcefully opposed to détente. Neither Jackson nor Reagan had wanted the United States to sign the Helsinki Accords in 1975, and both used the accords as a campaign issue. Reagan believed that the Soviets gained a lot more than the United States with formal recognition of communist rule in Eastern Europe and that trade agreements supported the continuation of the communist system. Jackson believed the human rights issues were basically ignored on both sides. By the spring of 1976, President Ford and Kissinger knew public opinion was turning against détente, and Ford quit using the term in his run for the presidential election. Further SALT negotiations stalled.

Democrat Jimmy Carter, the governor of Georgia, was the ultimate victor in the presidential race. President Carter vowed to eliminate nuclear arms from the world, but he had no foreign policy expertise. Quickly, he sent to Moscow a plan to radically reduce arms; the plan went far beyond anything ever discussed before. Soviet leaders thought it was outrageous and did not take it seriously. They flatly rejected it. Carter also immediately set out on his campaign for human rights around the world, citing the third part of the Helsinki Accords, the human rights "basket" that had riled the Soviets before they signed the agreement. (At the signing in 1975, Kissinger did not press the human rights section of the accords, aware it was a Soviet sticking point.) Carter's human rights effort was also based on the United Nations Declaration of Human Rights (1948), whose principal author was Eleanor Roosevelt (1884–1962), widow of the late U.S. president Franklin D. Roosevelt (1882–1945; served 1933–45). Included in Carter's early actions was a letter of support to Andrey Sakharov (1921–1989), noted Soviet nuclear physicist and father of the Soviet hydrogen bomb. Sakharov had fallen out of favor with the Soviets because of his outspokenness and went into exile in early 1980. Human rights advocate Carter admired Sakharov and believed he had been persecuted for his antinuclear arms race views.

Dissidents, or protesters, in several Eastern European countries demanded compliance with the human rights initiatives that the Soviets flatly rejected. Many dissidents were jailed. With the signing of the Helsinki Accords, many groups worldwide (even within the Soviet Union) more aggressively pressed the communist bloc regarding the lack of personal freedoms within their countries; it put the spotlight much brighter on the nature of communist rule. Brezhnev charged the Carter administration with meddling in internal Soviet affairs. Soviet-U.S. relations sank very low, and détente came to a close.

Ultimately, détente was not an alternative to the Cold War but a less belligerent way to wage it. A competitive relationship still existed between the United States and the Soviet Union. Both countries pursued a strategy of regular communication, which lessened tensions; both enjoyed claiming credit for the apparent progress in relations. However, both countries continued to build up their military strength, and each country remained vigilant about the activities of the other side. Despite official policies and treaties, neither country could bring itself to fully trust the other.

For More Information

Books

Garthoff, Raymond L. *A Journey through the Cold War: A Memoir of Containment and Coexistence.* Washington, DC: Brookings Institution Press, 2001.

Gates, Robert M. *From the Shadows: The Ultimate Insider's Story of Five Presidents and How They Won the Cold War.* New York: Simon and Schuster, 1996.

Isaacs, Jeremy, and Taylor Downing. *Cold War: An Illustrated History, 1945–1991.* Boston: Little, Brown, 1998.

Isaacson, Walter. *Kissinger: A Biography.* New York: Simon and Schuster, 1992.

Kissinger, Henry. *Diplomacy.* New York: Simon and Schuster, 1994.

Litwak, Robert S. *Détente and the Nixon Doctrine: American Foreign Policy and the Pursuit of Stability, 1969–1976.* New York: Cambridge University Press, 1984.

Thornton, Richard C. *The Nixon-Kissinger Years: Reshaping America's Foreign Policy.* New York: Paragon House, 1989.

Web Sites

Gerald R. Ford Library and Museum. http://www.ford.utexas.edu (accessed on August 12, 2003).

The Richard Nixon Library and Birthplace. http://www.nixonfoundation.org (accessed on August 12, 2003).

"SALT II Treaty." *U.S. State Department.* http://www.state.gov/www/global/arms/treaties/salt2-1.html (accessed on August 12, 2003).

A Freeze in Relations

14

"The reality is that we must find peace through strength. A freeze [on nuclear weapon development] would reward the Soviet Union for its enormous and unparalleled military buildup. I urge you to [not] ... ignore the facts of history and the aggressive impulses of an evil empire ... and thereby remove yourself from the struggle between right and wrong and good and evil." U.S. president Ronald Reagan (1911–; served 1981–89) spoke these words on March 8, 1983, in Orlando, Florida, at the National Association of Evangelicals Convention. His statement reflected a return to the tough Cold War talk of the 1950s and increasing tensions between the United States and the Soviet Union.

The Cold War was primarily a battle of social/political theories and goals: communism versus democracy and capitalism. The Soviet Union adopted communism as its system of government in 1917. In a communist society, a single political party, the Communist Party, controls nearly all aspects of people's lives. In a communist economy, private ownership of property and business is not allowed; instead the government controls business and production so that

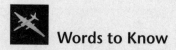

Words to Know

Capitalism: An economic system in which property and businesses are privately owned. Prices, production, and distribution of goods are determined by competition in a market relatively free of government intervention.

Cold War: A prolonged conflict for world dominance from 1945 to 1991 between the two superpowers, the democratic, capitalist United States and the communist Soviet Union. The weapons of conflict were commonly words of propaganda and threats.

Communism: A system of government in which the nation's leaders are selected by a single political party that controls all aspects of society. Private ownership

of property is eliminated and government directs all economic production. The goods produced and accumulated wealth are, in theory, shared relatively equally by all. All religious practices are banned.

Democracy: A system of government in which several political parties compete.

Détente: A relaxing of tensions between rival nations, marked by increased diplomatic, commercial, and cultural contact.

Strategic Arms Limitation Talks (SALT): Discussions between the United States and the Soviet Union aimed at lessening the threat of nuclear war by bringing the arms race under control.

goods produced and wealth accumulated can be shared relatively equally by all. The United States has a democratic system of government; this means the people govern themselves, through elected representatives. Multiple political parties represent differing points of view and different political and economic goals. Candidates from these various parties are voted into office by the people. In the United States, democracy is paired with capitalism, an economic system that allows property and businesses to be privately owned. Production, distribution, and prices of goods are determined by competition in the marketplace, and there is relatively little government intervention. Those who compete successfully can accumulate individual wealth.

The Cold War rivalry between the two superpowers steadily heated up through the administration of President Jimmy Carter (1924–; served 1977–81). Then in the early 1980s, President Reagan further escalated the rivalry through a heightened arms race. Military budgets for both nations would dramatically rise, significantly affecting the economies of both countries.

A Carter perspective

Jimmy Carter was inaugurated as the thirty-ninth U.S. president in January 1977. Like Cold War presidents Harry S. Truman (1884–1972; served 1945–53), John F. Kennedy (1917–1963; served 1961–63), and Lyndon B. Johnson (1908–1973; served 1963–69) before him, Carter arrived at the White House with little experience in foreign affairs. His main exposure to foreign issues came through a committee named the Trilateral Commission, which he had served on since 1973. Its role was to direct U.S. foreign policy more toward Western Europe and Japan and less toward combating communism. Zbigniew Brzezinski (1928–) was director of the commission. Harold Brown (1927–) and Cyrus Vance (1917–2001) were other members along with Carter. They would all serve in important positions in Carter's administration: Brzezinski as national security advisor, Vance as secretary of state, and Brown as secretary of defense.

Although they all served on the same commission, these members of the Carter cabinet, or group of top advisors, had differences that would become a key factor in Carter's presidency. Brzezinski and Vance in particular held opposing views over how to deal with the Soviets. This difference would lead President Carter to change course in foreign policy strategies during his single term of office. Vance heavily promoted diplomacy, whereas Brzezinski favored military responses to Soviet actions, such as the Soviet Union's attempts to expand its influence in Third World nations. (The term *Third World* refers to poor underdeveloped or economi-

People to Know

Leonid Brezhnev (1906–1982): Leader of the Soviet Union Communist Party, 1964–82.

Zbigniew Brzezinski (1928–): U.S. national security advisor, 1977–81.

Jimmy Carter (1924–): Thirty-ninth U.S. president, 1977–81.

Deng Xiaoping (1905–1997): Leader of communist China, 1976–90.

Andrey Gromyko (1909–1989): Soviet foreign minister, 1957–85.

Mao Zedong (1893–1976): Chairman of the People's Republic of China and its Communist Party, 1949–76.

Ronald Reagan (1911–): Fortieth U.S. president, 1981–89.

Cyrus Vance (1917–2001): U.S. secretary of state, 1977–80.

U.S. president Jimmy Carter (third from left) meets with members of his cabinet: (from left) Cecil Andrus, secretary of the interior; Cyrus Vance, secretary of state; and Harold Brown, secretary of defense. *Reproduced by permission of the Corbis Corporation.*

cally developing nations in Africa, Asia, and Latin America. Many of these nations were seeking independence from the political control of Western European nations.)

Détente (lessened international tensions) characterized U.S.-Soviet relations through the early 1970s. Therefore, Carter at first favored Vance's approach of diplomacy for resolving problems. Carter wanted the United States to serve as a model for the world by promoting human rights, freedom, democracy, and peaceful coexistence. (*Human rights* refers to certain economic and political freedoms that all people, simply by being human, deserve. Examples of human rights include freedom from oppression, freedom from unlawful imprisonment and execution, and freedom from torture, persecution, and exploitation.) Unlike his predecessors in office, Carter did not care for covert, or secret, operations carried out by the U.S. Central Intelligence Agency (CIA), and he did not want to support oppressive military dictatorships. Instead, he wanted to build a cooperative relationship with the Soviets by establishing nuclear arms control agreements and jointly fighting world poverty and hunger.

Soviet leader Leonid Brezhnev (1906–1982) was ready to work with Carter on the new Strategic Arms Limitation Talks, called SALT II. Brezhnev had led the Soviets in a major arms buildup, and now he felt the Soviets could bargain from a position of strength. However, U.S. senator Henry Jackson (1912–1983), a powerful Democrat from the state of Washington, led an effective effort to block arms control talks. He demanded that the Soviets make deep cuts in their arsenal, or collection, of ballistic missiles before talks could begin. Because the Soviets had more missiles, Jackson believed that the United States would become vulnerable to a Soviet first strike if both countries began reducing their arsenals from their existing levels. Not surprisingly, Brezhnev and Soviet foreign minister Andrey Gromyko (1909–1989) were not pleased with Jackson's demands. As a result, arms control talks under Carter did not progress well and led to no formal agreements. The two countries sat in a stalemate on arms control talks until May 1977, when Secretary of State Vance met with Gromyko in Geneva, Switzerland. They made significant progress on how to approach several key arms issues. Progress on nuclear arms limitations, however, would not come for another two years.

Carter's human rights campaign

A devout Christian, President Carter strongly believed in promoting human rights on a global scale. Human rights issues played a significant role in his administration, and this became a prime factor in the deterioration of U.S.-Soviet relations. At first, Brezhnev did not realize how sincere Carter was about promoting human rights. However, in March 1977, shortly after taking office, Carter increased funding and support for Radio Free Europe, Radio Liberty, and Voice of America. These U.S.-supported radio organizations beamed broadly into Eastern Europe and the Soviet Union and served to educate listeners in communist countries about basic human freedoms. When the Soviets realized the seriousness of Carter's intent, they considered it a real threat. The Soviets charged that the United States was interfering in the domestic affairs of the Soviet Union and Eastern European nations. In an attempt to punish the United States and deter Carter's efforts, Brezhnev increased the oppression of Russian Jews, who were critical of Soviet communist rule. Andrey Sakharov (1921–1989), a Soviet nuclear physicist who had become a dissident, or an individual who disagrees with the ideas of those in power, encouraged Carter to stick with his human rights campaign. Pushing harder in November 1977 at the Conference on Security and Cooperation in Europe, the United States openly accused the Soviets and Eastern European nations of human rights abuses.

Carter also focused on Latin American countries and South Korea during his human rights campaign. Latin America includes the entire Western Hemisphere south of the United States. It consists of all nations in Central and South America as well as Mexico and the islands of the West Indies. Carter believed that Latin America was safe from communist expansion, and he wanted to end the U.S. policy of supporting anticommunist dictatorships there. Carter decided to apply pressure to the military dictatorships of Argentina, Brazil, and Chile; they each had very bad human rights records. Carter blocked existing loans, stopped arms deals, and reduced other economic assistance to these countries. Unfortunately, Carter's strategy brought antagonism from the Latin American dictators.

The government of South Korea was a very oppressive regime. However, because South Korea was a noncommunist nation, the U.S. military had supported it since the end of the Korean War in 1953 (see Chapter 2, Conflict Builds). On January 26, 1977, shortly after entering office, Carter announced that he would begin withdrawing U.S. troops from South Korea. Government leaders worldwide and many regular citizens were alarmed. They feared that a reduction in U.S. forces would encourage an invasion of South Korea by communist North Korea, like the invasion in 1950 that started the Korean War. Facing strong congressional opposition, Carter decided to back off and soften his criticism of South Korea. Even when new government leadership put South Korea under martial law (military rule over civilians) in 1980 and violently suppressed student rioters, Carter and his administration said little.

Carter's human rights campaign had a very chilling effect on U.S. relations with the Soviet Union and many pro-U.S. Third World countries. They did not want the United States interfering in their internal affairs and encouraging uprisings within their populations against the ruling governments. However, his efforts essentially legitimized human rights as an international political issue. Human rights would gain increased attention through the following decades.

Containing communism in Africa

While U.S.-Soviet relations cooled over human rights issues, the Third World continued to be a key stage where the Cold War rivalry would play out militarily. Unlike his predecessor, Nikita Khrushchev (1894–1971), Soviet leader Leonid Brezhnev saw Africa as a key region where communist influence could expand.

In September 1974, communist factions seized control of Ethiopia from Emperor Haile Selassie (1892–1975). Somalia, Ethiopia's neighbor to the east, was aligned with the United States. Somalia and Ethiopia are strategically located in the Horn of Africa, a region bordering the Red Sea, the key access route for shipping Middle East oil to the West. In May 1977, Somalian soldiers invaded Ethiopia while the country was experiencing severe civil unrest and gained control of a disputed province. In November 1977, the Soviets began airlifting arms and Cuban troops into Ethiopia to help repel the Somalian attack and stabilize the pro-Soviet government. Somalia asked for U.S. assistance in responding to the Soviet-supported Ethiopian counteroffensive. Seeking to contain the spread of Soviet influence, U.S. national security advisor Brzezinski proposed sending a U.S. aircraft carrier into the region. He argued that if the United States did not respond in such a forceful way, it would encourage Soviet expansion elsewhere. Secretary of State Vance wanted to treat the situation as a local border conflict and recommended using a diplomatic solution. Carter opted for diplomacy; he got Somalia to promise not to attack Ethiopia again or else risk jeopardizing U.S. assistance. It worked: By March 1978, the Somalis withdrew from Ethiopia. With the Somalian forces out, the Ethiopians turned to domestic issues and, contrary to the pre-

Western Somalia Liberation Front guerrillas unite in Ethiopia in April 1981.

Photograph by Alain Nogues. Reproduced by permission of the Corbis Corporation.

dictions of some U.S. government leaders, did not try to attack Somalia, so there was no spread of Soviet influence.

The next incident in Africa would show that Carter's patience with Soviet activity on the continent was running thin. In Angola, communist revolutionaries had ousted Portuguese rulers in 1975 and established a communist government. The Soviets provided the new leadership with arms and thousands of Cuban troops to stabilize the government. Then in the spring of 1978, procommunist soldiers from Zaire (now known as the Democratic Republic of the Congo) who had been exiled in Angola invaded the Zaire province of Katanga. They wanted independence for the province. Carter confronted Soviet foreign minister Gromyko, asking whether the Soviets had supported the invasion of Katanga. Though Gromyko denied any support, Carter decided to help the pro-West Zaire government, which was led by Colonel Joseph Mobutu (1930–1997). U.S. transport planes flew in French, Belgian, Moroccan, and other African troops. Carter had U.S.

soldiers poised as well, but the international troops were able to send the refugees back into Angola from Zaire without the assistance of the American force. At this point, Carter began emphasizing containment of Soviet influence (restricting the territorial growth of communist rule) in Africa, making it a priority over the promotion of human rights and democracy on the continent.

Improving relations with communist China

While U.S.-Soviet relations were cooling, the Communist People's Republic of China (PRC) expressed an interest in improving relations with the United States. In the 1930s and 1940s, Mao Zedong (1893–1976) had led communist forces in a long civil war against the government of China. Mao finally won in 1949 and established the PRC. The overthrown government leaders fled to the island of Taiwan and established the Republic of China (ROC). The United States immediately recognized the ROC as the only legitimate government of China. For years, the United States blocked the PRC's entry into the United Nations (UN), an international peacekeeping organization.

Following Mao's death in 1976, Deng Xiaoping (1905–1997) emerged as the new leader of communist China. By the spring of 1978, Deng was ready to take a major step in improving relations with the United States. The PRC had a difficult relationship with the Soviet Union, especially at the time. PRC leaders feared that the Soviets would become increasingly involved in Southeast Asia. The Soviets were already supporting Vietnam in a border dispute with Cambodia. The PRC supported Cambodia, not wanting a stronger Vietnam on China's southern border. The United States also backed Cambodia. With these tensions mounting, PRC and Soviet troops clashed in combat to the north along the border between the Soviet Union and China.

U.S. presidents normally send the secretary of state to pursue discussions with a foreign nation. However, instead of sending his secretary of state, Cyrus Vance, to talk with Deng, Carter sent national security advisor Brzezinski, an anti-Soviet hard-liner. Arriving in Beijing, the PRC's capital, in May 1978,

Brzezinski reached a major agreement with Deng. The United States would recognize PRC as the sole government of China but would continue to sell defensive military arms and maintain trade relations with the ROC. On December 15, 1978, the PRC and the United States publicly announced that formal relations between the two would begin January 1, 1979. Deng followed this normalization of relations with a trip to the United States to personally meet with Carter.

In angry reaction to the agreement between the United States and China, the Soviets backed out of strategic nuclear arms control talks with the United States. They also signed a more formal treaty with Vietnam. Vietnam launched a major attack on Cambodia on December 25, 1978, overrunning the country and establishing a new communist government. In response, the PRC decided to flex its muscles in Vietnam. PRC troops moved across Vietnam's border on February 17, 1979, and fought for sixteen days before withdrawing. While U.S. relations with communist China had improved, U.S.-Soviet relations continued downward.

Camp David Accords

With the creation in 1948 of the state of Israel in the Palestinian homelands, a region on the east coast of the Mediterranean inhabited by Arab peoples who had been under British colonial rule, an intense conflict between the Jewish and Arab populations erupted. Jews are believers of Judaism who trace their descent from Hebrews of the ancient biblical kingdom of Israel. Arabs are the inhabitants who occupy Southwest Asia and Northern Africa, including Saudi Arabia, Yemen, Oman, and Egypt. President Carter became the first U.S. president to publicly suggest the creation of a Palestinian state as part of the long-term solution. Carter also invited a broad range of nations to help negotiate a resolution. Former secretary of state Henry Kissinger (1923–) had included only Egypt, Syria, and Israel in talks. Carter brought in other Arab nations, including the Palestine Liberation Organization (PLO), as well as the Soviet Union.

The Israeli government and the American Jewish community strongly protested the inclusion of the PLO because of its strong anti-Israel position, which favored the entire removal of Jews from the Middle East region. Israel decid-

ed to negotiate a peace settlement separately with Egypt. Israel offered to return the Sinai Peninsula region to Egypt if Egypt would formally recognize Israel. The Israelis had seized the very large Sinai area in a 1967 war with Egypt. Egyptian president Anwar Sadat (1918–1981) was very interested in this deal and traveled to Jerusalem, the capital of Israel, in November 1977 to discuss it. He was the first Arab leader to travel to Israel. Carter supported the negotiations, but the Soviets and other Arab countries were greatly disappointed because the Israelis had managed to divert the possibility of a broader resolution, one that would include the Palestinians. Israeli prime minister Menachem Begin (1913–1992) and Egyptian president Sadat met with Carter in the United States at Camp David, the presidential retreat in nearby Maryland, in September 1978 to complete the peace treaty, known as the Camp David Accords. The accords ended a state of war that had lasted almost thirty years. However, Egypt and its president, Sadat, lost favor with the rest of the Arab world.

Egyptian president Anwar Sadat (left), U.S. president Jimmy Carter, and Israeli prime minister Menachem Begin stand for their nations' national anthems during ceremonies associated with the Camp David Accords in March 1979. *Photograph by Wally McNamee. Reproduced by permission of the Corbis Corporation.*

Though it was a historic achievement, the peace treaty between Egypt and Israel essentially furthered Cold War politics by splitting the Middle East into pro-West and pro-Soviet countries. The pro-West bloc, or group, included Israel and Egypt as well as Iran and Saudi Arabia. The United States now felt more secure, knowing that the critical Middle East oil fields were being defended by friendly countries in the region.

More arms control talks

In early 1979, the Soviets decided they were ready to conclude strategic arms limitation talks, two years after U.S. senator Henry Jackson had derailed arms control discussions. On June 18 in a meeting in Vienna, Austria, Carter and Brezhnev agreed on strategic nuclear weapons restrictions. This agreement, called SALT II, placed limits on the numbers and types of missiles and missile launchers each country could develop. This included intercontinental ballistic missiles (ICBMs) and aircraft-launched cruise missiles. The two leaders also agreed on a method to inspect how well both sides were following the restrictions. They even discussed a future SALT III agreement that would actually reduce the number of existing stockpiled nuclear weapons, though this never happened.

Returning to the United States, Carter spoke to a joint session of Congress, made up of both the House of Representatives and the Senate, seeking approval of SALT II. In an effort to win the support of anti-Soviet hard-liners in Congress, Carter approved production and deployment of two hundred mobile MX ICBMs. Because these were part of a defensive missile system, they were not limited by the agreement. Congress debated approval of the arms control treaty.

Support for the contras

Amidst the SALT II activities, in July 1979, the Sandinista National Liberation Front, a largely communist organization, overthrew Nicaraguan dictator Anastasio Somoza (1925–1980). Despite Somoza's very poor human rights record, Carter had requested that the Organization of Ameri-

can States (OAS) provide support for the dictator against the Sandinistas. (The OAS is a Cold War–inspired organization of Western Hemisphere nations. Established in 1951 to maintain political stability in the region, it provides a forum for resolving disputes.) For the first time, the OAS refused to support a U.S. proposal.

U.S. president Jimmy Carter (left) shakes hands with Soviet leader Leonid Brezhnev at the SALT II talks in Geneva on June 18, 1979. *Reproduced by permission of AP/Wide World Photos.*

The Sandinistas soon gained control of the Nicaraguan government. Carter tried to establish friendly relations by offering over $300 million in loans and other forms of economic assistance. However, the Sandinistas turned to the Soviets instead and signed a trade agreement. They also suspended future general elections in Nicaragua. When the Sandinistas began supporting a revolutionary army in El Salvador that was attempting to overthrow a military dictatorship, Carter began to take action against the Sandinistas. He provided funds to an anti-Sandinista group in Nicaragua; this group was known as the contras (short for the Spanish word *contrarevolucionarios,* or in English, counterrevolutionaries).

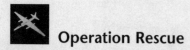

Operation Rescue

Throughout his presidency, Ronald Reagan had a particularly keen interest in political developments in the Latin American country of Nicaragua. In 1981, not long after taking office, Reagan cut off U.S. and international aid to the increasingly pro-Soviet Sandinista government led by Daniel Ortega (1945–). Reagan then provided $19 million to a small force known as the contras, five hundred soldiers who were attempting to overthrow Ortega. The money was to be used to disrupt the Nicaraguan economy by causing civil disorder as a show of opposition to Ortega's policies.

Ortega went to the World Court, an international organization that addresses grievances of one nation against another, to protest U.S. intervention in Nicaraguan internal affairs. The Court condemned the U.S. activities in Nicaragua. Though President Reagan ignored the finding, Congress did not. Congress moved to limit U.S. involvement through legislation known as the Boland Amendments. The first amendment

was passed by a House of Representatives vote of 411 to none. It limited CIA aid to the contras to $24 million and prohibited the overthrow of the Nicaraguan government by the CIA. In response, Reagan switched to more covert operations.

In April 1984, it was discovered that the CIA had secretly mined the harbors of Nicaragua in order to cripple its economy by cutting off trade. This led to the second Boland Amendment, an even stricter congressional limitation on U.S. involvement in Nicaragua. Reagan nevertheless pressed on with "Operation Rescue," a covert operation to funnel funds to the contras in the spring and summer of 1986. The funds came from a secret sale of weapons to Iran. Several members of Reagan's National Security Council (NSC) led the operation, including Marine Corps Lieutenant Colonel Oliver North (1943–), NSC director Robert McFarlane (1937–), and Admiral John Poindexter (1936–), McFarlane's successor. The arms Iran received in the deal were to be used in free-

---

Support of the contras would become a major endeavor of President Ronald Reagan (1911–; served 1981–89) and a source of much controversy through the 1980s (see box).

Americans held hostage

On January 16, 1979, Shiite Islamic fundamentalists, those in the Muslim religious faith of Islam who believe in strict adherence to the strictures, or guidelines, of the Koran, overthrew the pro-U.S. Iranian leader, Shah Mohammad Reza

Nicaraguan president Daniel Ortega.
Reproduced by permission of Getty Images.

ceived. Some $16 million of that sum went to the contras, and the rest went to other covert activities. Congressional hearings led to grand jury indictments against McFarlane, Poindexter, and North. (Grand jury indictments are formal accusations of a crime by a jury gathered to determine if sufficient evidence exists to justify a trial.)

In 1992, reports from later investigations revealed that President Reagan, Vice President George Bush (1924–), Secretary of State George Shultz (1920–), Defense Secretary Caspar Weinberger (1917–), and CIA director William Casey (1913–1987) had also been directly involved in the illegal covert operation. Casey suffered a severe stroke and died before he could testify at congressional hearings. Vice President Bush became president in 1989, but he was defeated in his reelection bid in 1992. However, Congress had no desire to pursue further legal action against Bush, Reagan, or the others.

ing seven American hostages seized by terrorists in Lebanon. The secret operation was exposed when a U.S. transport plane was shot down by Sandinistas on October 5, 1986.

Iran paid the United States approximately $48 million for the weapons it re-

Pahlavi (1919–1980). Reza had been the king of Iran since assuming the throne in 1941 from his father. A power struggle developed in 1951 with a nationalist seeking to take control of businesses and oil companies from outside influences such as the British. Reza was forced out of the country in 1953 but soon was reinstated, apparently with CIA assistance. Reza was pro-Western and pushed for modern economic development in Iran.

Shiite religious leader Ayatollah Ruhollah Khomeini (c. 1900–1989) became the new Iranian leader on February 9. The

Iranian leader Ayatollah
Ruhollah Khomeini.

Shiites were opposed to the shah's oppressive tactics toward political opposition, his efforts at Western modernization of Iran, and his close ties to the United States. The United States had a definite interest in keeping Iran friendly: Iran was a major source of oil for the West and strategically located along the southern Soviet border. It essentially blocked potential Soviet expansion southward toward the Persian Gulf. The United States had supported the shah (monarch) with billions of dollars, and as a result, Iran's military was the most powerful in the region. Carter had maintained this relationship with the shah despite Iran's miserable human rights record.

After being overthrown, the shah went into exile. Months later, he requested entry into the United States so he could undergo cancer treatments. Carter consented. In reaction, on November 4, Shiite Iranian militants stormed the U.S. embassy in Tehran, the capital of Iran, and took sixty-six Americans hostage, fourteen of whom were soon released. For the release of the six remaining hostages, the militants demanded that Carter return the shah to be tried for actions under his harsh rule. Carter refused. Instead, he froze Iranian assets, which meant Iranians could not withdraw their money from U.S. banks, and restricted U.S. trade with Iran. After several months, Carter approved a secret military operation to rescue the hostages. However, in April 1980, the operation failed when the rescue helicopters were caught in a sudden sandstorm. Eight U.S. soldiers died. Secretary of State Vance, who had opposed the risky operation, resigned in protest. The hostage crisis essentially doomed Carter's chances at reelection in November 1980. Iran did not release the hostages until January 20, 1981, the very day Ronald Reagan was inaugurated as president. Losing Iran as an ally was one of the major setbacks in the Cold War for the United States.

Afghanistan and the Carter Doctrine

In early July 1979, while the Senate was debating approval of the arms control treaty with the Soviet Union, U.S. intelligence discovered Soviet combat troops in Cuba. Though they were supposedly there only to train Cuban troops, Congress was incensed and less willing to approve the arms treaty. Then in December 1979, six weeks after Shiite Islamic militants seized the U.S. embassy in Iran and took American hostages, the Soviets invaded Afghanistan. Following a bloody coup (short for coup d'état; an illegal or forceful change of government) in April 1978, an unpopular pro-Soviet government was put in place. An Afghan Islamic militant group, the Mujahedeen, started an antigovernment resistance movement. The Soviets feared that the Islamic unrest in Iran and Afghanistan could spread to the numerous Islamic populations within the Soviet Union. To support the Afghan government and put down the Islamic rebellion before it could spread, the Soviets invaded Afghanistan on Christmas Day 1979.

Many scholars consider the Soviet invasion of Afghanistan as the ultimate end to détente, which had been sharply declining for the previous two years. U.S. national security advisor Brzezinski claimed the Soviets were trying to fill a power void in the region, created by the overthrow of the Iranian shah. Perhaps, he added, the Soviets intended to eventually capture the Persian Gulf oil fields. Reacting to these fears, Carter took swift action. He immediately restricted any further sale of U.S. high technology to the Soviets. He also stopped a major grain sale and announced that the United States would boycott the upcoming Olympics in Moscow. Carter also withdrew the SALT II agreement from further Senate consideration; it was never approved.

Next, in his State of the Union address on January 23, 1980, Carter announced the Carter Doctrine. The doctrine declared that it was in the vital interests of the United States to protect the Persian Gulf region from outside forces with whatever force was necessary. He asked Congress to boost military spending and resurrected the requirement that all American men between ages eighteen and twenty-six register for the military draft, meaning they would be eligible to serve in the military if required. President Richard Nixon (1913–1994; served 1969–74) had ended draft registration in 1973 near the end of the Vietnam War (1954–75).

Carter then turned to the PRC and Pakistan to further improve the U.S. position. He sold to the PRC the high technology he denied to the Soviets and granted the PRC most-favored-nation trade status, which the Soviets had been seeking. Most-favored-nation trade status lowers taxes on goods exported to the United States, making it much easier for a foreign country to sell goods to American consumers and U.S. businesses. Carter offered economic aid to Pakistan, a country that borders Afghanistan. Carter was willing to overlook that Pakistan's military leader had overthrown the democratically elected government and executed its leader in 1978. Pakistan would become the staging area for funneling U.S. weapons to the Mujahedeen, who were fighting the pro-Soviet government in Afghanistan. It was the first time during the Cold War that the United States would supply arms to directly fight Soviet forces. In reaction, the Soviets signed a new arms agreement with India in December 1979.

A costly arms race takes off

December 1979 marked the start of a spiraling escalation of the nuclear arms race. Soviet leader Leonid Brezhnev (1906–1982) announced he would place new SS-20 intermediate-range nuclear missiles in Eastern Europe. In response, the North Atlantic Treaty Organization (NATO), which was formed for the mutual protection of the United States and

Western European nations, decided to deploy the new U.S. intermediate-range tactical nuclear weapons: the Pershing 2 ballistic missile and the Tomahawk ground-launched cruise missiles. The Soviets threatened to target their new missiles on any Western European nations that accepted the new U.S. missiles. The threats were ignored as NATO countries received over five hundred Pershing 2 and Tomahawk nuclear missiles. In July 1980, Carter announced a renewed period of nuclear arms development, including continued development of the MX mobile missile system in the western United States. The Soviets responded by threatening to further increase their nuclear arms production as well.

The new U.S. missiles were welcomed by some in Western Europe but despised by many others. In general, the Western European nations were not pleased with Carter's new hard-line approach to the Soviets. They wanted to continue détente, which had brought peace and stability to Europe. Instead of reducing their trade with the Soviets as the United States had, Western European nations actually increased trade, but many feared war was now imminent. To ease Europe's fears of an impending war by further deterring any possible future aggression by Soviet bloc countries, Carter sent an additional thirty-five thousand U.S. troops to Europe.

The renewed arms race had grave economic implications for the Soviet Union. During the late 1970s, the Soviet economy was already struggling. Costs had mounted from the Soviets' involvement in Angola, Ethiopia, Indochina, and finally Afghanistan. In addition, Brezhnev's earlier disinterest in arms talks led to continued heavy military spending; domestic economic needs were going unaddressed. To make matters worse, Carter had withdrawn critically needed U.S. assistance because of the Soviets' invasion of Afghanistan.

Reagan escalates the arms race

Republican candidate Ronald Reagan defeated Carter in the November 1980 presidential election. The Iranian hostage crisis, the struggling U.S. economy, and a severe energy crisis all contributed to Carter's unsuccessful bid for re-election. Relations with the Soviet Union were at a new low. All these issues resulted in Carter receiving a record low presidential popularity. Like most of the Cold War presidents before him, Reagan entered office with little foreign affairs experience. The former actor and ex-governor of California did bring a very strong anticommunist perspective, however, reaching back to the late 1940s and 1950s. As president of the Screen Actors Guild from 1947 to 1951 and again in 1959, he had fought supposed communist infiltration of the U.S. movie industry (see Chapter 5, Homeland Insecurities). As U.S. president, Reagan wanted to restore America's international prestige by rebuilding the military to wartime levels.

Reagan had no desire to improve relations with the Soviets. He opposed reviving détente and the unapproved SALT II agreement. Instead, he chose to challenge the Soviets with an even greater arms buildup. Many of his key advisors had previously been members of the Committee on the Present Danger, a conservative group opposed to strategic nuclear arms talks. Rather than maintaining the policy of parity, or equality, in regard to nuclear weapons, they sought U.S. superiority in nuclear weapons. As a result, Reagan oversaw the largest peacetime military buildup in U.S. history. The defense budget increased from $171 billion in 1981 to $376 billion in 1986. Major strategic nuclear weapons systems were promoted, including the MX mobile missile system, the Advanced Technology Bomber (ATB) known as the Stealth, the B-1 bomber, antisatellite weapons, new ballistic missile systems, and the nuclear Trident submarine. Conventional forces were also boosted. For example, the number of naval ships increased from 454 to 600. To the Soviets it was clear the new U.S. administration preferred intimidation to negotiation. The United States appeared to be arming for war.

Reagan intended to use the increased arms buildup to further stress the Soviet economy. While the Soviets developed new weapons systems to keep up, they continued to suffer from former president Carter's ban on high-technology exports and from other trade restrictions that Reagan maintained. As a result, the Soviet economy would come under increasing strain. In addition, Soviet youths were increasingly learning about Western popular culture, and they were challenging Communist Party control of information and communist restrictions that affected their daily lives. The social and economic strains were mounting. However, the U.S. economy also suffered from the arms race. With defense spending increased 40 percent, tremendous budget deficits built up. The U.S. national debt tripled from $1 trillion in 1980 to $3 trillion in 1989, and fears of nuclear war had once again been heightened by the government's hardline approach.

Reagan Doctrine, dictatorships, and foreign policy

Not interested in Carter's human rights campaign, the Reagan administration adopted a new approach. Jeane Kirkpatrick (1926–), a former member of the Committee on the Present Danger and one of Reagan's appointed ambassadors to the United Nations, developed it. She argued that the human rights initiative was harmful to otherwise friendly anticommunist military dictatorships. She proclaimed that these governments had potential for democratic reform, whereas communist-controlled countries did not. Therefore, she stated, it was appropriate for U.S. aid to go to these dictators; U.S. aid would not only combat communist expansion but potentially encourage the growth of democracy. This policy, called the Reagan Doctrine, legitimized U.S. aid for military dictatorships in El Salvador, Guatemala, Chile, Haiti, the Philippines, and Pakistan, despite rampant human rights abuses in those countries. For example, Reagan sought congressional approval for U.S. aid to the pro-U.S. government of El Salvador led by José Napoleón Duarte (1925–1990). Despite El Salvador government paramilitary death squads murdering perhaps sixty thousand civilians, including a Roman Catholic bishop, between 1979 and 1986, the Reagan administration downplayed the violence and emphasized social reforms promoted by Duarte. As part of the Reagan Doctrine, Reagan supported establishment of the National Endowment for Democracy in 1983. Its purpose was to promote free elections in Latin America and the growth of democracy in the region.

Little democratic change would actually occur in Latin America, where military dictatorships continued to thrive. Like many other Cold War presidential administrations, Reagan and his advisors interpreted almost all nationalist movements in Third World countries as communist-inspired. They failed to consider that these movements might

Two U.S. soldiers stand in front of an American tank as they guard three Grenadian prisoners in October 1983. *Reproduced by permission of AP/Wide World Photos.*

be inspired by local poverty and local political corruption. Instead of providing economic assistance to relieve poverty, Reagan's administration provided military aid to anticommunist dictatorships so the dictators could maintain tight control and combat revolts.

Reagan wanted to go beyond containing communism and actually support anticommunist forces attempting to overthrow pro-Soviet governments. However, after painful experiences in Korea and Vietnam, the American public was in no mood for new military involvements (see Chapter 2, Conflict Builds, and Chapter 11, An Unsettled World). Reagan therefore focused on covert operations. For example, the U.S. Central Intelligence Agency (CIA) provided $2 billion in weapons and economic assistance to the Mujahadeen guerrillas to help them fight the pro-Soviet government in Afghanistan.

One very visible military action did occur during Reagan's presidency. In October 1983, the U.S. military invaded the island nation of Grenada, located in the Caribbean. Fighting had been going on there between two communist groups. One group overthrew and executed Grenada's communist leader, Maurice Bishop (1944–1983), who had gained power in 1979. President Reagan took the occasion to send nineteen hundred U.S. troops to liberate the country from fighting between communist factions. U.S. forces quickly took control and installed a pro-U.S. democratic government. Though the United States claimed victory over communist expansion in the Western Hemisphere, much criticism came from other countries, including Britain. The British charged that the United States had acted without United Nations (UN) approval. The invasion amounted to armed aggression against a sovereign (fully independent) nation. However, Reagan and Kirkpatrick had become very critical of the UN because it did not support U.S. actions as much as it had in the past. Therefore, Reagan saw no need to first obtain UN approval, and he would ultimately withhold U.S. funding support for the UN. He also withdrew the United States from its involvement in the United Nations Educational, Scientific, and Cultural Organization (UNESCO).

War in the Middle East

The Reagan administration interpreted Islamic nationalist movements in the Middle East in the same way it viewed nationalist movements elsewhere: Reagan and his advisors believed these movements were driven by outside communist influences rather than local issues such as poverty. Therefore, the United States was quick to get involved in Middle East conflicts. In the Middle East, Islamic opposition was building against lingering foreign influence such as ownership of companies, particularly oil companies, and there was constant unrest over the unresolved Israel-Palestine controversy.

Then in September 1980, Iraq attacked Iran, beginning a ten-year war. Iraq's leader, Saddam Hussein (1937–), wanted to acquire a rich oil-producing region in western Iran; he also wanted to weaken the new Shiite Islamic government in Iran so it would not have a chance to incite an Islamic rebellion in his country. The Soviets could not afford to help Iraq, because their war in Afghanistan was not going well. For this reason, and with instability in the region increasing, the Soviets approached Reagan shortly after he took office in early 1981, asking whether the Soviet Union and the United States could work together to ease tensions in the region. However, because the area was so important to U.S. interests, Reagan did not want to share the responsibility—or the benefits—of negotiating a Middle East solution. He declined to work cooperatively with the Soviets and instead began providing pro-Soviet Iraq with economic assistance as well as intelligence information on Iranian troop placements. Through this assistance, Reagan hoped to break the relationship between Iraq and the Soviets. However, the Soviets responded with increasing assistance to Iraq as well.

Star Wars

The nuclear arms buildup by the Reagan administration caused increasing public protests in Europe as well as the United States. In June 1982, over a half million protesters jammed New York City's Central Park, demanding an end to the Cold War arms race. The Roman Catholic bishops in the United States wrote a pastoral letter in 1983 calling for a nuclear freeze. The changing public attitudes began having an influence on Congress. Congress considered proposals to restrict testing and deployment of new nuclear weapons. Pressure from Congress, the public, and NATO allies finally pushed Reagan into arms control talks with the Soviets. However, negotiations did not go far.

A key reason for the stalled arms talks was a proposed new U.S. missile system. In March 1983, Reagan announced a five-year, $26 billion program to research and develop a ballistic missile defense system called the Strategic Defense Initiative (SDI). The system was more commonly called "Star Wars," after a popular science fiction movie (*Star Wars*, 1977), because it included a protective shield of laser-aimed satellites in space. Together, missiles, rockets, and laser beams would destroy enemy missiles fired toward U.S. targets. Critics claimed that the system was prohibitively costly and complex and would likely be ineffective in destroying all missiles fired toward the United States. Potentially, enough missiles to cause devastation could still penetrate. Reagan responded that the SDI approach was more humane than the earlier U.S. strategy of mutual assured destruction—that is, the guar-

The KAL Tragedy

On the night of August 31, 1983, Korean Air Lines (KAL) Flight 007, a 747 passenger plane carrying 269 people, wandered far off course—as much as 365 miles (587 kilometers). It was flying from Anchorage, Alaska, to Seoul, South Korea. During its flight, the commercial airliner began straying over Soviet territory, approaching a secret Soviet missile test site on the Kamchatka Peninsula of eastern Siberia. A Soviet fighter plane intercepted the wayward passenger plane. The Soviet pilot followed international procedures in trying to catch the attention of the airliner, but no response ever came back. After shooting tracers (ammunition with a visible trail) across the front of the airliner as a final warning and receiving no response, the Soviet pilot shot the plane down.

For several days, the Soviets denied any knowledge of the incident. Reagan charged the Soviets with barbarism, or cruelty, and condemned the Soviet Union for the incident. He used the episode to argue before Congress for a greater U.S. military buildup. As later investigations revealed, Soviet air defense tracking the

The wreckage of Korean Air Lines (KAL) Flight 007 sits in a field after being shot down by a Soviet pilot in August 1983. *Photograph by Allan Barnes. Reproduced by permission of the Corbis Corporation.*

plane believed it was a U.S. spy plane that had earlier been flying near Soviet airspace. To many, the incident dramatized the poor relations between the two superpowers and the Soviets' heightened state of alert during President Reagan's massive military buildup.

anteed destruction of both superpowers in the event of a nuclear war (see Chapter 10, Mutual Assured Destruction).

In keeping with the general tradition of the arms race, a key U.S. goal in developing SDI was to force the Soviets to develop a similar system in order to keep up. This would severely strain the already weak Soviet economy. However, critics said that the Soviets could make the U.S. SDI system ineffective without a great deal of expense. Firing numerous unarmed missiles among many nuclear-armed missiles would overwhelm the SDI system; it would be difficult to detect which missiles had real warheads. The Soviets charged that Reagan's SDI proposal would decrease world stability by ending nuclear parity, equality in the number of nuclear weapons each country held. New Soviet leader Yuri Andropov (1914–1984), who took charge when Leonid Brezhnev died in October 1982, charged that the space-based part of the system violated several arms control treaties signed since 1963, including the Outer Space Treaty of 1967. He exclaimed that the arms race would now have no bounds.

By late 1983, U.S. military leaders were increasingly talking of winning a limited nuclear war, which would limit a nuclear weapons conflict to a specific geographic area as opposed to a massive exchange of nuclear weapons with global implications. Soviet fears naturally heightened; it seemed that the United States might actually consider launching a first strike. In November 1983, the United States conducted a nuclear war training exercise that truly scared the Soviets. The United States put missile facilities on heightened readiness and deployed nuclear submarines. It was during a time of particular tension, as the United States had just invaded Grenada and Reagan was talking tough about the Soviets. Reagan forged ahead and would spend $17 billion on SDI research between 1983 and 1989. However, development proved difficult because of the system's technological complexity.

The SDI program and other arms developments gave Reagan a feeling of security. He could now be more accommodating toward the Soviets, because the United States appeared to have nuclear superiority. The presidential election was approaching in November 1984, and he needed to broaden his appeal by reaching out to Americans who had been clamoring for arms control. Secretary of State George Shultz (1920–) took the lead in pushing the Reagan administration away from its hard-line anti-Soviet position. The earliest outward signs of softening came in January 1984, when Reagan offered a plan for arms control talks. However, Andropov, the Soviet leader, died on February 9, 1984. Konstantin Chernenko (1911–1985), another aging leader in the Soviet Communist Party, assumed power. Chernenko was not eager to accept Reagan's plan, for various reasons. For one, he wanted to wait and see if Reagan was going to win reelection that fall.

As the election approached, the Democratic presidential candidate, former Vice President Walter Mondale (1928–), pressed the arms control issue, charging that Reagan had made no progress during his presidential term. Public pressure was mounting, and Reagan realized that to win reelection and ensure continued congressional funding for his massive arms development program, he would have to show increased commitment to arms control talks. On September 24, 1984, Reagan spoke before the United Nations General Assembly and outlined a new plan for arms negotiation. Called the Nuclear and Space Arms Talks (NST), the plan included a range of nuclear weapons. Reagan won reelection, and shortly afterward, Chernenko agreed to the newly proposed talks. But in early 1985, a sweeping change in Soviet leadership would dramatically alter U.S.-Soviet relations.

For More Information

Books

Brzezinski, Zbigniew. *Power and Principle: Memoirs of the National Security Adviser, 1977–1981.* New York: Farrar, Straus and Giroux, 1983.

Carter, Jimmy. *Keeping Faith: Memoirs of a President.* Fayetteville: University of Arkansas Press, 1995.

FitzGerald, Frances. *Way Out There in the Blue: Reagan, Star Wars, and the End of the Cold War.* New York: Simon and Schuster, 2000.

Shultz, George P. *Turmoil and Triumph: Diplomacy, Power, and the Victory of the American Ideal.* New York: Charles Scribner's Sons, 1993.

Sick, Gary. *October Surprise: America's Hostages in Iran and the Election of Ronald Reagan.* New York: Times Books, 1991.

Slavin, Ed. *Jimmy Carter.* New York: Chelsea House Publishers, 1989.

Vance, Cyrus. *Hard Choices: Critical Years in America's Foreign Policy.* New York: Simon and Schuster, 1983.

Wade, Linda R. *James Carter: Thirty-Ninth President of the United States.* Chicago: Children's Press, 1989.

Winik, Jay. *On the Brink: The Dramatic, Behind-the-Scenes Saga of the Reagan Era and the Men and Women Who Won the Cold War.* New York: Simon and Schuster, 1996.

Web Sites

The Cold War Museum. http://www.coldwar.org (accessed on August 12, 2003).

Jimmy Carter Library and Museum. http://www.jimmycarterlibrary.org (accessed on August 12, 2003).

Ronald Reagan Presidential Library. http://www.reagan.utexas.edu (accessed on August 12, 2003).

End of the Cold War

15

On December 25, 1991, U.S. president George Bush (1924–; served 1989–1993) proclaimed the end of the Cold War, calling the occasion a "victory for democracy and freedom." Bush credited Soviet leader Mikhail Gorbachev (1931–) for his "intellect, vision, and courage" in ending the rivalry and seeking much-needed economic and political reforms as the Soviet Union's empire dwindled. Gorbachev had attempted to reform the Communist Party and create a limited democracy in Eastern Europe and the Soviet Union, but his efforts caused a much more dramatic change: the collapse of communism. Communism is a system of government in which a single party, the Communist Party, controls almost all aspects of society. In a communist economy, private ownership of property and businesses is not allowed. Instead, the government controls business and production so that goods produced and wealth accumulated can be shared equally by all.

The struggling Soviet economy

U.S. president Ronald Reagan (1911–; served 1981–89) was inaugurated for his second term of office in January

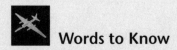

Words to Know

Capitalism: An economic system in which property and businesses are privately owned. Prices, production, and distribution of goods are determined by competition in a market relatively free of government intervention.

Cold War: A prolonged conflict for world dominance from 1945 to 1991 between the two superpowers, the democratic, capitalist United States and the communist Soviet Union. The weapons of conflict were commonly words of propaganda and threats.

Communism: A system of government in which the nation's leaders are selected by a single political party that controls all aspects of society. Private ownership of property is eliminated and government directs all economic production. The goods produced and accumulated wealth are, in theory, shared relatively equally by all. All religious practices are banned.

Conference on Security and Cooperation in Europe (CSCE): Alliance of the thirty-five member nations of the former NATO and Warsaw Pact countries.

Glasnost: A plan for greater freedom of expression put into place by Soviet president Mikhail Gorbachev in the mid-1980s.

North Atlantic Treaty Organization (NATO): A peacetime alliance of the United States and eleven other nations, and a key factor in the attempt to contain communism; the pact meant that the United States became the undisputed global military leader.

Perestroika: A plan for economic and governmental reform put into place by Soviet president Mikhail Gorbachev in the mid-1980s.

Warsaw Pact: A mutual military alliance between the Soviet Union and the Eastern European nations under Soviet influence, including East Germany.

1985. Soon after, on March 10, Soviet leader Konstantin Chernenko (1911–1985) died. The Soviet leadership had changed hands a number of times during the previous three years. A series of aging leaders—Leonid Brezhnev (1906–1982), Yuri Andropov (1914–1984), and Chernenko —had all died in office. These leaders all represented old-guard, or conservative, communism. The Communist Party had grown out of touch with Soviet society. Under old-style communism, the Soviet Union was sliding into economic stagnation. Industries were in desperate need of modernization.

Brezhnev suffered from increasing senility, a loss of mental faculties due to old age, the last few years of his rule. The next two leaders, Andropov and Chernenko, were both in ill health and only held the Soviet leadership position for about one year each. Without dynamic leadership, major Soviet social problems—such as increasing worker absenteeism, alcoholism, and infant mortality rates—went unaddressed and led to low public morale and rising discontent. Unsympathetic in regard to these issues, the Communist Party continued to silence critics within Soviet society, even as their numbers grew. For example, award-winning novelist Aleksandr Solzhenitsyn (1918–) was deported, or legally expelled from the country, and nuclear physicist Andrey Sakharov (1921–1989) was placed in exile in an isolated region of the Soviet Union, each for criticizing the government.

People to Know

George Bush (1924–): Forty-first U.S. president, 1989–93.

Mikhail Gorbachev (1931–): Soviet president, 1985–91.

Ronald Reagan (1911–): Fortieth U.S. president, 1981–89.

Eduard Shevardnadze (1928–): Soviet foreign minister, 1985–90.

Boris Yeltsin (1931–): Russian president, 1989–99.

The aging Soviet leaders continued to emphasize expansion of Soviet influence in far-flung areas of the world. Maintaining the Soviet empire, which consisted of Eastern Europe and many Third World countries, was expensive; many of these countries heavily relied on the Soviets for economic aid. (The term *Third World* refers to poor underdeveloped or developing nations in Africa, Asia, and Latin America. Economies in Third World countries are primarily based on agriculture, with few other industries.) Besides their large foreign economic assistance budget, the Soviets had a very large budget for nuclear weapons development because they wanted to keep up with the United States in the arms race. These major expenses, combined with little economic growth, caused a rapid decline in the Soviet economy. Continual shortages of raw materials and supplies, caused by wasteful manufacturing processes, led to very low industrial productivity.

With the decline in so many areas, public acceptance of communist rule among Soviet and Eastern European citizens was at a new low. One result was increased ethnic ten-

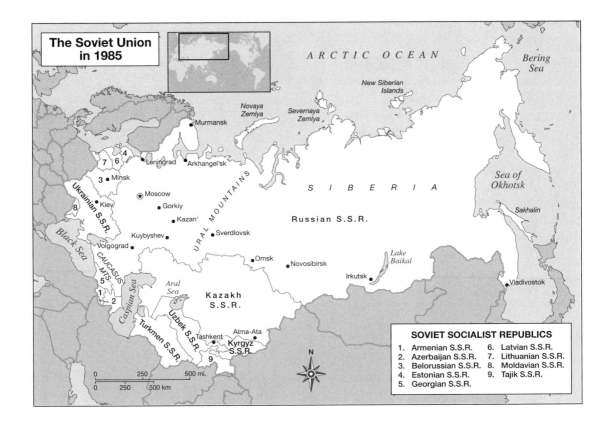

The Soviet Union in 1985.
The Kazakh, Kyrgyz,
Russian, Turkmen,
Ukrainian, and Uzbek
socialist republics are
identified on the map; the
nine smaller ones
correspond with numbers in
the key. *Map by XNR
Productions, Inc. Reproduced
by permission of the
Gale Group.*

sions within the ethnically diverse Soviet Union, which had
included one hundred nationalities when it was formed.

A major obstacle to economic growth was the Soviets'
inability to keep pace with the Western world in developing
computer technology. High technology was proving to be the
basis for substantial economic expansion in other advanced
industrial countries, such as the United States, West Germany,
and Japan. Such technological innovation could not flourish
under communist rule. The Eastern European nations and the
Soviet Union were becoming more detached from the newly
forming global economy. They continued to rely on arms sales
and exports of oil and natural gas to sustain their economies.

A new Soviet vision

Following Chernenko's death in March 1985, Mikhail
Gorbachev assumed Soviet leadership. At fifty-four years of age,

Gorbachev was much younger than the previous three leaders, and unlike the others, he was college-educated and personally dynamic. Outgoing, intelligent, and articulate, Gorbachev presented a new kind of Soviet leadership. However, he faced a difficult task, because the Soviet Union needed extensive reforms, or widespread changes. In May 1985, Gorbachev appointed Eduard Shevardnadze (1928–) as foreign minister. Shevardnadze replaced Andrey Gromyko (1909–1989), another aging member of the Soviet Communist Party. Gromyko had been Soviet foreign minister since 1957, when Nikita Khrushchev (1894–1971) was the Soviet leader. Shevardnadze would play a crucial role in promoting Soviet reform by improving international relations and reducing military competition—in other words, by ending the Cold War. His goal was to reduce Soviet military spending so Gorbachev could direct more funds to critical domestic needs.

Soviet leader Mikhail Gorbachev. *Reproduced by permission of Getty Images.*

Gorbachev adopted a plan for economic reform, called perestroika, and a plan for greater freedom of expression, called glasnost. Because it allowed people to speak up in favor of his reforms, glasnost would help Gorbachev overcome hard-line communist opposition to perestroika. However, the new policy allowing freer speech also extended to Gorbachev's opponents. Glasnost also pardoned past offenses against the old-style communist regime. For example, Andrey Sakharov, an exiled scientist, was allowed to return from exile. As part of perestroika, Gorbachev reduced military spending and cut back economic aid to Third World countries, including Nicaragua, Cambodia, Angola, and Ethiopia. He also began withdrawing Soviet forces from Afghanistan, where the Soviet Union had already suffered over thirty thousand casualties. Gorbachev even proposed to end the arms race and renew talks with the United States, with the hope of receiving much-needed technological assistance.

Gorbachev accepted that communism was the basic cause for falling Soviet productivity and lack of economic growth. But he did not want to end communist rule; instead he wanted to redefine communism. This meant pushing the Soviet economy toward capitalism. (Capitalism is an economic system in which property is privately owned. Production, distribution, and prices of goods are determined by competition in an open market that operates with relatively little government intervention.) Shifting to capitalism meant selling state-owned properties and businesses, eliminating some government control of prices, and becoming more active in the world market with a new currency, or money.

Making peace

In trying to end the Cold War, Gorbachev began to distance himself from previous Soviet leaders by denouncing their communist policies. However, British prime minister Margaret Thatcher (1925–) was the only Western leader who was initially receptive. President Reagan was at first suspicious of Gorbachev's intentions. But with strong encouragement from Secretary of State George Shultz (1920–), Reagan began to listen more to Gorbachev's offers of arms reduction and trade. While pursuing a hard-line anticommunist approach in his first four-year term of office (1981–85), Reagan did not meet with any Soviet leader. However, Reagan and Gorbachev would meet on at least four occasions between 1985 and 1988 to resolve differences between the two superpowers.

The first meeting between Reagan and Gorbachev took place in Geneva, Switzerland, in November 1985. It primarily served to build a personal relationship between the two leaders, and they agreed to continue talks. The next meeting was in October 1986 in Reykjavík, Iceland. To the Americans' surprise, Gorbachev brought a sweeping, detailed plan for arms reductions, a Soviet response to the Strategic Arms Reduction Talks (START) proposed by President Reagan in the early 1980s. Reagan's Strategic Defense Initiative (SDI) program, however, continued to be a major obstacle to these early talks. The SDI was a system of missiles, rockets, and a protective shield of laser-aimed satellites in space that would destroy enemy missiles fired toward U.S. targets. Reagan cre-

U.S. president Ronald Reagan (center) celebrates five years of his Strategic Defense Initiative program with physicist Edward Teller (left) and Lt. Gen. James A. Abrahamson, director of the program, on March 14, 1988. *Photograph by Charles Tasnadi. Reproduced by permission of AP/Wide World Photos.*

ated another obstacle in 1986, when he decided to quit conforming to the informal Strategic Arms Limitation Talks (SALT II) and begin arming B-52 bombers with cruise missiles. Nonetheless, Reagan and Gorbachev discovered some common goals at Reykjavík. These goals included a desire to eliminate all intermediate-range missiles from Europe, eliminate all ballistic missiles in a ten-year period, and make other major reductions involving bombers and tactical weapons.

U.S. president Ronald Reagan meets with Soviet leader Mikhail Gorbachev at their December 1987 summit in the Oval Office of the White House.
Photograph by Wally McNamee. Reproduced by permission of the Corbis Corporation.

When the two leaders left Iceland, they each went home to figure out how to achieve these goals.

Four months later, in February 1987, Gorbachev dropped his demands for Reagan to abandon SDI. That cleared the way for eliminating all intermediate-range nuclear force (INF) missiles in Europe. These included the controversial Pershing and cruise missiles in Western Europe and the Soviets' SS-20s in Eastern Europe. Reagan and Gorbachev signed the INF treaty on December 8, 1987, in Washington, D.C., at their third meeting.

The INF treaty was truly historic. For the first time, the two rivals not only agreed to reduce the number of nuclear weapons in existence but to eliminate certain types altogether. Under INF, the United States would destroy approximately 850 missiles and the Soviet Union almost 1,800 missiles. In total, the United States would dismantle almost one thousand warheads and the Soviet Union over three thousand. The U.S. Senate approved the treaty on May 29,

1988. In another startling development, Soviet foreign minister Shevardnadze declared on July 25, 1988, that both the arms race with the United States and the invasion of Afghanistan were mistakes.

For the fourth meeting, Reagan traveled to Moscow in June 1988, after Senate approval of the INF treaty, to show support for Gorbachev's reforms. He was the first U.S. president to visit Moscow since Richard Nixon (1913–1994; served 1969–74) went there in 1972. While visiting, Reagan gave a speech in front of the tomb of Communist Party founder Vladimir Lenin (1870–1924), a striking image that indicated the Cold War was at an end. The two leaders discussed many topics, from religious freedom in the Soviet Union to civil strife in Latin America.

Gorbachev proposed that the next step in arms reduction was to decrease conventional forces deployed, or strategically spread, in Europe. The negotiations to achieve this reduction, called the Conventional Forces (CFE) in Europe, included twenty-three North Atlantic Treaty Organization (NATO) and Warsaw Pact countries. Established in 1949, NATO is a military defense alliance of Western European nations and the United States and Canada. The Warsaw Pact was an alliance of Eastern European nations under Soviet influence, including East Germany. It was created in 1955 for the mutual defense of its members.

In December 1988, Gorbachev traveled to New York City to meet with Reagan and President-elect George Bush and to speak before the United Nations (UN) General Assembly. Gorbachev gave a dramatic speech to the UN, promoting democracy and individual liberty. To get momentum going on CFE, on December 7, 1988, Gorbachev announced that the Soviet Union on its own would reduce 10 percent of the Soviet forces in general, or about five hundred thousand troops and ten thousand tanks, including those in East Germany, Hungary, and Czechoslovakia. Reagan pressured Gorbachev to do more: While visiting West Berlin earlier in the year, Reagan had challenged Gorbachev to tear down the Berlin Wall, withdraw all Soviet forces from Eastern Europe, withdraw all remaining support for the largely communist Sandinista government in Nicaragua, and complete the Soviet troop withdrawal from Afghanistan. In his UN speech,

Gorbachev responded by announcing that all Soviet troops would be completely withdrawn from Afghanistan by February 1989.

In July 1986, while seeking to improve relations with the West, Gorbachev had also begun efforts to improve relations elsewhere. He had proposed talks to settle a longstanding border dispute with the People's Republic of China (PRC) and reduce Soviet troops stationed in Mongolia along the lengthy border between the PRC and the Soviet Union. In May 1989, Gorbachev visited the PRC, the first Soviet leader to do so since Nikita Khrushchev. Gorbachev also restored diplomatic relations with Israel and Egypt.

A cautious new president

George Bush, Reagan's vice president from 1981 to 1989, was inaugurated as president on January 20, 1989. Though the Cold War was clearly winding down, Bush had taken a hard-line stance against Gorbachev during the 1988 U.S. presidential campaign. Bush was reluctant to bargain with the Soviets; he believed Reagan had gone too far too fast in his discussions with the Soviet leader. Bush's secretary of defense, Richard Cheney (1941–), predicted in April 1989 that Gorbachev's reforms would fail and the Soviet Union would revert to hard-line communist policies. Meanwhile, former secretary of state Henry Kissinger (1923–) and former president Reagan worried that the Bush administration was missing key opportunities to create major world change. George Kennan (1904–), a longtime U.S. Cold War advisor, testified before the U.S. Senate Foreign Relations Committee that the Soviets were no longer a military threat. In Western Europe, French president François Mitterrand (1916–1996) and West German chancellor Helmut Kohl (1930–) also pressured Bush to be more supportive of Gorbachev.

To follow up on the progress he had made with Reagan, Gorbachev asked Bush to discuss further nuclear arms control measures. Gorbachev wanted to tackle the issue of short-range nuclear force (SNF) weapons still stationed in Europe. Bush rejected the proposal to remove them because it would leave NATO without any nuclear deterrents. Gorbachev responded by making cuts in Soviet SNFs without

U.S. participation. This brought Bush under increasing pressure from Western allies to do the same. By late May 1989, Bush responded with a plan that focused on reductions in conventional forces stationed in both the NATO and Warsaw Pact countries. Though his plan did not address SNFs, the European countries eagerly accepted it.

Strategic Arms Reduction Talks (START) resumed in mid-1989, and in early December 1989 Bush and Gorbachev traveled to the European nation of Malta for a summit meeting. On his way to the meeting, Gorbachev stopped in the Vatican City and made a historic visit to the leader of the Roman Catholic Church, Pope John Paul II (1920–), a major foe of communism, and promised religious freedoms for Soviet citizens. The Malta meetings covered a wide range of topics, from nuclear arms control to trade relations to Third World conflicts. Many historians consider the Malta meetings as marking the end of the Cold War. Both Gorbachev and Bush came away from the meetings with an understanding that they were no longer enemies.

The fall of communism in Eastern Europe

President Bush began more actively supporting Gorbachev's reform efforts when fears arose that stalled reform might create impatience, turn into rapid revolt in the Soviet empire, and lead to severe political instability in Europe and elsewhere. Nonetheless, change did come quickly in Eastern Europe, in a sort of reverse "domino effect," as reforms rippled from one country to the next. By the end of 1989, communism was out in Eastern Europe. Gorbachev and people all around the world were stunned by the rapidity of these major events.

Change first came in Poland. In early 1989, as part of perestroika, Polish leader General Wojciech Jaruzelski (1923–) invited Solidarity, the popular workers' union, to become part of a coalition, or combination, government still to be led by the Communist Party. Solidarity accepted the offer. General elections for the Polish parliament were set for June. The communists were stunned when Solidarity's candidates won 160 of the 161 seats up for election in the lower house of the Polish parliament and 99 out of 100 in the upper house.

Given the overwhelming victory, Solidarity leader Lech Walesa (1943–) excluded communists from the new government and named Tadeusz Mazowiecki (1927–) as the new Polish prime minister. Mazowiecki became the first noncommunist government leader in Eastern Europe since the Czech democratic government was overthrown in 1948 (see Chapter 2, Conflict Builds). Walesa himself was elected the new president of Poland in 1990. Rather than sending in Soviet forces to restore the Communist Party to power as past Soviet leaders would have done, Gorbachev encouraged the Polish Communist Party to support the new government. Gorbachev realized that the use of force would likely trigger riots and jeopardize the Soviet Union's chances of getting much-needed economic aid from the West. The Brezhnev Doctrine, which declared the Soviet Union's right to intervene in the affairs of other nations in order to support communism, had lost its force. Eastern European nations were now free to pursue their own course of reform.

Poland was a model quickly followed by other Eastern European countries, at a far faster pace than Gorbachev ever envisioned. Hungary, East Germany, Bulgaria, Czechoslovakia, and Romania would all undergo rapid governmental changes. Gorbachev and other communist leaders greatly underestimated the popular disdain for communist rule. Rather than reforming communism, perestroika was leading to a complete communist collapse.

In February 1989, the Hungarian parliament dropped prohibitions against noncommunist political organizations. In March, Hungary became the first Eastern-bloc country to open its borders to Western Europe by opening border crossings to Austria. Sixty thousand East Germans flooded into Hungary, most intending to cross into Austria and continue on to West Germany. In April, János Kádár (1912–1989), who had gained power in a bloody communist revolution in 1956, was removed by the Communist Party. Communist leaders more supportive of perestroika were installed. Free elections in Hungary were held in 1990. The Communist Party, renamed the Socialist Party, received less than 10 percent of the vote. A noncommunist government took over.

On October 7, 1989, Gorbachev visited East German leader Erich Honecker (1912–1994) to promote reform in East

Germany. East Germans cheered for Gorbachev as they demonstrated against their strict communist government. On October 18, the East German Communist Party replaced Honecker and opened East German borders to West Germany. Thousands poured into West Germany. The most dramatic moment came on November 9, when the East German government opened the Berlin Wall. Hundreds of thousands of East Germans jubilantly streamed into West Berlin (see Chapter 3, Germany and Berlin). On that same day, Bulgarian Communist Party leader Todor Zhivkov (1911–1998), who had led Bulgaria since 1961, was removed. Demonstrations in East Germany steadily increased; the people were demanding free elections. The communist leaders finally promised elections for March 1990. Like the communist candidates in Poland and Hungary, the East German communists suffered an overwhelming defeat, and a noncommunist coalition government was installed.

Similar events unfolded in Czechoslovakia. On November 17, 1989, a massive demonstration took place in

Hundreds of thousands of Czechs gather in Prague, Czechoslovakia, to demand free elections and greater freedoms. *Photograph by Peter Turnley. Reproduced by permission of the Corbis Corporation.*

Prague, the capital city; Czechoslovakians gathered in the city's main square and demanded greater freedoms. Two days later, two hundred thousand protesters demanded free elections and the resignation of hard-line communist leaders. Milos Jakes (1922–) resigned from his leadership position five days later. After millions of Czech workers went on strike on November 28, the Czech government gave in and legalized noncommunist political parties. A new cabinet, or group of top advisors, led by noncommunists, was formed on December 10 as part of an interim government; a noncommunist president was installed on December 29, 1989. Free elections held in June 1990 brought victory by large margins for the noncommunists. Noted author and human rights activist Václav Havel (1936–) became the new Czech president and would serve in that role until early 2003. As in Poland, communists were not elected to any government positions.

Communism came to a violent end in Romania. In December 1989, Romanian communist authorities sought to evict from his church a priest who was a dissident, an individual who disagrees with the ideas of those in power. Thousands of demonstrators protested the government's decision. In response, Romanian security forces killed hundreds of the protesters, triggering even larger demonstrations. The highly unpopular Romanian president Nicolae Ceausescu (1918–1989) began losing control of the military; the soldiers were starting to support the demonstrators instead of defending the government. On December 22, Ceausescu and his wife attempted to flee but were captured and executed on December 25.

Communism challenged in the Soviet Union

Shortly before the cascade of events in Eastern Europe, Gorbachev pressed for political reform in the Soviet Union. He revised the Soviet constitution in early 1989. The revisions established a new parliament called the Congress of People's Deputies. Elections were held in March 1989 to elect representatives from the various Soviet republics. As in Eastern Europe, old-guard communist candidates lost badly. Among the newly elected officials was Boris Yeltsin (1931–), who represented the Moscow district of the republic of Russia.

Though a communist, Yeltsin was not a supporter of the old-guard, ultra-conservative Communist Party establishment. The elections immediately decreased the influence of the Communist Party, something Gorbachev had not anticipated.

The new Congress of People's Deputies now took precedence over the Communist Party. By February 1990, demonstrations against Communist Party domination were growing; hundreds of thousands of Russians in Moscow gathered to protest communist rule. Like some Soviet leaders before him, Gorbachev was both leader of the Communist Party and leader of the Soviet Union's government. This dual role put him in a very difficult position: Therefore, Gorbachev created a Soviet presidency that was separate from the Communist Party. Gorbachev moved into the president position which gave him more distance from his Communist Party association. He also legalized noncommunist political parties.

By mid-1990, it was clear Gorbachev's perestroika had failed to preserve communist control; neither had it revived the Soviet economy. Still, Gorbachev tried to keep the economic change somewhat in control. He feared too rapid of a shift to a free market economy, or economic conditions dictated by open competition, would cause a rapid rise in prices and in unemployment; this could cause even greater public unrest. He left many government price supports in place to keep prices from going up further. Nonetheless, with the collapse of the old communist-controlled economic system and no new system in place, the Soviet economy was headed for crisis. Productivity was declining, prices were escalating, and shortages were occurring more frequently. Meanwhile, Gorbachev was enjoying great popularity abroad; in 1990, he received the Nobel Peace Prize for his reform efforts and *Time* magazine's "Man of the Year" award. Moscow was chosen as the location for a human rights conference for the following year. However, Gorbachev's popularity at home was plummeting.

Through 1989, Gorbachev had witnessed the loss of the Soviet empire—all the communist-controlled countries in Eastern Europe had ultimately rejected communism. And tensions were rising within the borders of the Soviet Union itself. In the Soviet republic of Estonia, citizens had attempted to declare independence in 1988. Though Gorbachev was willing to let Eastern European countries break free from Soviet control, he felt differently about the Soviet republics. An early indication of this came in April 1989 when Soviet troops killed nineteen demonstrators, including sixteen women, in the republic of Georgia. Gorbachev's resolve to keep the Soviet Union together was tested again in early 1990. On March 11, the parliament of the republic of Lithuania declared independence from the Soviet Union. Gorbachev sent Soviet troops, established an economic blockade, and threatened to disband the government.

By mid-1990, President Bush and his advisors were still debating how hard they should try to keep Gorbachev in power and maintain the Soviet system. A primary concern was the stockpile of nuclear weapons scattered about the Soviet Union. The various ethnic factions within the Soviet Union could start a civil war in their quest for independence, and the security of the weapons could be jeopardized. (The Baltic States—the Soviet republics of Estonia, Latvia, and Lithuania— had been the most active in opposition to Soviet rule. These former independent nations had been forcibly brought into the Soviet Union by Joseph Stalin [1879–1953] in the 1940s.) However, as nationalist independence movements within the Soviet Union began to grow, Bush found it harder to justify helping Gorbachev maintain the Soviet Union. In response to Gorbachev's military actions against Lithuania, Bush placed economic trade restrictions on the Soviet Union and warned Gorbachev against further use of force. Still seeking a most-favored-nation trade status with the United States, Gorbachev responded by lifting economic restrictions on Lithuania. (Most-favored-nation trade status lowers taxes on goods exported to the United States, making it much easier for a foreign country to sell goods to American consumers and businesses.) However, Bush still denied Gorbachev improved trade conditions, yet he granted the privilege to the PRC, even though PRC forces had massacred more than two hundred pro-democracy demonstrators in Tiananmen Square in Beijing on June 4, 1989. Gorbachev was angered by Bush's decision to limit economic aid to the Soviet Union and Eastern Europe, but Bush had little choice in the matter: The United States was suffering an economic recession, or reduced economic activity, and the public was unlikely to support sending substantial aid to an inept Soviet government. The Soviet Union did not receive most-favored-nation trade status until 1992.

German reunification

Gorbachev traveled to Washington, D.C., for a summit meeting with Bush on May 31, 1990. A key topic was the reunification of Germany. Gorbachev was not pleased with the trend toward reunification since the fall of the Berlin Wall the previous November. Like Stalin and other former Soviet leaders, Gorbachev feared having a strong, unified Germany near the Soviet western border. Gorbachev proposed reunifying Europe instead—that is, dissolving the NATO and Warsaw Pact divisions—and keeping Germany divided into two nations. However, the major election defeat of communist candidates in East Germany in March 1990 made eventual reunification with the noncommunist West Germany a certainty. The new, noncommunist East German government immediately pressed for reunification with West Germany.

Conceding that reunification was inevitable, Gorbachev wanted guarantees that a reunified Germany would not become a member of NATO. However, Bush insisted that

Soviet leader Mikhail Gorbachev extends his hand to U.S. president George Bush at the Washington, D.C., summit on June 1, 1990. *Photograph by Peter Turnley. Reproduced by permission of the Corbis Corporation.*

only Germany, reunified, could make that decision. At the Washington summit meeting, Bush did provide Gorbachev several other key assurances. He promised that (1) NATO forces would not be placed in the former East Germany; (2) Germany's borders would not be moved back to pre-World War II (1939–45) locations; (3) the former West Germany would not be allowed to possess nuclear weapons; (4) Germany would provide economic assistance to the Soviets; and (5) arms control talks concerning European conventional and nuclear forces would proceed.

The NATO member nations held a meeting in July 1990 to make additional assurances to Gorbachev. They offered formal relations with Warsaw Pact countries and pledged not to attack the Soviet Union or Eastern European countries. In response to Gorbachev's proposals to limit short-range nuclear force weapons (SNFs), NATO offered to eliminate nuclear artillery shells if the Soviets would agree to do the same. NATO also agreed to further reduce conventional forces. Given the various assurances from Bush and NATO, on July 14, 1990, Gorbachev agreed to accept a reunified Germany and accept its membership in NATO. In return, German chancellor Helmut Kohl promised substantial economic aid to Gorbachev. Gorbachev set a timetable of four years for withdrawal of all Soviet forces from the former East Germany. Also in July, the two German governments agreed to an economic merger. In August, the East German parliament voted to merge East Germany and West Germany on October 3, 1990.

A new Europe

The collapse of communism in Eastern Europe paved the way for major changes in the region. In yet another momentous event, the four allied powers of World War II (the United States, the Soviet Union, France, and Great Britain) and the two German governments signed a peace treaty on September 12, 1990, bringing an official end to World War II. The emerging Cold War rivalry between the United States and the Soviet Union in the late 1940s had blocked final negotiations at that time (see Chapter 1, Origins of the Cold War). The new treaty was called the Treaty on the Final Settlement with Respect to Germany.

New Allies

On the heels of the collapse of communism in Eastern Europe in 1989 and while the Soviet Union was struggling for survival, the first major post–Cold War military conflict erupted. On August 2, 1990, Iraq invaded Kuwait and gained control of that nation. Fearing Iraqi control of larger amounts of Middle East oil, President George Bush condemned the invasion and vowed to push the Iraqis out of Kuwait. In the new post–Cold War world, the United States looked to the Soviets for assistance in responding to Iraq. Eager to receive U.S. aid, Soviet leader Mikhail Gorbachev readily agreed to help. However, remaining Communist Party hard-liners sharply criticized Gorbachev for siding with the United States against Iraq, a longtime ally of the Soviets. In response to his critics, Gorbachev provided support through the United Nations (UN) rather than directly to the United States. The UN established embargoes, or trade restrictions, against Iraq. Soviet military leaders refused to provide the United States military assistance.

On August 6, Bush launched Operation Desert Shield, sending two hundred thousand U.S. troops to protect Saudi Arabia from any further Iraqi aggression. The American soldiers were stationed only seven hundred miles (1,126 kilometers) from the Soviet border, which caused uneasiness among the Soviet military. Unable to convince Iraq's ruler, Saddam Hussein (1937–), to withdraw from Kuwait, Gorbachev supported a November 29 UN resolution to use force to free Kuwait from Iraq occupation. Supported by the UN, the United States launched an air attack on January 17, 1991. That was followed by a ground invasion on February 23 known as Operation Desert Storm. In less than seventy-two hours, U.S. soldiers forced Iraqi troops out of Kuwait and southern Iraq. Iraq lost thousands of troops and tanks. Bush refrained from completely destroying Iraqi forces and capturing Iraq because he did not want to bring stronger Soviet criticism on Gorbachev or make Iraq vulnerable to a takeover by Iran.

A new European organization was formed and began taking quick action on several issues. The thirty-five member nations of NATO and the Warsaw Pact joined in the Conference on Security and Cooperation in Europe (CSCE). The CSCE signed a Conventional Forces in Europe (CFE) Treaty on November 21, 1990, reducing conventional forces of both NATO and Warsaw Pact nations. However, the agreement allowed NATO nations to maintain larger military forces than the Warsaw Pact nations. The military rivalry of the Cold War was clearly over. The CFE Treaty reduced a broad range of weapons, including tanks, armored combat vehicles, ar-

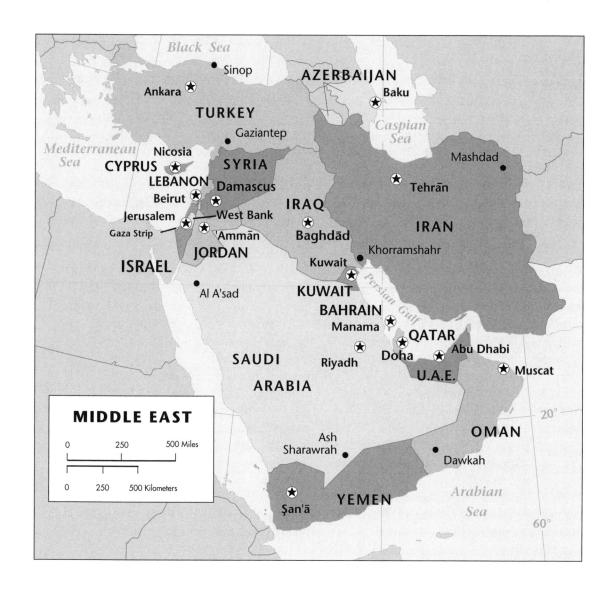

MIDDLE EAST

| 0 | 250 | 500 Miles |

| 0 | 250 | 500 Kilometers |

A regional map of the Middle East, including Iraq, with whom the United States went to war in 1991.
Map by Maryland Cartographics. Reproduced by permission of the Gale Group.

tillery, combat aircraft, and combat helicopters. The CSCE also signed the Charter of Paris, which declared an end to the old Cold War split and proclaimed a new Europe. The charter declared support for democracy, human rights and fundamental freedoms, social justice, and economic liberty. These common values would give the nations of Europe a sense of shared security.

In another major change, the Warsaw Pact began dissolving during 1990. In June, Hungary became the first country to announce it would pull out by the end of 1991. Other countries soon followed, leading the Warsaw Pact to suddenly decide on February 25, 1991, that it would disband, effective in one month.

Gorbachev under fire

By late 1990, following the collapse of communism in Eastern Europe and growing tensions in the Soviet Union, Gorbachev was struggling to maintain his leadership position. On the one hand, he was trying to please the reformers led by Boris Yeltsin; they were pushing hard for a free market economy. On the other hand, he was also trying not to alarm the old-guard communists who were becoming very upset with the direction Gorbachev's reform efforts were going. Yeltsin kept pushing. He introduced a plan calling for the Soviet republics to become more independent and individually control their own economies, including taxation, natural resources, currencies, and trade.

Russian leader Boris Yeltsin.
Photograph by Greg Gibson. Reproduced by permission of AP/Wide World Photos.

Gorbachev could not support Yeltsin's plan because if he did, there would be no further need for a centralized economic structure—the very thing the Communist Party had always provided. Deciding to reassure his communist critics, Gorbachev backed off from his reforms and appointed communist hard-liners to several key government positions. In protest, Soviet foreign minister Eduard Shevardnadze resigned on December 20, 1990. In January 1991, Gorbachev approved a plan to overthrow the new Lithuanian pro-independence government. While reeling back glasnost, he also reestablished restrictions on Soviet television and radio news programs. Gorbachev even attempted to remove Yeltsin as president of Russia. However, mass public demonstrations blocked Yeltsin's removal. The large size and angry mood of the demonstrations convinced Gorbachev that there was no way to turn back from reform.

Borrowing from Yeltsin's idea, Gorbachev now decided to salvage the Soviet Union by redefining it as a federation of republics. He proposed a new national cabinet elected by the republics and a more democratic Soviet Communist Party. However, Yeltsin continued to press for full democracy and capitalism. Gorbachev finally gave in to Yeltsin's pressure: In early July 1991, Gorbachev promoted privatizing (selling to private owners) most of the Soviet-owned industries. The nine Soviet Slavic and Muslim republics were allowed to develop their own economic reform plans.

An attempted Soviet coup

On July 17, 1991, at a London meeting of world leaders, Bush and Gorbachev finally came to an agreement on arms control. Bush traveled to Moscow two weeks later to sign the treaty with Gorbachev. The treaty required a reduction in the nuclear warheads already deployed by each country; each country was limited to six thousand.

Noting Gorbachev's renewed push for sweeping reforms and his participation in a substantial arms control agreement in July 1991, Soviet communist hard-liners decided to take action against Gorbachev. In late August, Gorbachev left for Crimea, on the Black Sea, for an annual vacation. While he was away, the hard-liners attempted a coup (short for coup d'état; an illegal or forceful change of government). On August 19, they placed Gorbachev under house arrest (confinement in one's home rather than prison) in his vacation home and publicly announced that he was being removed for health reasons. They then declared a six-month state of emergency to "restore law and order." However, the highly popular Yeltsin came to Gorbachev's rescue. On August 21, Yeltsin denounced the emergency government as illegal. Despite orders from the coup leaders, Soviet troops refused to arrest Yeltsin or the Russian parliament. Deciding their efforts were futile, the coup leaders gave up and were placed under arrest, except for one who committed suicide.

Ironically, the coup by the communist hard-liners led to the end of Communist Party rule in the Soviet Union. A rapid sequence of events followed the failed coup: On August 22, a weary Gorbachev returned to Moscow and reasserted control over the government to continue his reforms. However, the last credibility of the Communist Party had vanished with the failed coup. On August 23, Yeltsin suspended Communist Party activities in the Russian republic and seized its property. He also dismissed Russian ministers appointed by Gorbachev and appointed new ones. Other Soviet republics followed, banning the Communist Party in their regions. Seeing the dramatic change, Gorbachev resigned from the Communist Party and suspended further party participation in the Soviet government. Communism in the Soviet Union had essentially come to an end. On August 24, Yeltsin extended formal recognition of independence to the Baltic States—Estonia, Latvia, and Lithuania. The Ukraine declared independence on the same day. In September, Gorbachev extended Soviet recognition of independence to the three Baltic nations also; these were the first nations to leave the Soviet Union.

Throughout the coup attempt, President Bush was slow to respond. He did not condemn the attempted coup until Yeltsin begged him to. Then he chose not to join Yeltsin in recognizing the independence of the Baltic States, waiting for more nations, and Gorbachev in particular, to do so first. Bush expressed preference for the more cautious Gorbachev to Yeltsin. This led to criticism that he was supporting a communist leader over the leading Russian advocate for democratic reform.

Collapse of the Soviet Union

Through the fall of 1991, political developments in the Soviet Union were getting increasingly beyond Gorbachev's control. In reaction, Bush began making bolder moves by late September. With the ongoing decline of the Soviet Union, Bush feared that nuclear weapons could end up in the hands of terrorists or a remaining out-of-control hard-line communist. He announced that the United States would remove or destroy all tactical nuclear weapons deployed in Europe and Asia and on U.S. warships. He also suspended deployment of the MX missile system and ended the twenty-four-hour alert status of the Strategic Air Command, a unit established by the U.S. military with the goal of identifying targets in the Soviet Union and being ready to deliver nuclear weapons to those targets. Bush also proposed a plan to reduce ICBMs and other nuclear weapons. Gorbachev responded to Bush's actions with similar reductions of tactical nuclear weapons. The Baltic States and the twelve remaining Soviet republics formed an alliance for defense and control of the Soviet nuclear arsenal. By October, they had also formed a new economic union. In November, the U.S. Congress provided up to $400 million to assist the union in destroying its nuclear weapons.

In a last effort to salvage a political union, Gorbachev went to work creating a new transitional government, with himself and the presidents of the various republics as its leaders. However, acceptance of the new union depended on the approval of the Ukraine, the most populous former Soviet republic aside from Russia. In a public vote on December 1, the Ukraine voted for full independence rather than joining the new proposed government. The other former republics followed suit, voting for independence instead of Gorbachev's union. The Ukraine and Belarus (and later Kazakhstan) transferred their nuclear missiles to Russia, which took on a new official name, the Russian Federation.

After Gorbachev's failed attempt to create a new union of countries, Yeltsin moved to create a new alliance, called the Commonwealth of Independent States (CIS). Unlike the Soviet Union, it would not act as a formal government. Eleven of the former Soviet republics joined the CIS. Yeltsin also requested that NATO accept Russia as a new member, but he was turned down. On December 25, Gorbachev resigned as president of the Soviet Union and transferred the Soviet nuclear arsenal over to Yeltsin, president of Russia. The Soviet Union ceased existence on December 31, 1991. All Soviet embassies around the world became Russian embassies, and Russia took over the Soviet seat in the United Nations. Even with the breakup of the Soviet Union, Russia still had the largest conventional military force in the world.

The swift collapse of the Soviet empire stunned everyone worldwide, even foreign policy experts. The Cold War and the Soviet Union had lasted for so long that everyone had believed it would last at least decades more. Now it was replaced with a loose alliance of countries that had large conventional and nuclear forces and critical economic and political problems.

A regional map of post–Cold War Europe, with Russia inset. *Map by Maryland Cartographics. Reproduced by permission of the Gale Group.*

Expensive Weapons

During the Cold War, nuclear military systems came with no clear price tag. However, estimates in 1998 revealed that the United States spent $2 trillion (in 1996 dollars) for nuclear technology during the Cold War years, from 1945 to 1991. Nuclear submarines took a good part of that total, costing over $320 billion.

Almost single-handedly, Gorbachev had peacefully ended the Cold War. He had made major cuts in the size of the Soviet military, renounced past foreign policies of expanding Soviet influence, and encouraged basic economic reform. He pressured U.S. presidents Reagan and Bush into two arms control treaties, the INF Treaty and START. However, he had certainly not intended to end Communist Party rule in the Soviet Union or dismantle the Soviet Union itself.

Cold War costs

U.S. leaders claimed victory in the Cold War. However, the United States paid a heavy price in the long, four-decade struggle. First and foremost, tens of thousands of American troops were killed in Cold War–related conflicts, particularly in Korea and Vietnam. Careers were ruined from suspicion of communist involvement. Many U.S. citizens lived in continual fear and suspicion of communist infiltration or nuclear war. The country went to the brink of nuclear war at least once, during the 1962 Cuban Missile Crisis, and had threatened nuclear war on several other occasions.

Financial costs were also large. By the late 1980s, the United States had become a debtor nation. During the Cold War, the U.S. government was restructured with an emphasis on national security rather than domestic needs. The arms race and economic aid to friendly countries were expensive priorities, creating a debt of $4 trillion. The U.S. infrastructure of roads, bridges, and public buildings suffered from too little funding. Inner cities began to decay, slums spread, and unemployment and crime increased. With much of its budget dedicated to Cold War costs, the United States lost some of its lead in new technology development; Germany and Japan, countries that were unable to spend on their militaries because of the conditions of their surrender in World War II, made major technical gains. Considering both the human and financial costs the United States incurred, Gorbachev commented that the Soviet Union and the United States had both lost the Cold War.

Russian citizens suffered severe economic hardships, especially following the collapse of the Soviet Union. Yeltsin moved to sell state-owned businesses and remove market and trade restrictions. However, the change to a free market economic system proved much more difficult than expected. The highly inefficient Russian businesses proved noncompetitive in world markets. With the economy suffering, the Russian parliament rebelled against Yeltsin's economic policies in 1993, but Yeltsin maintained control. He disbanded the parliament and created a new Russian constitution that gave him expanded powers.

Widespread economic hardships and frustrations with capitalism continued in Russia. Political support for the Communist Party increased as the Russian parliamentary elections approached in December 1995. The communists received the largest percentage of seats—22 percent —among the competing political parties. Despite disappointment with his economic programs, Yeltsin managed to win reelection in 1996 as Russian president over the challenge of Gorbachev. Continued financial problems led to increased bankruptcies among Russian businesses, and the country defaulted on, or was unable to pay back, foreign loans in 1998. Yeltsin's popularity finally began to decline, and on December 31, 1999, he resigned. Vladimir Putin (1953–), a former KGB (secret police) intelligence officer, replaced him as interim president and then secured the office in a public election in 2000. The country began experiencing some economic growth, but concerns rose over Putin's increased exercise of control in some troublesome regions and his new restrictions on media outlets.

 Where Are They in 2003?

Nuclear weapons development and buildup was a major feature of the Cold War. Though the Cold War ended, nuclear weapons had come to stay. By early 2003, seven nations were known to have nuclear weapons: the United States, Russia, Great Britain, France, Pakistan, India, and the People's Republic of China. Israel was on the verge of having nuclear weapons. South Africa had nuclear weapons but claimed to have destroyed them. Three former republics of the Soviet Union—the Ukraine, Belarus, and Kazakhstan—had nuclear weapons but had either destroyed them or turned them over to Russia. Three nations either had or were still developing nuclear weapons: Iraq, Iran, and North Korea. Some nations in the North Atlantic Treaty Organization (NATO) did not have nuclear weapons programs of their own but had U.S. nuclear weapons deployed in their countries. These nations included Belgium, Germany, Greece, Holland, Italy, and Turkey.

Crowds gather outside the Kremlin on October 7, 1998, to rally for the removal of Russian president Boris Yeltsin.
Photograph by Mikhail Metzel. Reproduced by permission of AP/Wide World Photos.

Ethnic conflicts and world terrorism

Ironically, with the end of the Cold War and the demise of the Soviet Union, global politics became less stable. Historians even began referring to the Cold War as the "Long Peace." During the Cold War, the balance of power between the Soviet Union and the United States, including their mutual fear of nuclear war, ensured a certain stability. By the late 1980s, ethnic rivalries kept in check by the Soviet

rule burst forward. In Yugoslavia, the four republics of Slovenia, Croatia, Bosnia and Herzegovina, and Macedonia declared their independence, leading to a bloody war between ethnic groups through the 1990s.

Ethnic conflicts also occurred elsewhere, such as in Azerbaijan, Chechnya, and Armenia. Chechnya, a member of the Russian Federation, declared independence in 1991. Unwilling to recognize Chechnya's independence, Russia sent troops into Chechnya in late 1994 to reclaim control. The Russians captured Chechnya's capital, Grozny, in 1995. However, in 1996, Chechen forces pushed the Russians out of Grozny, and a cease-fire resulted. After several bombings in Russia were attributed to Chechen rebels, Russia reasserted control over Chechnya and sent forces in once again. Guerrilla warfare followed.

Left as the lone superpower, the United States began serving as a peacekeeper in various violent internal conflicts around the world—in the African nation of Somalia, for ex-

A Russian soldier looks down at huddled Chechen prisoners in February 1995. *Photograph by Nikolay Galiayev. Reproduced by permission of the Corbis Corporation.*

ample, in Haiti (part of the West Indies), and in Bosnia and Herzegovina. International terrorism also escalated through the 1980s, marked by the sabotage of a Pan Am 747 airliner in flight over Scotland in December 1988, which killed 270 people. Terrorists supported by Iran, Libya, and Syria had carried out the bombing in response to a U.S. ship mistakenly shooting down an Iranian airliner carrying more than one hundred civilians. The threat of terrorism became a major global concern in the 1990s. With the terrorist attacks on New York City and Washington, D.C., on September 11, 2001, the United States assumed a leading role in fighting terrorism globally.

For More Information

Books

Ash, Timothy G. *The Magic Lantern: The Revolution of '89 Witnessed in Warsaw, Budapest, Berlin, and Prague.* New York: Random House, 1990.

Ashlund, Anders. *Building Capitalism: The Transformation of the Former Soviet Bloc.* New York: Cambridge University Press, 2002.

Ciment, James. *The Young People's History of the United States.* New York: Barnes and Noble Books, 1998.

Kaplan, Robert D. *The Coming Anarchy: Shattering the Dreams of the Post Cold War.* New York: Random House, 2000.

Kelly, Nigel. *Fall of the Berlin Wall: The Cold War Ends.* Chicago: Heineman Library, 2001.

Litwak, Robert S. *Rogue States and U.S. Foreign Policy: Containment after the Cold War.* Baltimore, MD: Johns Hopkins University Press, 2000.

Mandelbaum, Michael. *The Ideas That Conquered the World: Peace, Democracy, and Free Markets in the Twenty-First Century.* New York: PublicAffairs, 2002.

Matlock, Jack F., Jr. *Autopsy of an Empire: The American Ambassador's Account of the Collapse of the Soviet Union.* New York: Random House, 1995.

Newhouse, John. *Europe Adrift.* New York: Pantheon Books, 1997.

Stokes, Gale. *The Walls Came Tumbling Down: The Collapse of Communism in Eastern Europe.* New York: Oxford University Press, 1993.

Web Sites

George Bush Presidential Library and Museum. http://bushlibrary.tamu.edu (accessed on August 13, 2003).

President Mikhail Sergeyevich Gorbachev. Website: http://www.mikhail gorbachev.org (accessed on August 13, 2003).

Where to Learn More

Books

Barson, Michael, and Steven Heller. *Red Scared! The Commie Menace in Propaganda and Popular Culture.* San Francisco: Chronicle Books, 2001.

Brubaker, Paul E. *The Cuban Missile Crisis in American History.* Berkeley Heights, NJ: Enslow, 2001.

Ciment, James. *The Young People's History of the United States.* New York: Barnes and Noble Books, 1998.

Collier, Christopher. *The United States in the Cold War.* New York: Benchmark Books/Marshall Cavendish, 2002.

FitzGerald, Frances. *Way Out There in the Blue: Reagan, Star Wars, and the End of the Cold War.* New York: Simon & Schuster, 2000.

Gaddis, John L. *We Now Know: Rethinking Cold War History.* New York: Oxford University Press, 1997.

Gates, Robert M. *From the Shadows: The Ultimate Insider's Story of Five Presidents and How They Won the Cold War.* New York: Simon & Schuster Trade Paperback, 1997.

Glynn, Patrick. *Closing Pandora's Box: Arms Races, Arms Control, and the History of the Cold War.* New York: Basic Books, 1992.

Grant, R. G. *The Berlin Wall.* Austin, TX: Raintree Steck-Vaughn, 1999.

Herring, George C. *America's Longest War: The United States and Vietnam, 1950–1975.* 2nd ed. New York: Knopf, 1988.

Huchthausen, Peter A., and Alexander Hoyt. *October Fury*. Hoboken, NJ: Wiley, 2002.

Isaacs, Jeremy, and Taylor Downing. *Cold War: An Illustrated History, 1945–1991*. Boston: Little, Brown, 1998.

Jacobs, William Jay. *Search for Peace: The Story of the United Nations*. New York: Atheneum, 1996.

Keep, John L. H. *A History of the Soviet Union, 1945–1991: Last of the Empires*. New York: Oxford University Press, 1995.

Kelly, Nigel. *Fall of the Berlin Wall: The Cold War Ends*. Chicago: Heineman Library, 2001.

Kort, Michael G. *The Cold War*. Brookfield, CT: Millbrook Press, 1994.

LaFeber, Walter. *America, Russia, and the Cold War, 1945–1996*. 8th ed. New York: McGraw-Hill, 1997.

Parrish, Thomas. *Berlin in the Balance, 1945–1949: The Blockade, the Airlift, the First Major Battle of the Cold War*. Reading, MA: Addison-Wesley, 1998.

Parrish, Thomas. *The Cold War Encyclopedia*. New York: Henry Holt, 1996.

Pietrusza, David. *The End of the Cold War*. San Diego, CA: Lucent, 1995.

Sherrow, Victoria. *Joseph McCarthy and the Cold War*. Woodbridge, CT: Blackbirch Press, 1999.

Sibley, Katherine A. S. *The Cold War*. Westport, CT: Greenwood Press, 1998.

Smith, Joseph. *The Cold War, 1945–1991*. 2nd ed. Malden, MA: Blackwell, 1998.

Stein, Conrad. *The Korean War: "The Forgotten War."* Springfield, NJ: Enslow, 1994.

Walker, Martin. *The Cold War: A History (Owl Book)*. New York: Henry Holt, 1995.

Magazines

Hoover, J. Edgar. "How to Fight Communism." *Newsweek,* June 9, 1947.

Levine, Isaac Don. "Our First Line of Defense." *Plain Talk,* September 1949.

"X" (George F. Kennan). "The Sources of Soviet Conduct." *Foreign Affairs,* July 1947.

Novels

Brunner, Edward. *Cold War Poetry*. Urbana: University of Illinois Press, 2000.

Clancy, Tom. *The Hunt for Red October*. New York: Berkley Publishing Group, 1985.

Clancy, Tom. *Red Storm Rising*. New York: Berkley Publishing Group, 1987.

Clancy, Tom, and Martin Greenberg. *Tom Clancy's Power Plays: Cold War*. New York: Berkley Publishing Group, 2001.

George, Peter. *Dr. Strangelove, or How I Learned to Stop Worrying and Love the Bomb.* New York: Bantam Books, 1964.

Le Carre, John. *Spy Who Came in from the Cold.* New York: Coward, McCann & Geoghegan, 1978.

Littell, Robert. *The Company: A Novel of the CIA.* New York: Overlook Press, 2002.

Web Sites

The Atomic Archive. http://www. atomicarchive.com (accessed on September 26, 2003).

CNN Interactive: The Cold War Experience. http://www.CNN.com/SPECIALS/cold.war (accessed on September 26, 2003).

"Cold War History: 1949–1989." *U.S. Air Force Museum.* http://www.wpafb.af.mil/museum/history/coldwar/cw.htm (accessed on September 26, 2003).

The Dwight D. Eisenhower Library and Museum. http://www.eisenhower.utexas.edu (accessed on September 26, 2003).

George Bush Presidential Library and Museum. http://bushlibrary.tamu.edu (accessed on September 26, 2003).

Gerald R. Ford Library and Museum. http://www.ford.utexas.edu (accessed on September 26, 2003).

International Spy Museum. http://spymuseum.org (accessed on September 26, 2003).

John F. Kennedy Library and Museum. http://www.cs.umb.edu/jfklibrary/index.htm (accessed on September 26, 2003).

Lyndon B. Johnson Library and Museum. http://www.lbjlib.utexas.edu (accessed on September 26, 2003).

The Manhattan Project Heritage Preservation Association, Inc. http://www.childrenofthemanhattanproject.org (accessed on September 26, 2003).

National Atomic Museum. http://www.atomicmuseum.com (accessed on September 26, 2003).

National Security Agency. http://www.nsa.gov (accessed on September 26, 2003).

President Mikhail Sergeyevich Gorbachev. http://www.mikhailgorbachev.org (accessed on September 26, 2003).

The Richard Nixon Library and Birthplace. http://www.nixonfoundation.org (accessed on September 26, 2003).

Ronald Reagan Presidential Library. http://www.reagan.utexas.edu (accessed on September 26, 2003).

"Secrets, Lies, and Atomic Spies." *Nova Online.* http://www.pbs.org/wgbh/nova/venona (accessed on September 26, 2003).

Truman Presidential Museum & Library. http://www.trumanlibrary.org (accessed on September 26, 2003).

U.S. Central Intelligence Agency (CIA). http://www.cia.gov (accessed on September 26, 2003).

Woodrow Wilson International Center for Scholars. *The Cold War International History Project.* http://wwics.si.edu/index. cfm?fuseaction= topics.home &topic_id=1409 (accessed on September 26, 2003).

Index

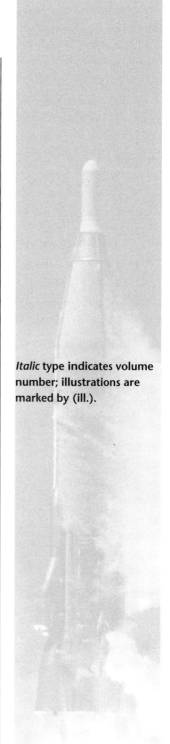

Italic type indicates volume number; illustrations are marked by (ill.).

Burgess, Guy, *1:* 128, 142, 143
Bush, George, *2:* 363 (ill.)
　Baltic States and, *2:* 369
　China and, *2:* 362
　Cold War and, *2:* 347
　democracy and, *2:* 369
　economy and, *2:* 362
　election of, *2:* 356
　Germany and, *2:* 363–64
　Gorbachev, Mikhail, and, *2:* 347, 356–57, 362–64, 368, 369, 372
　Iran-Contra scandal and, *2:* 332–33
　Iraq and, *2:* 365
　Kissinger, Henry, and, *2:* 356
　North Atlantic Treaty Organization (NATO) and, *2:* 363–64
　nuclear weapons and, *2:* 356–57, 362, 368, 369–70, 372
　Reagan, Ronald, and, *2:* 256
　Soviet collapse and, *2:* 369–70
　Soviet Union and, *2:* 369–70
　Strategic Air Command (SAC) and, *2:* 369
　Strategic Arms Reduction Talks (START) and, *2:* 357
　Yeltsin, Boris, and, *2:* 369
Bush, Vannevar, *1:* 83
Byrnes, James, *1:* 3, 16, 18, 20, 31

C

Cambodia, *1:* 181–82; *2:* 327, 328
Cambridge Spies, *1:* 135, 140–44
Cameras, *1:* 136, 137 (ill.)
Camp David, *2:* 201, 328–30, 329 (ill.)
Campaign for Nuclear Disarmament (CND), *2:* 245–46
Candy, *1:* 66
Capitalism
　Cold War and, *1:* 25, 60
　communism and, *1:* 19, 23–24, 25, 29, 33, 129, 169–70, 188; *2:* 215–16, 352
　definition of, *1:* 28, 56, 126, 168; *2:* 192, 214, 298, 320, 348
　democracy and, *2:* 299, 320

　economy and, *1:* 4, 27, 28, 56, 58, 104, 126, 168, 169–70; *2:* 192, 214, 216, 298, 299, 320, 348, 372–73
　Germany and, *1:* 58–59
　Gorbachev, Mikhail, and, *2:* 352
　Great Depression and, *1:* 104
　imperialism and, *2:* 208, 215
　Khrushchev, Nikita S., and, *1:* 188
　Marshall Plan and, *1:* 31–32
　nation building and, *1:* 177, 178–79
　property and, *1:* 4, 27, 28, 56, 58, 101, 126, 128, 168, 169; *2:* 192, 214, 216, 298, 299, 320, 348
　Russia and, *2:* 373
　Soviet Union and, *2:* 304, 352, 361, 367–68
　Yeltsin, Boris, and, *2:* 367–68
Carmichael, Stokely, *2:* 276, 281
Cars, *1:* 137
Carter Doctrine, *2:* 336
Carter, Jimmy, *2:* 322 (ill.), 329 (ill.), 331 (ill.)
　Afghanistan and, *2:* 335–36, 337
　Africa and, *2:* 325–27
　Brezhnev, Leonid, and, *2:* 316, 330
　Brown, Harold, and, *2:* 321
　Brzezinski, Zbigniew, and, *2:* 321
　cabinet of, *2:* 321–22
　Camp David Accords and, *2:* 328–30
　Carter Doctrine and, *2:* 336
　Central Intelligence Agency and, *2:* 322
　China and, *2:* 301, 327–28, 336
　containment and, *2:* 327
　Deng Xiaoping and, *2:* 328
　détente and, *2:* 322–23, 335–36
　dictatorship and, *2:* 322–23, 324, 330–31
　Egypt and, *2:* 328–30
　election of, *2:* 315, 321, 335, 337–38
　foreign affairs experience of, *2:* 321
　Gromyko, Andrey, and, *2:* 326

causes of, *1:* 23–24, 29

communism and, *1:* 25, 60, 105

costs of, *2:* 372–73

death in, *2:* 372

definition of, *1:* 1–2, 28, 56, 80, 100, 126, 168; *2:* 192, 234, 252, 276, 298, 320, 348

democracy and, *1:* 25, 60, 105; *2:* 347

détente and, *2:* 297–300

economy and, *1:* 24–25

Eisenhower, Dwight D., and, *1:* 52

end of, *1:* 66, 160; *2:* 347, 351, 355, 357, 370–72

espionage and, *1:* 24, 127–29, 129–32

fear and, *1:* 105, 128–29

freedom and, *2:* 347

Germany and, *1:* 60–61

Khrushchev, Nikita S., and, *1:* 52

as Long Peace, *2:* 374

name of, *1:* 2–3

nuclear weapons and, *2:* 233–35

origins of, *1:* 3–25

peace and, *2:* 374

Red Scare and, *1:* 114

Stalin, Joseph, and, *1:* 25, 52

thaw of, *1:* 187–88; *2:* 192–93, 297–300

Truman, Harry S., and, *1:* 24, 25, 52

Colonialism. *See also* Imperialism

Africa and, *2:* 206–8

containment and, *2:* 206

France and, *2:* 206, 268–69

Great Britain and, *2:* 202, 206

Indochina and, *2:* 268–69

Middle East and, *2:* 202

Monroe Doctrine and, *1:* 186–87

nation building and, *1:* 176–78

Portugal and, *2:* 206

Combined Airlift Task Force, *1:* 65

Combined Development Trust (CDT), *1:* 143

Combined Policy Committee (CPC), *1:* 143

Comecon. *See* Council of Mutual Economic Assistance (Comecon)

Cominform. *See* Communist Information Bureau (Cominform)

Committee for State Security. *See* KGB (Soviet secret police)

Committee of 100, *2:* 245–46

Committee on the Present Danger, *2:* 338

Committee to Reelect the President (CREEP), *2:* 310

Commonwealth of Independent States (CIS), *2:* 370, 374–76

Communism. *See also* Communist Party

in Berlin, *1:* 57, 73

Bolshevik Revolution and, *1:* 2, 3–5, 6–7

capitalism and, *1:* 19, 23–24, 25, 29, 33, 129, 169–70, 188; *2:* 215–16, 352

Cold War and, *1:* 25, 60, 105

collapse of, *2:* 347, 357–60

in Cuba, *2:* 216–17

Cultural Revolution and, *2:* 277, 293–94

definition of, *1:* 2, 28, 56, 80, 99, 100, 126, 168; *2:* 192, 214, 234, 252, 276, 298, 320, 348

democracy and, *1:* 100–101, 128–29, 167–68; *2:* 215–16, 267–68, 319, 347

dictatorship and, *2:* 263

in East Germany, *1:* 30–31

in Eastern Bloc, *1:* 105

economy and, *1:* 2, 3, 27–29, 28, 56, 57, 80, 99, 100, 126, 128, 167, 168, 169–70; *2:* 192, 214, 215, 234, 251, 252, 262, 276, 290–92, 298, 299, 319–20, 348, 352

elections and, *1:* 2, 3, 27, 28, 56, 57, 80, 99, 100, 105, 126, 128, 168; *2:* 192, 214, 215, 234, 251, 252, 276, 298, 320, 348

fear of, *1:* 99–100; *2:* 372

freedom and, *1:* 5, 20–21, 77, 99, 100–101; *2:* 292

freedom of speech and, *2:* 292

Korean War and, *1:* 48
Lebanon and, *2:* 204
loyalty programs and, *1:* 171
Malenkov, Georgy M., and, *1:* 170–71
McCarthy, Joseph R., and, *1:* 118
missiles and, *2:* 198–99
Mosaddeq, Mohammed, and, *1:* 178
nation building and, *1:* 177, 178–80
nuclear energy and, *2:* 241
nuclear weapons and, *1:* 70, 170–71; *2:* 200–201
Open Skies and, *1:* 186–87
reconnaissance and, *1:* 148, 150; *2:* 211–12
Suez War and, *2:* 203
Taiwan and, *1:* 184
Vietnam and, *1:* 181–82; *2:* 283
West Berlin and, *1:* 70
Elections
of 1948, *1:* 107
of 1952, *1:* 48, 117, 118
of 1960, *1:* 70; *2:* 212, 251
of 1964, *2:* 270
of 1968, *2:* 273, 312
of 1972, *2:* 312
of 1976, *2:* 314–15
of 1980, *2:* 335, 337–38
of 1984, *2:* 344–45
of 1996, *2:* 373
of 2000, *2:* 373
communism and, *1:* 2, 3, 27, 28, 56, 57, 80, 99, 100, 105, 126, 128, 168; *2:* 192, 214, 215, 234, 251, 252, 276, 298, 320, 348
Communist Party and, *1:* 27
in Cuba, *2:* 216
in Czechoslovakia, *2:* 360
democracy and, *1:* 4, 27, 58, 128, 167–68; *2:* 192, 214, 216, 276, 298, 299, 320
in East Germany, *1:* 68; *2:* 359, 363
in Great Britain, *1:* 15
in Hungary, *2:* 358
in Poland, *2:* 357–58
Red Scare and, *1:* 106
in Russia, *2:* 373

in Soviet Union, *1:* 52; *2:* 255–56, 360–61
in Vietnam, *1:* 182
in West Germany, *1:* 67, 173
Yalta agreements and, *1:* 105
El Salvador, *2:* 331, 339
Elsey, George, *1:* 22
Empire Ken, 2: 203 (ill.)
Enola Gay, 1: 87–88
"Enormous," *1:* 90–91
Espionage, *1:* 136, 137 (ill.), 146 (ill.), 149 (ill.). *See also* Intelligence; Moles; Reconnaissance
Ames, Aldrich, and, *1:* 162
Berlin tunnel and, *1:* 145–46, 146 (ill.)
Boyce, Christopher, and, *1:* 154–55
Cambridge Spies and, *1:* 135, 140–44
Central Intelligence Agency (CIA) and, *1:* 34, 143, 145–46, 154, 158, 162
China and, *1:* 158–59
Churchill, Winston, and, *1:* 140, 142
Cold War and, *1:* 24, 127–29, 129–32
definition of, *1:* 125–26
Eisenhower, Dwight D., and, *1:* 152; *2:* 198, 240
execution and, *1:* 140, 152, 158, 162
Federal Bureau of Investigation (FBI) and, *1:* 131, 143, 163
Gorbachev, Mikhail, and, *1:* 157
Gordievsky, Oleg, and, *1:* 157
Great Britain and, *1:* 127, 131, 136–38, 140–44, 145–46, 151–52, 157
GRU (Soviet military intelligence agency) and, *1:* 154
Hanssen, Robert Philip, and, *1:* 162–63
Hiss, Alger, and, *1:* 44, 135
history of, *1:* 126–27
human element of, *1:* 150–51
Israel and, *1:* 159–60
Jordan and, *1:* 161
Kennedy, John F., and, *1:* 152

H

World War II and, *1:* 2, 8, 10, 12, 17, 39, 50, 86–88, 104–5

Jaruzelski, Wojciech, *2:* 357

JEN. *See* Junta de Energía Nuclear (JEN)

Jews, *1:* 121–23; *2:* 315, 324, 328–30. *See also* Israel

Job Corps, *2:* 282

Joe-1, *1:* 89–90

Joe-4, *1:* 95

John Paul II (pope), *2:* 357

Johnson, Louis, *1:* 95

Johnson, Lyndon B., *2:* 261 (ill.), 272 (ill.)
    Alliance for Progress and, *2:* 263
    communism and, *2:* 270, 283
    election of, *2:* 270
    Great Society of, *2:* 254, 272, 282
    Kosygin, Aleksy, and, *2:* 247
    Latin America and, *2:* 263–65
    nuclear weapons and, *2:* 247, 258
    Panama and, *2:* 263
    Vietnam War and, *2:* 270, 271–73, 282, 283, 289–90

Jordan, *1:* 161; *2:* 204

Jornada del Muerto, *1:* 79

Junta de Energía Nuclear (JEN), *2:* 242–43

K

Kádár, János, *2:* 196, 358

Kassem, Abdul Karim, *2:* 204

Kazakhstan, *2:* 370, 373

Kennan, George F., *1:* 19 (ill.), 19–20, 35–36; *2:* 356

Kennedy, John F., *2:* 227 (ill.), 229 (ill.), 230 (ill.), 259 (ill.), 261 (ill.)
    Alliance for Progress and, *2:* 262–63
    Bay of Pigs and, *2:* 217, 218, 258–59
    Berlin and, *1:* 72–73, 76–77; *2:* 259–60
    brinkmanship and, *2:* 256
    China and, *2:* 266
    communism and, *2:* 251–54, 262, 269

Cuban Missile Crisis and, *2:* 213–14, 221–27, 228, 229, 260
    death of, *2:* 254, 270
    election of, *1:* 70; *2:* 212, 251
    espionage and, *1:* 152
    Gromyko, Andrey, and, *2:* 224–25
    Hoover, J. Edgar, and, *1:* 109
    Khrushchev, Nikita S., and, *1:* 70–71; *2:* 226, 228, 251–54, 259–61
    McNamara, Robert S., and, *2:* 253
    military and, *2:* 256
    nation building and, *1:* 177
    nuclear weapons and, *2:* 246, 256–58
    Operation Mongoose and, *2:* 219
    Peace Corps and, *2:* 255
    Rusk, Dean, and, *2:* 253
    second-strike strategies and, *2:* 256–58
    space race and, *2:* 198–99
    Vietnam War and, *2:* 269–70, 283
    West Berlin and, *1:* 70–71

Kennedy, Robert F., *2:* 215, 222, 228–29, 229 (ill.)

Kent State University, *2:* 290

KGB (Soviet secret police)
    Ames, Aldrich, and, *1:* 162
    atomic spies and, *1:* 140
    Berlin tunnel and, *1:* 146
    Boyce, Christopher, and, *1:* 154–55
    Cambridge Spies and, *1:* 141–42, 144
    definition of, *1:* 127
    Dzerzhinski, Feliks, and, *1:* 160
    formation of, *1:* 132
    Hanssen, Robert Philip, and, *1:* 163
    Mitrokhin, Vasili, and, *1:* 163–64
    Penkovsky, Oleg, and, *1:* 151, 152
    Stalin, Joseph, and, *1:* 127, 132
    Walker spy ring and, *1:* 156–57
    Yurchenko, Vitaly, and, *1:* 158

Khomeini, Ayatollah Ruhollah, *2:* 333–35, 334 (ill.)

missiles and, *2:* 239–40, 244
  nuclear powered, *2:* 237
Subversives, *1:* 104, 107
Suez War, *2:* 203, 203 (ill.)
Summer of love, *2:* 287
SVR (Russian Foreign Intelligence
    Service), *1:* 132
Syria, *2:* 204, 309–10
Szilard, Leo, *1:* 81

T

Tactical Air Command (TAC), *2:*
    225
Tactical arms, *2:* 234, 235
Taft, Robert A., *1:* 48
Taiwan. *See also* China; People's
    Republic of China (PRC); Re-
    public of China (ROC)
  China and, *1:* 50, 183–85; *2:*
    205, 266, 301
  Communist Party and, *1:*
    184–85
  Eisenhower, Dwight D., and, *1:*
    184
  formation of, *1:* 41
  Nationalists in, *1:* 50
  Nixon, Richard M., and, *2:* 301
  Truman, Harry S., and, *1:* 50
Taiwan Resolution, *1:* 184
Taylor, Maxwell, *2:* 222
Teachers, *1:* 115
Teach-ins, *2:* 284, 285
Tehran Conference, *1:* 143
Television, *1:* 110
Teller, Edward, *1:* 81, 94; *2:* 353
    (ill.)
Terrorism, *2:* 376
Tet Offensive, *2:* 271–72
Thatcher, Margaret, *1:* 144; *2:* 352
Thermonuclear bombs, *1:* 88. *See
    also* Nuclear weapons
Third World
  in Africa, *2:* 206
  Carter, Jimmy, and, *2:* 325
  communism and, *1:* 176–78; *2:*
    193
  definition of, *1:* 168; *2:* 193,
    252, 307, 321–22, 349
  economy and, *2:* 252, 254, 307
  Four Point Program and, *1:*
    49–50

Khrushchev, Nikita S., and, *2:*
    210
  nation building and, *1:* 175–82;
    2: 254, 307–8, 325–27
  Peace Corps and, *2:* 255
  Soviet Union and, *2:* 210, 254,
    321–22, 349, 351
  United Nations and, *2:* 210
Threats
  asymmetrical response and, *1:*
    173–75
  Berlin airlift and, *1:* 64–65
  Cuban Missile Crisis and, *2:*
    226, 227
  Khrushchev, Nikita S., and, *1:*
    69–71
  nuclear weapons and, *1:* 32,
    64–65, 184; *2:* 205, 256, 338
  as weapon, *1:* 2, 28, 56, 80,
    100, 126, 127, 168; *2:* 192,
    234, 252, 276, 298, 320, 348
Thule Accident, *2:* 243
Tiananmen Square, *2:* 295 (ill.),
    362
Time, 2: 361
Tito, Josip Broz, *1:* 51, 51 (ill.),
    121, 188
Tocqueville, Alexis de, *1:* 1
Tradecraft, *1:* 136–37, 137 (ill.),
    141
Transportation, *1:* 68–69, 70, 71
Treaty on the Final Settlement
    with Respect to Germany, *2:*
    364
Trilateral Commission, *2:* 321
Trinity, *1:* 79, 82 (ill.), 85, 87
Trotsky, Leon, *1:* 4 (ill.)
Truman Doctrine, *1:* 2, 23–24, 107
Truman, Harry S., *1:* 14 (ill.), 16
    (ill.)
  Attlee, Clement, and, *1:* 86
  character of, *1:* 25
  China and, *1:* 40, 42
  Cold War and, *1:* 24, 25, 52
  containment and, *1:* 29–30,
    168–69, 173–74
  espionage and, *1:* 140, 142
  Executive Order 9835, *1:* 107
  Indochina and, *1:* 50
  Iron Curtain and, *1:* 20–21
  Korean War and, *1:* 46, 47, 48
  Mao Zedong and, *1:* 40, 42
  Marshall Plan and, *1:* 32

W

Y